THE DRAMA AND THEATRE
OF ANNIE BAKER

Amy Muse is Professor of English at the University of St. Thomas, USA. She is the author of *The Drama and Theatre of Sarah Ruhl* (Methuen Drama, 2018) and essays on dramatic literature, intimate theatre, and travel that have appeared in *The Journal of Dramatic Theory and Criticism*, *Text & Presentation*, *Romanticism: The Journal of Romantic Culture & Criticism*, *Frontiers*, and *The Journal of Greek Media and Culture*.

Also available in the Critical Companions series from Methuen Drama:

THE THEATRE OF PAULA VOGEL: PRACTICE, PEDAGOGY, AND INFLUENCES
Lee Brewer Jones

THE THEATRE OF SIMON STEPHENS
Jacqueline Bolton

CRITICAL COMPANION TO NATIVE AMERICAN AND FIRST NATIONS THEATRE AND PERFORMANCE: INDIGENOUS SPACES
Jaye T. Darby, Courtney Elkin Mohler, and Christy Stanlake

THE DRAMA AND THEATRE OF SARAH RUHL
Amy Muse

THE THEATRE OF AUGUST WILSON
Alan Nadel

THE THEATRE OF EUGENE O'NEILL: AMERICAN MODERNISM ON THE WORLD STAGE
Kurt Eisen

THE THEATRE AND FILMS OF CONNOR MCPHERSON: CONSPICUOUS COMMUNITIES
Eamonn Jordan

IRISH DRAMA AND THEATRE SINCE 1950
Patrick Lonergan

For a full listing, please visit https://www.bloomsbury.com/uk/series/critical-companions/

THE DRAMA AND THEATRE OF ANNIE BAKER

Amy Muse

Series Editors: Patrick Lonergan and Kevin J. Wetmore, Jr.

methuen | drama
LONDON • NEW YORK • OXFORD • NEW DELHI • SYDNEY

METHUEN DRAMA
Bloomsbury Publishing Plc
50 Bedford Square, London, WC1B 3DP, UK
1385 Broadway, New York, NY 10018, USA
29 Earlsfort Terrace, Dublin 2, Ireland

BLOOMSBURY, METHUEN DRAMA and the Methuen Drama logo are trademarks of Bloomsbury Publishing Plc

First published in Great Britain 2023
This paperback edition published 2025

Copyright © Amy Muse and Contributors, 2023

Amy Muse has asserted her right under the Copyright, Designs and Patents Act, 1988, to be identified as author of this work.

For legal purposes the Acknowledgements on p. viii constitute an extension of this copyright page.

Cover image: Maria Dizzia and Michael Shannon in the Soho Rep's production of Anton Chekhov's Uncle Vanya.
Photo © Julieta Cervantes.

All rights reserved. No part of this publication may be reproduced or transmitted in any form or by any means, electronic or mechanical, including photocopying, recording, or any information storage or retrieval system, without prior permission in writing from the publishers.

Bloomsbury Publishing Plc does not have any control over, or responsibility for, any third-party websites referred to or in this book. All internet addresses given in this book were correct at the time of going to press. The author and publisher regret any inconvenience caused if addresses have changed or sites have ceased to exist, but can accept no responsibility for any such changes.

A catalogue record for this book is available from the British Library.

A catalog record for this book is available from the Library of Congress.

Names: Muse, Amy, author.
Title: The drama and theatre of Annie Baker / Amy Muse.
Description: London ; New York : Methuen Drama, 2023. | Series: Critical companions | Includes bibliographical references and index.
Identifiers: LCCN 2022059702 (print) | LCCN 2022059703 (ebook) | ISBN 9781350319974 (hardback) | ISBN 9781350319981 (epub) | ISBN 9781350319998 (pdf)
Subjects: LCSH: Baker, Annie, 1981—Criticism and interpretation. | American drama–21st century–History and criticism.
Classification: LCC PS3602.A5842 Z77 2023 (print) | LCC PS3602.A5842 (ebook) | DDC 812/.6–dc23/eng/20230413
LC record available at https://lccn.loc.gov/2022059702
LC ebook record available at https://lccn.loc.gov/2022059703

ISBN: HB: 978-1-3503-1997-4
PB: 978-1-3503-2001-7
ePDF: 978-1-3503-1999-8
eBook: 978-1-3503-1998-1

Series: Critical Companions

Typeset by Deanta Global Publishing Services, Chennai, India

To find out more about our authors and books, visit www.bloomsbury.com and sign up for our newsletters.

To D—

For the long conversation

CONTENTS

Acknowledgments		viii
Foreword: *Mac Wellman on Annie Baker*		x
Preface: The Magic of Slow Theater		xi
1	Listening to the Lonely: Chekhov and Baker's *Uncle Vanya*	1
2	Botched, Beautiful Attempts at Communication: *Body Awareness*, *Nocturama*, and *Circle Mirror Transformation*	17
3	The Presence of Silence: *The Aliens* and *The Flick*	51
4	Stories of Complicated Desire: *John*, *I Love Dick*, and *The Antipodes*	73
5	**Critical Perspectives**	
	Caring about the Matter in Annie Baker's Drama *Thomas Butler*	99
	Annie Baker's Domestic Uncanny *Jeanmarie Higgins*	116
	Annie Baker: Building on Samuel Beckett *Katherine Weiss*	125
	Undressing the Wound of Theatergoing Whiteness in Annie Baker's *Nocturama* *Harrison Schmidt*	134
Afterword: The Fragility and Imperfection of Creating Theater		149
Notes		151
Bibliography		174
Notes on Contributors		185
Index		186

ACKNOWLEDGMENTS

I am grateful to Kevin Wetmore, series editor for Critical Companions, and Mark Dudgeon, Senior Publisher of Theatre and Shakespeare Studies at Bloomsbury, for entrusting me with another volume in the series. Ella Wilson was the perfect Editorial Assistant: kind, patient, friendly, diplomatic. Many thanks to Elizabeth Kellingley, Production Editor, Sharmila Mary, Project Manager, and those behind the scenes at Bloomsbury who worked with care to bring this book to physical life. Abby Bensen was a fabulous copyeditor for the notes and bibliography and creator of the index; she is lightning-fast, super-attentive, and cheering. Thomas Butler, Jeanmarie Higgins, Katherine Weiss, and Harrison Schmidt wrote wonderful essays to accompany and complement my own analyses. Jeanmarie, I am grateful for your design knowledge, and Katherine, for your Beckett expertise; Tom, I can always count on you to press and inspire my thinking about philosophy and drama and I appreciate having you on board again; Harrison, thank you for being my interlocutor for thinking about Baker, relationality, and contemplative practice. I am also indebted to the excellent essays on Annie Baker by scholars I have never met but whose work has meant so much to me and gets frequently cited in these pages: thank you, Sam Kahn and Jennifer Cayer.

Mac Wellman was as generous and kind as everyone says; thank you, Mac, for writing the foreword. Kelly Younger was my champion; thank you also, Kelly, for the listening-to-the-lonely Chekhov exercise that inspired my thinking about *Uncle Vanya*. Alan Berks and Leah Cooper, co-artistic directors of Wonderlust Productions, engaged me in crucial conversations about loss and care and realism and theater. My book-group circle of girlfriends watched *I Love Dick* and discussed women's desire with me; thank you, Nanette Hanks, Martha Johnson, Sarah Spencer, and Sarah Taffee. And I am always grateful to have such encouraging colleagues and friends in the English department at the University of St. Thomas: thank you, Kanishka Chowdhury, Alexis Easley, Young-ok An, Ray MacKenzie, Olga Herrera, and especially Liz Wilkinson, who had to hear the most about it.

Acknowledgments

I have been lucky with inspiring vistas and supportive friends while writing. Chapter 3 was drafted in Athens, Greece, my home away from home, between coffees and stimulating conversations with Martha Frangiadaki, who has been the most generous of friends for over a decade. Chapter 2 was drafted in Seward, Alaska, thanks to all the good people at the Seward Public Library who provided such a peaceful space for thinking and writing. I also want to thank my sister-in-law, Paige Johnson, for our contemplative talk one evening along Resurrection Bay, during which she asked me the kinds of caring, probing questions that pushed me to clarify my purpose in writing this book. I am forever grateful to have been raised in a home that prized reading and theatergoing, and thank my parents, Marlene and Bill Muse, my brother Van, and especially my sister Ellen for their many years of involvement in my theater explorations and for accepting my own quiet style.

The last and greatest thanks go, as always, to Doug Phillips. He pulled books for me from our epic home library, thought of the next book I should read, and listened to the same half thoughts over and over. Every idea, every philosophical reference, every grace note in this book was mulled over with him in our quiet morning writing time, during the long conversation.

FOREWORD
Mac Wellman on Annie Baker

Annie Baker is the most remarkable of theater writers: she is knowledgeable and, most importantly, thoughtful. I remember her thoughtful words and conversation in one of the most difficult of my elective courses at Brooklyn College: the one on Wittgenstein and new writing.

This was a project I had long ago considered to help me through Wittgenstein's difficult thought and scribbling. The various texts we discussed were wonderful and awfully baffling at the same time; but I had hoped the discussions would promote a more thoughtful discussion among my students.

Many of them thought the discussions were silly and ridiculous—that is to say, useless for serious theater folk, playwrights in particular. But Annie Baker was very serious about the discussions and frequently came up with startling and wonderful thoughts. Baffling to many, but splendidly invigorating for those few willing to take on the unusual consequences of the resulting discussion. I knew then that she was that rarest of theater writers—a profoundly thoughtful one.

She was to take on the role of docent for the course in the following semester on the work and terrifying thought of Martin Heidegger; but around that time her career began to take off and she was unable to do the course.

I realized my job was, in a sense, to get out of her way. And I did!

Lastly, I recall when I went to see her play *The Flick* at Playwrights Horizons, I was at first terrified by its very, very long length as I have a profound dislike of long plays, particularly those longer than an hour-and-a-half. But! But I sat through the entire play delighted and hypnotized by her passionate and thoughtful questioning of all matters she addressed.

There is really no one like her in our time. Sadly so.

Mac Wellman
Donald I. Fine Professor of Playwriting, Brooklyn College
December 2022

PREFACE
THE MAGIC OF SLOW THEATER

Annie Baker isn't interested in drama. She's interested in life. Or maybe we should put it this way: Annie Baker creates dramas with such precise, vivid attention to language and gesture and space that through them we are able to experience life in its full, glorious, strange, painful wonder.

In an oft-repeated story, she recalls having a breakdown about playwriting—feeling oppressed by cause-and-effect structure and advice to move plot along, and pressed to position herself among either the slick uptown commercial theater or the arty downtown expressionist theater, neither of which felt quite like her. Talking with her graduate school mentor, playwright Mac Wellman, she told him, what I *really* want to write would be "a play that was just my mom and her hippie friends sitting around and talking about spirituality for two hours." His response: "Do that! That sounds great!"[1] The result: *Body Awareness*, her first professional production.

Wellman's advice to Baker to follow her own inclinations and write what she would like to see onstage has proven wise. Her close observations of relating, her "patient fascination with humans doing the work of living,"[2] has earned her critical acclaim and a devoted following. Since 2008, Baker has had seven plays premiere in New York, most followed by international productions, and she has piled up awards that include three Obie Awards (for *Circle Mirror Transformation*, *The Aliens*, and *The Flick*), the Susan Smith Blackburn Prize (for *The Flick*), and the Pulitzer Prize (for *The Flick*), along with the Steinberg Playwright Award for career excellence, a Guggenheim Fellowship, and a MacArthur "genius" grant. She is only getting started.

As I have struggled to put into words what I experience in Baker's plays, I have taken some comfort in seeing others similarly struggling to articulate that "uncanny mixture of wonder, elation and despair" that her plays conjure up in us.[3] The psychoanalyst and essayist Adam Phillips said in his *Paris Review* interview that it doesn't matter to him if people remember the content of his essays; he wants readers to have an experience, even if they don't quite know why or can't recall the details afterward: "what I want is for people to enjoy the experience of reading the books and then forget about them," to read and enjoy and then "discover what you find yourself thinking, feeling, in the reading of it."[4] Baker's plays feel like this to me. To itemize their content, to describe what they are about, is to make them sound mundane, even trifling. For they are about the consequential in the seemingly inconsequential, the extraordinarily particular ordinariness of our ordinary lives. She is Emily Webb at the end of *Our Town*, calling to us to realize life, every minute of it, while we're living it.

Nathan Heller wrote in a *New Yorker* profile of Baker that "she wants life onstage to be so vivid, natural, and emotionally precise that it bleeds into the audience's visceral experience of time and space. Drawing on the immediacy of overheard conversation, she has pioneered a style of theatre made to seem as untheatrical as possible, while using the tools of the stage to focus audience attention."[5] As playwright Alan Berks said in a conversation with me, "most theater feels more 'essentialized' like you're getting an injection of insight about life in a pure, mainline form. Shakespeare is like that. It's not realism, it's better"; but Baker, like Chekhov, "is not 'realism,'" it's just "real—and it's even better."[6] With all this talk of "real," should we label her work "realism"? Adam Greenfield points out although Baker's plays "employ detailed, life-like stage designs, and though her characters speak in well-observed patterns, the properties of her plays, when you look at them, are actually very weird, erratic, subversive. They question our reality, rather than affirm it, making our lives seem more complicated and astonishing, not more knowable."[7] In other words, Baker's "scrupulous attention to detail" defamiliarizes the world; instead of finding order in it, we find "greater mystery, wonder, beauty, despair."[8] "Art exists that one may recover the sensation of life," goes Viktor Shklovsky's famous notion of defamiliarization. Art helps us resee what we think we know. Baker's plays help us feel more alive. Her plays "take elements of the everyday and infuse them with transcendence."[9] Surrender to the rhythms of life, her plays call out to us; that is where aliveness dwells.

Her style is often described as "quiet" and "slow." As Sam Kahn wrote in a marvelous essay, "The Triumph of the Quiet Style," Baker's success has been "so sweeping" that we forget "how *weird*" her quiet style seemed to audiences at first, "how much it ran against all the prevailing headwinds of playwriting, which, for decades, had been all about making plays faster, more shocking, *edgier*."[10] Baker "created a revolution," Kahn explains, "by slowing everything down, inserting long pauses, setting plays at room temperature." She describes herself as having a "slow theatrical metabolism" (and a slow metabolism for art in general—she loves Thomas Mann novels and other such long, quiet, densely detailed works) and finds silence and stillness "very exciting."[11] She is sometimes criticized for not writing plays that directly address the political moment and therefore seem apolitical. Like in Chekhov's plays, her politics are quietly entwined into life; "I think every time a group of people are in a room talking it's a social and a political event."[12] (Though cryptically she once said, "I do have a secret political project with every play I write.[13]) The quiet of Baker's work is, as Kevin Quashie puts it in *The Sovereignty of Quiet*, "a metaphor for the full range of one's inner life—one's desires, ambitions, hungers, vulnerabilities, fears"; it is "not apolitical," but in fact, "the interior—dynamic and ravishing—is a stay against the dominance of the social world; it has its own sovereignty."[14] I agree with Kahn that the quiet style is fundamentally "a mode of religious expression and it leans heavily on its confessional aspect, its blind faith that the moments of most abject, most senseless humiliation are also the moments when we are at our funniest and truest and (ultimately) most divine."[15]

To Baker "the theater is a place for contemplation,"[16] and I would extend that further to propose that Annie Baker's theater is its own form of contemplative practice. We usually think of contemplative practices being things like yoga or meditation or prayer: tools designed to slow us down, regulate our breathing, bring us into attention. What is less discussed is that they are practices designed to bring us *into relation*, as is indicated in yoga's root in "yoke" or unite. Contemplative practices help us develop our relationship to ourselves as well as our relationship to other human beings, other creatures, the world, the divine. I am hesitant to propose a unifying thesis for a playwright whose work has already proven so variegated, and even more, to use a unifying thesis from quantum physics, which gets applied slapdash to everything we can't explain, but we might find it illuminating to view Annie Baker's work in light of relationality, of the theory that the world is a "dense web of interactions."[17] We are all entangled. *Of course*, I hear you saying; *isn't that drama at its core? Everything and everyone exists in relation to everything else.* Annie Baker is a playwright who puts us in contemplative spaces to notice this, to notice ourselves, and to feel the interconnectedness. This is what audiences experience that makes them so ecstatic, I have come to believe. At the same time, the challenge of this relation is what makes some people get up and walk out of her plays; the attentiveness is too much to bear.

Preface

Annie Baker grew up in the college town of Amherst, Massachusetts, in an intellectual household. She has often credited her mother, therapist and retired psychology professor Linda Baker, for making her a playwright, and her early plays (called the Vermont Plays) all have a character who feels like a tribute to her mother: spiritual, warm, well-intended, a bit intrusive but lifesaving. Her father, Conn Nugent, was an administrator for the Five Colleges consortium (Amherst College, Hampshire College, Mount Holyoke, Smith, and the University of Massachusetts-Amherst). Her older brother, Benjamin Nugent, is also a writer—a novelist and journalist. (She is Annie Nugent Baker, he Benjamin Baker Nugent. As Baker describes it, "My parents did this hilarious patrilineal and matrilineal naming thing."[18]) Her parents divorced when she was six. Baker and her brother continued living with their mother in Amherst and visited their father in New York City. "It was intense to go back and forth, especially because my parents have very different personalities that required very different things from me and my brother," she has said; "I would train myself to be a very sassy, super-assertive person around my dad. Then I'd get back to my mother's house, and she'd be like, 'Why did you just speak to me that way?'"[19] Observing the lifestyles and relationship expectations in the two very different households—earnestly discussing sexuality and spirituality with her mother, reading *The Importance of Being Earnest* aloud with her father—shaped Baker's acumen for playwriting.

While Baker never envisioned being a professional playwright—it just wasn't something that seemed realistic—like many people who go into the theater, she did a lot of "theater kid" things, including taking a creative drama class at the local community center, which served as an inspiration, over a decade later, for *Circle Mirror Transformation*. She was first drawn into theater by seeing a high school production of *Guys and Dolls* when she was in fifth grade: "I had that experience of just being totally swept up by something and the high-schoolers seeming like Olympian gods, and afterwards I learned all the songs and made up little dances in my bedroom."[20] (She later played the role of Miss Adelaide in *Guys and Dolls* when she got to high school.) At the age of fourteen, on a visit to her father, she

> somehow ended up in New York City's East Village at the Ontological-Hysteric Theatre for a production of Richard Foreman's *Permanent Brain Damage*, which was pretty much as avant-garde as you could get in 1995. So somehow Oscar Wilde plus *Guys and Dolls* plus people behind a glass wall hitting each other on the heads with plastic hammers made me love theatre.[21]

Preface

She moved to New York to study dramatic writing at NYU's Tisch School of the Arts, where she graduated with a BFA in 2003. She found traditional methods of dramatic structure (from Aristotle to Robert McKee) stifling with their instructions for "writing plays that had clear PROTAGONISTS and QUESTS and TURNING POINTS and INSTIGATING EVENTS and THIRD ACT REVERSALS but not one believable or truthful line of dialogue"[22] and took more interest in studying religion and history. For graduate school she went to Brooklyn College to study with Mac Wellman, who was then the director of their famed MFA program in Playwriting. When asked later for advice to young playwrights, Baker responded, along with "Don't give up. Don't love everything you write, be hard on yourself, but don't become so crippled by self-hatred that you can't finish a draft," that if "you're interested in grad school and you like weird plays, go study with Mac Wellman at Brooklyn College. He is one of the smartest and most generous people on the planet."[23]

When she moved to New York City, productions that particularly excited and influenced her included Daniel Aukin's production of Maria Irene Fornes's *Molly's Dream*, Big Dance Theater's production of Mac Wellman's *Antigone*, James Macdonald's production of Caryl Churchill's *A Number* at New York Theatre Workshop ("That play just killed me," she said; "I cried and shook through the whole thing. I reacted to that piece more strongly than I'd ever reacted to a movie or novel"[24]) and Young Jean Lee's *The Appeal*.[25] Chekhov has been her most obvious and enduring influence, but she also cites "William Shakespeare, Mac Wellman, Caryl Churchill, Vladimir Nabokov, Emily Dickinson, Virginia Woolf, Samuel Beckett, Edward Albee, Thomas Mann, Jane Austen, Fritz Perls, Eric Rohmer, and my mother," adding, "I realize only half of those people are playwrights."[26]

Understandably, she's reluctant to explain her writing. "The writing is best for me when I feel mindless," she says, "which is so weird and so creepy and such a contradiction that it's hard to talk about, so I always get stopped up."[27] But she does talk freely about process. She tends to start with a long incubation period (from nine months to two years) of wide and deep reading, in history and theory, psychology and theology, as well as fiction. She describes it as like entering "a maze, like I know eventually I'll hit the heart of my play if I read enough books."[28] She writes long, detailed biographies of each character as though she's a novelist. Then, when she begins to conceive of a play for those characters, she begins with form—each time seeking to transcend and break the conventions of her previous play. "On every project, I realize that I've boxed myself into a corner, or that the play necessitates some sort of theatrical convention that I realize I hate while I'm making it," she has said; "So then the next play is always a rebellion. Or like, the thing I didn't even realize I was doing last time I will make sure I don't do this time. But there's always some other blind spot. And then that blind spot inspires the play that comes after."[29] She starts with space, figuring out the stage picture, what she calls the "container" for the play, "the space container and the time container, what the play needs and what's going to make it a deep and complex experience for the audience."[30]

When she writes, it's always on the computer rather than longhand, and always in Times font, as she's "obsessed with typography" (if she used a different font she'd write a different play).[31] Her accurately rendered dialogue comes about through a painstaking process. When she's got a first draft, she records herself reading it aloud, line by line, pause by pause, because, as she says, "it's so important to capture the cadences of painful, ordinary speech, and it's hard to tell if it's believable when it's on the page"; when she listens to it, if she can "hear the writer writing, like if there's thinly-disguised exposition or a nudge to the audience or some kind of obvious point made," she changes it. This particular strategy was sparked when she was seventeen and "started surreptitiously tape-recording people's conversations and transcribing them, trying to understand how people really spoke," and it was a revelation to see, laid out on paper, not "how people spoke their minds but how they *failed* to—all the filler, the obliqueness, the false starts."[32] Today, when she teaches playwriting (she's taught at NYU and Hunter College and is currently Associate Professor of Practice in Playwriting and Directing at the University of Texas at Austin), she gives students a similar assignment, though instead of recording and transcribing, she has them listen carefully and transcribe in the moment, writing down what they hear. "I can hear my students' voices through just the way they listen," she says. "I always tell them, If you lose track of your voice as a writer, go back, eavesdrop, write down everything you hear, and that's it. That's you listening to the world."[33]

As you read this book, you'll notice that my method is similar in that, rather than making a lot of interpretive claims of my own (which often close down a text), I am primarily trying to listen to Annie Baker—to listen to her world, "in order to learn from it how to think about it"[34]—and to open up a clearing of thought for you, the reader, to enter. My approach is to guide you through the nooks and crannies of her plays and convey the experiences of reading and viewing them. I try to see the plays as the playwright herself does; Baker waves away notions that her work is directly autobiographical ("Unlike some other playwrights, the characters in my plays are not based

Preface

upon people I've met. They really do feel like products of my imagination, or different pieces of my consciousness in dialogue with each other," she says[35]), and for the most part I leave it to others to psychoanalyze or to investigate the possible real-life connections, and instead attempt to illuminate the plays by contextualizing them in the other works of theater, art, theology, and psychology that Baker read while writing.

A couple of notes. First is a technical one about ellipses. Baker is very precise with her language and I want to represent that as clearly as I can. She often uses ellipses in dialogue to indicate thinking or grasping for a word. Therefore, whenever you see three ellipsis points (. . .) in a character's speech, you can know that these are Baker's and that they are a part of the character's dialogue. They do not indicate a gap in the text. When I *do* want to indicate a gap in quoting, you will see square brackets around the ellipsis points, like this: [. . .].

The second is a note on how this book is organized. There's a fascinating book to be written that explores Annie Baker's work in dialogue with Thomas Mann's: their intensity of detail, their compression of time, their inexhaustible curiosity. I hope someone will write that soon; I look forward to reading it. In the end, I've designed this one so that each chapter follows the same pattern and you can dip into and out of the plays in any order, and chose a traditional, mostly chronological unfolding. However, I begin out of chronology, with Baker's adaptation of *Uncle Vanya*. It was the fourth of her plays to have been professionally produced, but Chekhov has been such a longtime influence that putting her adaptation of his work in Chapter 1 allows us to see their shared continued compassion and empathy for lonely, flawed people. It then allows us to hear the Chekhovian resonances, and the patience with everyday interactions, in Baker's earliest plays, *Body Awareness, Nocturama,* and *Circle Mirror Transformation* (all set in the town she invented, Shirley, Vermont), which are the subject of Chapter 2. In Chapter 3, I pull aside the fourth Vermont Play, *The Aliens*, to discuss it alongside *The Flick* (Baker's Pulitzer play) because these two feel like companions in their innovative attention to silence and the unfolding of time onstage. Chapter 4 tackles Baker's more recent excursions past realism into the surreal and numinous to explore stories of complicated desire in *John*, her episode of the TV series *I Love Dick*, and *The Antipodes*. The opening pages of each of those four chapters situate Baker in larger intellectual conversations about (among other things) loneliness, empathy, attention, patience, silence, boredom, and desire. As with all the books in the Critical Companions series, other scholars have written essays expressly

Preface

for this volume, countering and fleshing out my considerations with critical perspectives of their own: Thomas Butler on the ethical demands Baker makes on her audiences, Jeanmarie Higgins on how the scenic design for *John* pulls us into an uncanny world, Katherine Weiss on how Beckett's and Baker's plays speak to the lost ones among us, and Harrison Schmidt on how Baker's naturalism makes white audiences uncomfortable with whiteness. The Afterword speculates on how Annie Baker will amaze us next, in the upcoming plays and film projects of her still-very-much-in-progress career, and mulls over her remarkable talent for helping us really see and appreciate the fragility and imperfection of life.

CHAPTER 1
LISTENING TO THE LONELY
CHEKHOV AND BAKER'S *UNCLE VANYA*

An interviewer once asked Annie Baker, "Who are your heroes?" Her response: "Chekhov. Chekhov. Chekhov. Chekhov."[1] So when, in 2012, Baker and her frequent collaborator, director Sam Gold, decided to create a new version of *Uncle Vanya*, fans of Baker thought: *Of course*. Baker had already been called—by audience members in Moscow, no less—"the American Chekhov."[2] His name had already been used as an adjective to describe her: "There is something distinctly Chekhovian," Charles Isherwood wrote, "in the way her writing accrues weight and meaning simply through compassionate, truthful observation."[3]

Like Chekhov, Baker writes plays about people who are afraid that life is passing them by, that they aren't really living. Chekhov's notebooks are filled with brief notes, for possible stories or plays, of observations of human weakness, frailty, and shame—how we limit ourselves and close ourselves in. Baker is also finely attuned to human frailty. But both playwrights' incisive observations resist cruelty. They are enormously compassionate and patient with characters the rest of us might give up on and choose to walk away from. While both work in a naturalistic vein, reproducing the cadences and inarticulation of everyday speech and behavior, neither adheres to traditional naturalism's economic determinism, and thus both Chekhov and Baker have had critics scrambling to find the right genre labels for their plays. Neither is a tragic playwright. Both write plays that would be more precisely called comedies, but in the sense of the "human comedy," plays that gently but honestly reveal the "heartbreaking ridiculousness of our everyday behavior."[4] In Chekhov's words, "A play must be written in which people can come, go, dine, talk about the weather, and play cards, not because that's the way the author wants it, but because that's the way it happens in real life."[5]

"What happens onstage should be just as complicated and just as simple as things are in real life," he insisted; "People are sitting at a table having dinner, that's all, but at the same time their happiness is being created, or their lives are being torn apart."[6] It is the contradictions, in both his plot and characters, that Baker particularly admires. She loves that the conflicts in his plays (which is true of her own plays as well) are "ultimately about inner conflict, not outer conflict"; she reflects that his plays show us "people in dialogue with themselves. Almost all the outer conflict between people is actually about competing narratives."[7] Chekhov does so much that is "initially counterintuitive to writers who have learned a lot about plot and action," such as that his characters "aren't *listening* to each other. People will be statement-and-response for twenty seconds, and then someone else will be like, 'Oh, look what's in the newspaper!'"[8]

In *Uncle Vanya*, Chekhov "seemed to have turned the conventional play inside out, having decided" (as Rosamund Bartlett puts it) "to create a drama out of the seams and stitch work one is not supposed to see."[9] His major plays, influenced by the growth of Symbolism in Maeterlinck and Strindberg, became "increasingly plotless, in conventional terms," with his dialogue often "consisting of mutually incomprehensible pieces" of speech; the "interplay between action and stillness, sound and silence" became more fascinating to him.[10] As we will see over the course of this book, the same could be said of the career of Annie Baker; her plays evolve from a precisely-observed naturalism to more irrealistic territory. The "enduring questions" of Chekhov's late plays are "the everyday reaches of human speech," the "silences of missed opportunity, the nonsense phrase that suddenly seems laden with meaning, the jealousies and envies and despairs that drive people to drink instead of expressing their feelings—all are revealed in an increasingly fragmentary language. The commonplace words and phrases in the plays function as replacements for the passions that unite or separate us."[11]

Louis Malle's 1994 film *Vanya on 42nd Street* was Baker's introduction to Chekhov. She saw it at the Academy of Music in Northampton, Massachusetts, when she was thirteen, and remarks that "it changed my life. I think I went into the theater in large part because of this movie."[12] She continues,

> I didn't see much theater as a kid, and this was my first clue as to what it could be like. They really nailed what's so great about Chekhov, and it made total sense to a thirteen-year-old girl in Massachusetts. Then all the Chekhov I saw after that as a young adult that was so terrible and haughty and faux-British . . . I'm just really grateful that this was my first encounter with his work. Wally Shawn's performance is incredible, too.[13]

Listening to the Lonely

She has said that the choice to create an *Uncle Vanya* was first, an opportunity to write something for actors she loves, including Reed Birney and Maria Dizzia (who played Vanya and Yelena in her production). She and Sam Gold had done a read-through of *Uncle Vanya* in 2008 while taking a break during the Sundance Theater Lab session (he played Vanya, she Sonya) and kept thinking of it over the years of developing Baker's *Circle Mirror Transformation* and *The Aliens* together. When Soho Rep commissioned the work, she decided to develop a new translation because, as she says, "I just had a lot of ideas about it, and I also found myself dissatisfied with all of the translations and adaptations of Chekhov I read, with Paul Schmidt being the exception," plus there was also "the pure pleasure of investigating the play. I studied Russian in high school, and it was a way to revisit the language and to go to Russia" for research.[14] She worked with a literal translator, Margarita Shalina, "but I also did a pass with my Russian dictionary, which was so fun. I don't have fun writing my other plays. It's usually a very painful, horrifying process."[15]

The title page of Baker's *Uncle Vanya* calls it "a new version" of the play and her preface mulls over whether the word "translation" or "adaptation" is the more accurate. Initially she thought,

> Maybe I'll do some crazy version of *Uncle Vanya*, where they're not talking about getting their horses ready, they're getting their car. But once I looked at the original text, I thought, No, this is totally strange and perfect and the problem is people just cleaning it up too much. We have to do the weird, specific, original, dirty Uncle Vanya.[16]

She resolutely refrained from modernizing the references: there are still samovars; all the place and name references remain Russian; and she retains Russian words such as "verst"—a term for measurement of distance—so instead of Americanizing to "mile," she has Astrov say that he rode "thirty versts" to get to the estate, which provides just the right amount of defamiliarization for the audience. The magic of Baker's adaptation lies in its being a version "that sounds to our contemporary American ears the way the play sounded to Russian ears during the play's first productions in the provinces in 1898."[17] She paid particular attention to "the grammar of the original text—endless run-on sentences, ellipses, the awkward repetition of words" (v), which Chekhov used to reflect how people actually speak. As Ben Gassman wrote for *American Theatre*, "Chekhov's characters don't respond to one other—they struggle to say what they mean and aren't quite

3

able to. Nor do they listen. They reach for each other or verbally push each other away. They trip over their words. They get stuck between themselves and the possibilities beyond themselves"; such "conversational veritas" and "communicative disintegration" is essential to Baker's *Uncle Vanya*.[18]

Its premiere was at New York City's Soho Rep, directed by Gold. In a joint interview between Baker and Gold for *Interview* magazine, he said of their approach to the play:

> I think we're trying to be evocative; we're trying to pull everyone in the room and do as minimal a job of interpretation as possible, so the interpretation happens in the minds of the audience. People are wearing contemporary clothing [in our production], but the reason they're wearing contemporary clothing is not because we're setting it in contemporary America, it's because to me, neutral is contemporary clothing.[19]

He observes, "I think the American theater tradition is fairly narrow in how it thinks about the act of translation of the old texts and their reproductions, there's a lot of convention about how an old play is allowed to be staged in a contemporary setting." Baker adds, "I feel like, from my experience of seeing Chekhov plays, there's either the 19th-century, corset version, spoken in pseudo-British accents, or there's the 'updating' of it where [the characters] live in Cleveland, in 1982. [Our production] is not in the 19th century, but it's not-not in the 19th century, either."

Comparing their version to *Vanya on 42nd Street*, which is similarly intimate, Baker says, "That was about rehearsing 'Uncle Vanya,' but this is more about implicating the audience. That's very exciting to me."[20]

Implicating the audience, making us feel a bit voyeuristic, as though we are eavesdropping, was just the kind of discomfort-mixed-with-fascination that they were going for in their very intimate production. Andrew Liebermann's set design settled the cast and audience within the room of an A-frame house, with audience members seated on the floor, on beige-carpeted risers around the stage, as though they were in a living room. Gold and Baker took "pains to make their production as low-frills, intimate and homemade as possible."[21] Baker served as the costume designer as well, observing what the actors wore to rehearsal and creating costumes that blended actor and character. She joked, "I'm up late at night wondering what color socks people should wear."[22] (The look of their *Uncle Vanya* was so deeply evocative of Baker's work that we chose an image of it for this book's cover.) Performing in a Chekhov play can make an actor feel naked. In Chekhov it's all "everyday realities"; "nothing extravagant in the costumes; no violent make-up; a complete absence of crowd scenes; no cascade of external tints—in a word, nothing with which the actor might protect himself against revealing his individuality to the point of nakedness."[23] Charles Isherwood wrote of the intensity of this experience, "The production can make you feel just how oppressive it would be to be trapped in a house with a handful of people who, despite their general good will, cannot stop rubbing one another's wounds raw. Fortunately you also experience the moments of fleeting communion among the characters with a luminous intensity that few productions can match."[24]

The Soho Rep production was a sold-out hit. Writing for *The Paris Review*, Clancy Martin noted, "what makes Baker's translation and adaptation superior—in the writing—to any other *Uncle Vanya* I've read or seen is her insistence on strictly following Chekhov's own maxim that the language should be as simple, authentic, and realistic as possible."[25] Isherwood concurs, calling Baker's language "easygoing, free of the stilted or formal locutions that clutter up some of the more antique-sounding translations."[26] Reviewing Robert Falls' 2017 production at the Goodman Theatre in Chicago, Chris Jones praised Baker's "warm translation" that conveys "real sympathy" with the characters and "plumbs the existential depths without ever taking itself too seriously."[27] It has since also been staged at the Shaw Festival in Ontario; Women Arts in Northampton, Massachusetts; Quintessence Theatre Group in Philadelphia; Round House Theatre in Bethesda, Maryland; Antaeus Theatre in Los Angeles; and The Court Theatre in Christchurch, New Zealand, among others.

Baker's *Uncle Vanya*

Were it not for the Russian references, *Uncle Vanya* would feel like an Annie Baker play. We see characters who are self-absorbed, anxious about having underachieved and not being known, concerned that they aren't really living, convinced that if they could just start over someplace else, they'd be a new person and live a better life. Astrov, the doctor and Chekhov surrogate, tries to destroy this illusion: "Look," he tells them, "there is no other new life out there" (96). It is this life that we are living, and we cannot hope to be remembered by those who come after us. *Uncle Vanya* is a play about degradation, of both humans and the environment. To contemporary audiences it, at first, seemed that Baker was embellishing Chekhov by inserting our own concerns about climate change; as it turns out, Chekhov was way ahead on observing humans' indifference to their destruction of the land and themselves.

The initial situation of the play is that of many classic dramas, in which a visitor disrupts the daily lives and routines of a group of people. The visitors in this case are two: Serebryakov, a self-regarding old professor, and his distractingly beautiful, much younger second wife, Yelena; they can no longer afford to live in the city and have thus moved out to the country house of Serebryakov's late first wife, where his brother-in-law Voinitsky (the Uncle Vanya of the title) and his daughter Sonya manage the estate. The professor is a hypochondriac; his wife is bored. Everyone on the estate has been tending to them. As the play opens, it is mid-afternoon and the sky is overcast. Astrov, the physician, has come to see about yet another complaint of Serebryakov's, but finds the professor out on a walk. Astrov works too hard, drinks too much, and has more faith in trees than in people. Life is generally boring, he reflects to Marina, the character they call Nanny; "You're surrounded by creeps, you spend all day hanging out with creeps, a few years go by and little by little, without even realizing it, you become a creep yourself" (9). (The word "creep" is Baker's word for "странно" in Russian. It sounds like "strange" but also connotes revulsion, and has challenged many translators. Paul Schmidt translates it as "freak"; Peter Carson uses "eccentric.") Astrov feels "numb" and sounds depressed as he tells Nanny that he feels as though he has no needs or desires anymore, though he of course loves her. He is disturbed because one of his patients recently died while under chloroform, and he fears that "maybe, just maybe, I had intentionally killed him" (9).

Vanya enters. Baker does not list his character name as "Uncle Vanya" but as "Voinitsky," his proper name. This is at first confusing to the reader, though it reflects Chekhov's script and reminds us that Vanya is a nickname, a diminutive for "Ivan," along the lines of "Johnny." The only characters who use the name Vanya are Telegin (Waffles), an old friend and impoverished landowner whose family once owned the estate, and Sonya, who is the only character to address him as *Uncle* Vanya. Astrov usually calls him Ivan Petrovich; his mother, Maria Vasilyevna, calls him Jean. For the ease of readers, however, I will call him "Vanya" or "Uncle Vanya" in my discussion.

When Vanya enters he is rumpled from having gotten up from a nap. His ordinary schedule has been upturned: he sleeps all day, stays up late drinking, eats rich food. He used to work all the time. Some of Chekhov's comedy comes from observing differences between people. Telegin, though impoverished, and having been left, many years ago, by his wife on their wedding day, has an extraordinary capacity for gratitude and enjoying life. He tells Marina that no matter the circumstance he is "capable of experiencing extreme bliss!" (13) Even when he is overlooked and misnamed by Yelena, he gently corrects: "Uh . . . miss . . . I'm so sorry to . . . but my name is not Ivan Ivanich. It's Ilya Ilyich. Ilya Ilyich Telegin. Or, as some call me on account of my pockmarked face, Waffles"; and patiently reminds her, "I live here now. I live with you. If you'd be kind enough to notice, I, uh, I eat meals with you every day" (17). At various points throughout the play, Telegin plays songs on his guitar. Baker's stage directions indicate that this is not mere background sound but that *"Everyone listens"* (21). The songs generate aura and also slow the audience down and pull them into the milieu.

In contrast to Telegin, Vanya describes himself as "bitter," "like a piece of horseradish" (13). Brimming with resentment at the professor because for twenty-five years Vanya has been managing the estate and supporting the professor's lifestyle in the city, he sputters that he had once admired Serebryakov but now realizes that he never had an original idea, that the professor has spent his entire career "writing what intelligent people already know and stupid people aren't even interested in"(14), and now that he's retired nobody will remember him, which means Vanya's own sacrifices mean nothing and he wasted his life energies that could have been spent on his own development. Being unknown, unseen, unremembered is the deepest horror expressed in the play: both one of the worst insults to hurl at another and one of the most painful revelations for oneself. Vanya's mother blames Vanya himself for neglecting his passions; she reminds him that he used to be "lit from within. . ." (19). Vanya replies, "I was lit from within, but nobody wanted any of my light" (19).

The doctor claims not to love anyone except Nanny but he is clearly attracted to Yelena, whom he invites to visit his estate and forest nearby. Yelena struggles to find the idea of tending a forest interesting in comparison with being a physician. To her, the forest, all those trees, seems boring. Sonya counters (and in so doing exposes her love for the doctor) with a rapturous recalling of what Astrov has told her about the forests: that they "teach us what beauty *is*" and inspire a "more spiritual mood" in us, that the forest not only soothes the climate, but soothes *us*, making us kinder, more elegant and graceful people (23–24). Vanya deflates her rhapsody and insists he'll continue to burn wood as he wishes. Astrov, disturbed, responds with a beautiful speech that sounds as though it comes from our own time, not one hundred years earlier: the "wonderful, sacred landscape is disappearing," he mourns (24). Humans have been "blessed with reason and creativity," yet are intent on "ruin," chopping down the forests, destroying the habitat for wildlife (24). "When I walk through a forest that I saved," Astrov tells them, "I realize that I have my own little bit of control over the climate" and he feels a wave of hope that perhaps his actions could bring happiness to people, even "one person," in the future (24). (Robert Falls' production at the Goodman Theater in Chicago kept this vision of Astrov's steadily in front of audiences. Todd Rosenthal's set, "an erstwhile stately manor that has been left to rot," centered the degradation, with "the only truly beautiful spot onstage" being "the glimpse of the forest seen through the open doors, perfectly lit through sunshine, clouds, and rain by Keith Parham."[28] Misha Kachman's set design for the Round House production visually echoed Astrov's concerns by dotting the set with tree stumps.[29]) After this stirring speech, Astrov deflates himself, self-deprecatingly, with "Maybe I'm just crazy" (25).

When Astrov leaves, Yelena turns to Vanya to criticize his petty disparaging of her husband. Just as humans chop away at the forests, destroying them, Vanya picks away at people to destroy anything noble in them. "The demon of destruction is inside all of you," she says (26). Act One closes with the seeds of romantic complication being planted, which in a melodrama, rather than a play by Chekhov or Baker, we would expect to see fulfilled in some way in the end: Yelena starts to think about the doctor's tired, caring face; she knows Sonya is in love with him but she is starting to find him attractive as well. Vanya interrupts this pleasant thought with a declaration of love for her, which she finds unbearable. They both exit into the house. Baker's final stage direction of this act calls the reader's attention to what theater audiences would have seen all along: that Telegin, playing his guitar, and Maria Vasilyevna, making notes in her book, have been onstage this entire time, quietly witnessing, and doing, the work of living.

The play shows intimately how people living together exhaust one another and how the smallest acts of attention can be reviving. Act Two opens late, past midnight, in the dining room, where Yelena and Serebryakov have fallen asleep in armchairs. His blanket slips and he complains of pain and of feeling repulsive because he's old, prattling on about how he still longs for fame and success. He wakes up the house, refusing to see the doctor (who has made another special trip to the estate), barking at Sonya to get his medicines, protesting that he doesn't want to be left with Vanya but no one cares except Marina, Nanny, who comforts him, guides him to his room, and assures him she'll make him some linden tea and say a prayer for him.

Yelena is feeling the claustrophobia, even though the estate is large. She insists that Vanya stop complaining; everyone needs to come to peace with one another. Vanya recognizes this yet can't get the thought out of his head that his life "has been . . . irretrievably lost" (38). He continues to proclaim his love for her but Yelena is unresponsive. She leaves, and Vanya, alone onstage, reflects aloud in a monologue that shows him in an unusual moment of tenderness and vulnerability, recalling having met Yelena ten years earlier and regretting that he didn't fall in love and propose to her then, fantasizing that they would now be married and he would console her during stormy nights. Then, working himself up again about being deceived by the professor, he fumes. There will be no reflected glory for Vanya to bask in, no encomiums for his years of labor and sacrifice. He is just a fool.

Astrov, tipsy, enters with Telegin, who is playing his guitar softly. When Sonya enters, he remembers himself and leaves to get his necktie. Sonya scolds Vanya for getting drunk with the doctor and abandoning his work, which has all fallen on her shoulders. "I'm running out of energy, you know" (44), she tells him. This moves Vanya to tears, as Sonya reminds him of her mother, his sister. "Akh, if she only knew!" he moans. "Knew what?" Sonya asks (45). But Vanya cannot articulate it and falls into silence.

Chekhov's work is famous for its "mood" (as Meyerhold put it[30]) but it would be more precise to say "moods" because the play is shaded with so many fine variations of mood. (And indeed, a primary reason so many productions of Chekhov plays have fallen flat over the years is their tendency to play just one unending dreary mood.) Sonya calls to the doctor, who comes back in wearing a waistcoat and necktie, to ask him not to get her uncle drunk anymore. Astrov answers (and repeats this throughout the next scene), "Fine. / We won't drink anymore" (46) which is invariably followed soon afterward with his drinking. They have a cozy late-night snack together, during which the doctor opens up to Sonya that he has no personal life and that he feels such despair because he can see nothing ahead for himself and has not experienced love for many years. He is most frustrated with those of his own class, the educated people who are petty and narcissistic and ready to label and analyze everyone as "strange" who doesn't follow the mainstream. Because Astrov loves the forest and doesn't eat meat, he is considered strange. What is wrong with people? We have no connection with our natural home or with one another. This feels like an opening for Sonya to help him. A bit gawkily, she draws up the courage to ask him, in a roundabout way, that if she happened to have a friend who loved the doctor, and he learned about this, what he would think. Astrov does her the courtesy of pretending he doesn't know who she's really referring to, or perhaps he's truly obtuse at this moment, as he states, kindly but firmly, that this person would have to understand that he is not interested in love anymore. He then takes his leave.

What follows is a monologue from Sonya that Baker crafts in all its awkwardness of Sonya working through her feelings to herself. In this translation it doesn't feel like a setpiece, a monologue that an actor would "perform." Sonya reflects, "His heart is closed off," yet she is filled with joy as she relives the way his voice affects her, as though "he's touching me when he talks" (51). But she keeps running up against the painful reality of her plain appearance, especially because Astrov has praised Yelena's beauty several times. Sonya, so vulnerable and open, overheard a woman at church lamenting how unfair it is that Sonya, so kind and sweet, isn't pretty.

Yelena comes in. In this gentle scene, which closes act two, Yelena asks Sonya to stop being angry with her, that they stop being enemies. Pouring wine, she proposes that they drink from one glass, "So. I can call you 'ты'?" she asks (53). Baker leaves this word, the familiar form of "you," in the Russian. Curiously, it is the only time she uses it in her translation, although there are several uses of it in Chekhov's original.[31] Reserving it for this scene calls attention to the intimacy of this encounter and how Yelena and Sonya grow closer through it. Both let down their defenses, which opens them up enough to cry. They confide in one another: Yelena admits that she is not happy, and that if it were possible, she would want a younger husband. Sonya is dying to talk about the doctor. As Yelena reflects upon Astrov, she seems to awaken to her own admiration and attraction, telling Sonya that "people like him are rare, and they deserve love" (56). She wishes Sonya happiness but calls herself a "minor character in a play," boring and inconsequential (56). Sonya, caught up in her own reverie, is laughing, and their criss-crossing of moods leaves us in a powerful mixed-emotion space as well. Yelena wants to play the piano because she's sad, and Sonya wants to hear her play the piano because she's happy. But they can't, because music irritates the professor when he is ill. End of act. (Isherwood described this moment in the Soho Rep production as "the warmth that suddenly suffused the room goes out like a snuffed candle."[32])

Act Three opens with what would appear to be a major plot point that will incite some action: the professor has requested that everyone gather to hear an announcement. This is not picked up until seventeen more pages into the script, halfway through the act. Instead, we are returned to the internal conflicts of Yelena, Sonya, Vanya, and Astrov—to the love triangle (of sorts) of Yelena, Vanya, and Astrov, complicated by Sonya's unrequited love for the doctor. Even though we have just seen Yelena's beautiful, moving evening with Sonya and we might expect her, as a character in a drama, to have been changed, she isn't. As Chekhov's biographer Michael Finke writes, "These are not plays in which people grow and change"; instead, characters—much like human beings—"remain themselves. Situations do not change because characters are unable to; but when a situation does change, that too results from characters being unable to break established patterns."[33] Vanya and Yelena are still tetchy and bored. She complains that she has nothing to do to alleviate her boredom. Sonya, earnest and puzzled, responds with a list of things that Yelena could do, such as helping out around the estate or helping sick and dying people, though none of that interests Yelena. Sonya points out that Yelena's "boredom is contagious"; she has cast a spell on the household. Vanya jumps in, excited, telling her, "You have mermaid blood flowing through your veins" (61), tries unsuccessfully to detain and kiss her, and then, apologizing, leaves, saying he'll bring her roses to make amends.

The mood shifts as he leaves, becoming less restless and more melancholy. Sonya is agonizing over her feelings for the doctor but feels unseen, unnoticed by him, and senses her hope fading away. Yelena proposes that she intercede and talk with Astrov to find out whether the doctor has feelings for Sonya, insisting that the truth will be settling. Sonya isn't so sure: "Maybe not knowing is better. Then at least you have hope" (65). Yelena then has a monologue in which her own desire for the doctor—and guilt in advance for hurting Sonya—is unfolded. She understands how dull Sonya's life is but recognizes that she has become attracted to the doctor. Astrov enters. He is creating a map of "gradual and undeniable degradation" (69) that marks the destruction of the forest and the consequent decline in birds and water fowl and elk and goats and all matter of plants to make way for the building of estates. While people might take this as a sign of "progress," it is actually "the result of man's pointless battle for survival" (69). This speech, delivered in Act Three in a play by Ibsen, would be stirring the audience and signaling the message of the play. It may still be Chekhov's message, but he follows it with a deflation, a moment of miscommunication. Astrov looks at Yelena and notes that she's not even listening. Yelena, unlike Sonya, does not share the doctor's passions, but at this moment she is preoccupied with her own desires for him and her promise that she'd ask him about his feelings for Sonya. When he says—though after a moment of hesitation—that he is not attracted to Sonya "as a woman" (70), Yelena takes his hand and tells him he'll have to stop coming to the house. Her action confuses him and then shifts him into action. Getting aroused, he calls her a "little vixen" and a "wild little minx" who knows that she is the one he is always coming to see (72). Pressing her to set a time for them to meet outside the estate, he kisses her just as Vanya arrives in the doorway with a bouquet of apology-roses. Seeing Vanya, the doctor switches to talk of the weather—the classic form of evasion—then exits. Yelena tells Vanya that she and her husband must leave the house that day.

It is at this point that the professor arrives to make his announcement. Sonya is eager to hear from Yelena about her talk with the doctor but can see from Yelena's face that the news is bad, and throughout this next scene Sonya *"stands, her head lowered, suffering"* (77). Serebryakov has a grand plan: "We," he says (ostensibly meaning himself and Yelena, but it seems quite clear that he's really just thinking of himself) are not country people (79). But they can no longer afford to live in the city on the profits from the estate. So he proposes that they sell the estate, convert the cash into interest-bearing securities that will give them a steady income, and buy a "not-too-large dacha in Finland" (79).

Vanya, having already been humiliated once today by Yelena, has reached his breaking point. Serebryakov has not considered that Vanya, Maria, and Sonya all live on the estate (not to mention Nanny and Telegin) and would be made homeless by his decision. Vanya's own livelihood—his inheritance—was given up for his father to buy the estate as a dowry for his sister, and he worked on it for many years, *"like an ox,"* to pay off the mortgage (82). He spirals out of control, returning to his earlier resentment of the professor and embarrassment of having admired someone who isn't worth admiring. "You ruined my life!" he yells at Serebryakov (84). "I never lived!" (84) He mourns that he wasted his talents: "I could've been a Schopenhauer or a Dostoyevsky" (84). (At this moment, in his self-aggrandizement and shame and loathing, Vanya sounds like KJ and Jasper in Baker's *The Aliens*, written right before her *Uncle Vanya*.) Desperate, Vanya warns Serebryakov that he will give him something to remember him by, and heads offstage. The professor responds, to those in the room, with the harshest of assessments: "He's a nonentity" (85). Sonya is the peacemaker, begging him to have mercy and to realize how unhappy she and Vanya are. Serebryakov, more self-absorbed than evil, goes off to reason with Vanya. Sonya breaks down and is comforted by Nanny. Gunshots are heard offstage. Has Vanya killed the professor? Shot himself? Serebryakov runs in, followed by Vanya and

Listening to the Lonely

Yelena, who is trying to get Vanya's gun. Vanya shoots again at the professor, and misses again. Another instance of deflation after a moment of high drama. Vanya, mortified and desolate, collapses, and Sonya cries to Nanny as the act ends.

Act Four opens quietly, calming the audience as well as the characters. It is evening and the setting is Vanya's room, both bedroom and office for the estate, where the doctor also has a small work table. Telegin and Marina have the job of delivering the exposition; as they sit peacefully winding wool, they talk about how the professor and Yelena are leaving to go live in Kharkov and how their life will now go back to a settled routine. Vanya and the doctor enter; Astrov will not leave until Vanya returns a vial of morphine that he's taken from the doctor's bag. Vanya is distraught that his gesture with the gun was a failure; he shot at the professor twice but didn't hit him. The doctor responds drily, "If you didn't want to miss, you should've aimed at your own forehead" (94). He assures Vanya that he is not crazy, he's just a "creep," and that, what's more, "we're all creeps. Everyone in the world, behaving naturally, is a complete creep" (95).

When Yelena and Serebryakov leave, Vanya and Sonya settle into their work, doing the accounts for the estate. Marina knits; Maria Vasilyevna reads a book. The doctor won't come regularly anymore; they probably won't see him again until the next summer. The small household sits around the table. Telegin quietly tunes his guitar. The play ends with Sonya. She has a beautiful final monologue that, unlike her earlier ones, is not filled with ellipses and half sentences. It sounds confident and assured, although the content of what she says is deeply sad and its only hope lies in some relief after death. "We'll live, Uncle Vanya," she tells him (113). They will endure many days and nights and years of toil, working for others, never really experiencing peace, and then they'll die. Though when they die, they will see "a radiant new life, beautiful, full of grace" (113). In the background, Telegin begins to play his guitar as Sonya's speech begins to soar. "We'll hear the angels," she says, and see the "sky lit up in diamonds" and "watch all of our suffering drown in a divine mercy" (113). The play ends with her repetition of "We'll rest" (114).

Sonya's final speech "provides the play with a grand and desperate rhetorical flourish that is uplifting, or is meant to be, a big moment in which happiness and sorrow, the past and the present, are combined."[34] And yet it doesn't ring true. Charles Baxter reads Sonya's monologue as an example of "double-voicing," when a person is trying to "engineer wish fulfillment," to convince themselves of an argument by convincing another.[35] She is dejected but must find a way to lift Vanya's spirits and her own. How do we live without hope? The entire play *Uncle Vanya* has been exploring this, but has no answers for us. Baxter finds that as Sonya's speech gets carried away, it begins to look "more and more like a symptom rather than a statement." Chekhov, he reminds us,

> was a doctor, and often his characters act and speak in what I'd call a symptomatic way. It is as if Chekhov were saying, "Look. This is what people say and do when they're in despair. Don't blame me if this is what Sonya says. It's beautiful, in a way, and besides, almost everyone talks like this or thinks like this sooner or later. All I'm doing is reporting on what someone says in the depths of this particular condition. That's my task."[36]

At the same time, as Chekhov is reporting how humans talk and think, he is also noticing how humans *don't* notice one another: how, as Baxter writes, "the world is ending in one room, and in the other room, people are playing cards and getting drunk or playing the guitar."[37] "There's something eerily, preternaturally *contemporary* about the way" Chekhov's characters interact with each other, Roger Copeland writes for *American Theatre*. "Even when seated at the same dinner table, they rarely feel fully 'present' to one another. They all seem to practice the sort of 'continuous partial attention' that's become the new normal for denizens of the digital age. Chekhov's characters are never more alone than when they're together."[38]

Writer Kelly Younger has developed an exercise that he uses for teaching Chekhov's *The Cherry Orchard*, though it would apply equally well to *Uncle Vanya*. Before class begins, he slips a note onto one student's desk, explaining that everyone will be doing an in-class writing exercise reflecting on their own experiences of loneliness, and that in the middle of that quiet writing time, this student is asked to "blurt out so everyone can hear you: 'I'm so lonely. I don't have anyone to talk to.'"[39] The note also explains, "Expect the whole class to be surprised and most likely look at you"; the instructor, however, will "act as if nothing has happened, and let everyone just continue in silence."[40] When the student blurts out that they're lonely, and when the rest of the students ignore them, it opens the way for a class discussion about Chekhov's painful realism: how he writes characters who are at every minute essentially telling us about their loneliness but are ignored by the others.

Loneliness manifests itself in so many ways that we may not immediately recognize it as loneliness. When people are lonely, it may look like they are:

irritable	angry	depressed	tired	bored
needy	indifferent	horny	weepy	callous
resentful	manic	desperate	anxious	solicitous

In *Uncle Vanya*, every character in the play is lonely. And they are each lonely in their own way and for their own reasons. Chekhov and Baker don't pity them; that would be condescending. They also don't laugh at them; that would be cruel. Instead, they *listen* to the lonely, and call us to feel the great and multifaceted loneliness that is the human condition. Baker was attuned to this from the earliest moments in her career. As we will discuss in the next chapter, her Vermont Plays set off on a Chekhovian path.

CHAPTER 2
BOTCHED, BEAUTIFUL ATTEMPTS AT COMMUNICATION
BODY AWARENESS, NOCTURAMA, AND *CIRCLE MIRROR TRANSFORMATION*

Following Chekhov's attunement to "the everyday reaches of human speech,"[1] our inarticulate communication, Baker's first three plays—*Body Awareness, Nocturama,* and *Circle Mirror Transformation*—center on humans trying and failing to communicate with those around them, failing especially hard with those closest to them. "The way human beings speak is so heartbreaking to me," Baker says;

> we never sound the way we want to sound. We're always stopping ourselves in mid-sentence because we're so terrified of saying the wrong thing. Speaking is a kind of misery. And I guess I comfort myself by finding the rhythms and accidental poetry in everyone's inadequate attempts to articulate their thoughts. We're all sort of quietly suffering as we go about our days, trying and failing to communicate to other people what we want and what we believe.[2]

The plays derive their theatricality, their watchability, from, as playwright Alan Berks puts it, "simply our ability to be compassionate, live. Because few things can be as powerful as the compassion you feel for another person in front of you."[3]

Body Awareness, Nocturama, and *Circle Mirror Transformation* (along with *The Aliens,* which we'll discuss in the next chapter) are all set in a town Baker invented: Shirley, Vermont, and have thus become known as "The Vermont Plays." (Baker has said she actually wrote six plays set in Shirley but two have never been—and, according to her, will never be—released.) There was no conscious, overarching plan to create a series of plays in Shirley, she says; "It just kind of happened—I fell in love with this imaginary town and suddenly all these imaginary Shirley residents were crowding into my brain."[4] The town of Shirley is modeled on a group of small towns, known for their liberal arts colleges and town-gown tensions, their historical house tours and politically liberal "crunchiness," that Baker has known, including Amherst, Massachusetts; Putney and Brattleboro, Vermont; and Bolinas, California, and feels so true to life that people have gone looking for it on maps. Baker imagines her places and characters deeply and writes biographies for them before she begins writing her plays. In an interview, when asked to write the town's Wikipedia profile, she responded with details going back to its Indigenous roots (it was a "fishing place for the Abenaki tribe of the Northeast") and its colonial history: it was settled by the English in 1754 by "Lord Henry Shirley, the man who was eventually responsible for one of the first acts of biological warfare in North America. In response to various Native American uprisings in the 1760s, Shirley approved a plan to distribute smallpox-infected blankets to the Indians, whom he referred to as 'an execrable race.'"[5] The whiteness of Shirley, its residents' "embracing of diversity and fear of diversity," their "good intentions and weird intentions,"[6] forms a deep background to the plays that was mostly left undiscussed, possibly even unnoticed, in the first round of productions in 2008–10 but will be more observable for later readers, audience members, and scholars. Harrison Schmidt launches that conversation in Chapter 5 of this book, where he addresses Baker's examination of whiteness in *Nocturama*.

The plays are not directly linked with one another—there are no common characters, for instance, or shared incidents, although you can imagine the characters knowing one another, and a name is occasionally dropped in one play that seems to refer to a character in another play. Two distinct character types show up in each: first, a maternal figure who is a kind of "earth mother," spiritual and advice-dispensing (Joyce in *Body Awareness*, Judy in *Nocturama*, the offstage character of Sandy Janos in *The Aliens*— all of whom are mothers—and Marty in *Circle Mirror Transformation*, a caring stepmother and the leader of the community center Creative Drama class). And second, an intelligent but underachieving young man who is depressed and flailing (Jared in *Body Awareness*, Skaggs in *Nocturama*, KJ and Jasper in *The Aliens*; Schultz in *Circle Mirror Transformation* is an older version of these younger men). We can also identify a third common character type significant by his absence: there are no involved fathers in these plays. Jared's and Skaggs' fathers have long been gone from the family and seem to have left unhappy memories, and there's no mention at all of the fathers of KJ or Jasper; James in *Circle Mirror Transformation* and Gary in *Nocturama* are estranged from their children. Thematic chords across the plays resonate with those in *Uncle Vanya*: the characters fear that life has passed them by and they missed their moment to shine; they are not fully living. This emerges in various ways, from gently comic to highly irritating to quietly tragic. Like Chekhov, Baker has an affection, a compassion for her characters' human foibles—their addictions, irritations, pretensions, biases—and there are no heroes or villains in her plays. "The distinction between ordinary and extraordinary is bogus," Baker insists; "I want to erase the line between the two, between good-guy and bad-guy, because, in the course of one day, everybody commits beautiful acts of nobility and does something small and terrible. Every day we make someone feel wonderful. Every day we fall from grace."[7]

Ben Brantley describes Baker as "the aural equivalent of a good photorealist painter, someone who makes us see the quotidian in such heightened detail that it looks almost shockingly new"; she not only captures how people really speak, "her plays are shaped by an understanding that all conversation is a compromise."[8] Her portraits come from a place of *care* rather than critique or satire. In these first three Vermont Plays—*Body Awareness*, *Nocturama*, and *Circle Mirror Transformation*—we'll see a lot of quiet suffering, frequent echoes of Chekhov's realism. Baker's striking departure is that she tends to leave us with more optimism for her characters' futures.

Body Awareness

Quietly suffering as we go about our days, trying and failing to communicate to other people what we want and what we believe, could be the subtitle of *Body Awareness*, Baker's first produced play. Written when she was twenty-six years old, it was developed at the Bay Area Playwrights Festival in 2007 and had its premiere production, directed by Karen Kohlhaas, at the Atlantic Theater Company in New York in 2008, when she was twenty-eight years old. For a first production it was well-received, winning Drama Desk Awards for both the play and for actor Peter Friedman, who played the character of Frank. Baker has said that she wrote *Body Awareness* "during a pretty weird stage in my life" after a "very scary period of self-hatred and crippling depression"; it was her first Vermont Play and creating "this imaginary town and its confused residents was not only a real comfort and escape but also an opportunity to forgive—or at least laugh at—myself for being such a flawed human being."[9] There are autobiographical echoes throughout it in the sense that the issues the characters face "were also all issues that I'd watched my mother grapple with while I was growing up" and she had a sudden realization during the rehearsals for *Body Awareness* that "the play was about me and my mother—if we were a lesbian couple. But luckily I wasn't aware of that while I was writing it."[10] It's also a play that explores intellectual issues but isn't an "issue play": "sort of like in 'The Magic Mountain,' which is full of people debating issues and talking about philosophy, but because Mann loves them in such detail, his characters are complete."[11] Issues that Baker explores throughout *Body Awareness* include lexicographers' debates between descriptivism and prescriptivism, the distinctions between pornography and erotic photography, the power of the viewer's gaze, the Theory of Mind, and what it means to have empathy for another. Because these issues are so inherent to the characters' work and lives, and so effortlessly woven into the dialogue and action, the play does not feel bogged down by them but gives us a "deceptively light treatment of heavy questions."[12] If philosophy examines the problem of other minds, or how we know others have minds and can think and feel like we do, *Body Awareness* takes us into the problem of other *bodies*, or more precisely, *body-minds*, and encourages us toward "a more nurturing awareness of the bodies and souls around us."[13]

The play centers on a couple, Phyllis (a psychology professor at Shirley State College) and her partner Joyce (a high school teacher), Jared (Joyce's 21-year-old son from a previous marriage, who lives with them), and the houseguest who shakes things up among them, Frank Bonitatibus, a photographer who is visiting the college for Body Awareness Week. *Body Awareness* is a one-act play divided into fifteen (unnumbered) scenes that move among three playing spaces: in the center is Joyce and Phyllis's bedroom; on stage left is their kitchen; and stage right contains a blackboard, which signifies the college, where Phyllis is leading Body Awareness Week. It unfolds over the course of five days, and the blackboard serves as a way of marking the time, with the days (MONDAY, TUESDAY, and so on) written on the blackboard; scenes of Phyllis at a microphone, publicly addressing the audience as though we have arrived for the week's events, are interspersed with private scenes in the home. The scenes presage and echo one another, and over the course of the week we watch Phyllis lose confidence in her convictions.

The title of the play most obviously refers to the festival organized and led by Phyllis. More subtly, it also refers to the awareness of body issues experienced by the characters: Phyllis has a twitching eye; Joyce has gray crud growing on her toenails, may have been sexually abused by her father, and is excited but self-conscious about posing for Frank, whose photographs focus on female nudes, including young girls. Both women are concerned about Jared, who may or may not have Asperger Syndrome.[14] He is not aware of socially appropriate behavior involving bodies; at the end of the play he has exposed himself to a high school girl, misunderstanding Phyllis's reassurance that "penises are beautiful" and Frank's advice to be "sexy." More subtly still, the play explores connections between body and mind—how we know or don't know what others are thinking or what we ourselves are thinking.

Or, as Thomas Butler discusses in his essay in Chapter 5, what might be most accurate is to say that *Body Awareness* is a play about *language*: the language we use to talk about, think about, and judge bodies. Baker has a keen and funny ear for the hypocrisies and self-importance of liberals who are self-conscious about their language. Phyllis, a college professor, refers to herself as an "academic" but denies that term to Joyce, a high school teacher. There's a lot of talk about being "open," but Phyllis accuses Joyce of being "the language police."[15] Jared is terrified of being thought "retarded." A key scene that brings the language and body awareness together is when Jared, who is interested in becoming a lexicographer, explains the prescriptivism versus descriptivism debate to Phyllis. "Prescriptivism is the dictionary telling you what the correct definition" of a word is (the Phyllis type), while descriptivism sounds much like Baker herself: those who strive to be a "Totally Neutral Observer" (422), recording how people actually use language.

The play opens with Phyllis at the blackboard, which is marked "MONDAY." Speaking to the audience, she introduces the goals of Body Awareness Week; we will not just develop a greater awareness of our own bodies but of how we think about and judge others' bodies. The festival, which used to be called National Eating Disorder Awareness Week, is now a mashup of events, art exhibits, and multicultural performances to help students develop "gaze awareness" (372). (This will be explored and cause tension later between Joyce and Phyllis when Joyce decides to pose for Frank and Phyllis accuses her of succumbing to the male gaze.) Phyllis's introductory comments about judging others' bodies and being aware of the gaze will shift contexts from art to pornography as the scene shifts. The light goes down on Phyllis and comes up on Joyce and Jared at the kitchen table. After "*a long silence*," Joyce states, "We're fine with you masturbating, Jared" (372). Jared has been racking up expensive phone bills with pay-perview porn. Joyce is careful not to shame him even as she tries to educate him about the unrealistic images of women in pornography and the need to accept and connect with people in real life.

The gaze of much of this play is on Jared. Even though Phyllis has just counseled us against doing so, it is hard not to judge him. He is twenty-one but has the sexual immaturity of a young teenager. Joyce and Phyllis think he has Asperger's because he has trouble relating to people and feeling empathy, has an extraordinarily strong sense of smell, and is attached to objects and rituals for comfort (he carries around an electric toothbrush and rubs it against his gums). Joyce has given Jared a book about Asperger's; Jared returns the book, vehemently denying it describes him. He singles out an example from the book in which a person with Asperger's sees someone crying and doesn't ask them what's wrong. He states unequivocally that he would ask. Joyce reminds him that when he saw her crying he told her "to stop and make you a snack." "You were crying for a stupid reason," Jared responds. She corrects him; she was crying because he "threatened to stab me in the eye" (376). Jared fears that his intelligence is being attacked; he equates "Asperger's" with "retarded." We are shown that his intelligence lies in etymology; he loves thinking about words, likes referring to himself as an autodidact, reads the OED (large volumes of which are included on the set), and calls the audience's attention to Baker's exploration of the language we use about bodies.

Frank, the guest artist photographer, is staying in Joyce and Phyllis's home. When the lights come up on the next scene, he is standing in the middle of the kitchen playing a recorder while Joyce watches. (A review of a 2022 revival at the Portland Theater Festival with Whip Hubley in the role captures Frank's quality: "Frank holds space and power effortlessly, almost unthinkingly, quite in contrast to everyone else in the house."[16]) We're not sure what to think about Frank in the beginning—or, perhaps, until the very last moment of the play. He tells Joyce that "politically correct" people tend to be threatened by his nude photos; they assume "If a woman is naked, you're a misogynist" (392) but he insists that the women in his photos have volunteered to pose "to, uh, reclaim their own body image" (401). Over the course of the play, Phyllis will get jealous that Joyce wants to pose for him and that she seems to be attracted to him; Joyce will be flattered by Frank's attention, as Phyllis has not been noticing her; and Frank will give Jared some ludicrously bad advice for meeting women.

At first Frank feels like a warm and uniting figure. As they all sit down to dinner, he asks if they say grace. Joyce explains that she's half Jewish but not observant, and Frank hits upon the idea that they do a Shabbas. There are initial hesitations—Phyllis points out that it's not Friday, Jared declares "religion is stupid" (405), and Joyce isn't sure she knows the right way to do the Shabbas ritual—but to please their guest, they do so. (Baker has mentioned taking a graduate course called "Risking Enchantment" with Martin Epstein at NYU, who would tell the students that in their plays "THERE HAS TO BE A RITUAL AND THAT RITUAL HAS TO BE DISRUPTED."[17] All of the Vermont Plays include a ritual of some sort, which serve to pull the audience into attention.) They set up the ritual elements: Joyce gets out grape juice and pours it into wine glasses, Frank plays his recorder and sings the Hebrew prayer for wine. He asks if they have candles. Phyllis observes drily, "This is great. A goy teaching a Jew how to do Shabbas. On a Tuesday" (407). Joyce lights the candles and follows Frank's instructions for waving her hands over the candle and then putting her hands over her eyes, while Frank plays his recorder and sings another prayer, asking that they all sing the final "Amein" together. When Joyce takes her hands away from her eyes, Phyllis is appalled that she's crying, that she's been moved by the ritual. The stage is dark, lit just by the candles, and the ritual aurally and spiritually opens the space for the conversation to loop back to the play's exploration of our ideas of *seeing*. Frank encourages them to make themselves open to visitations and tells them about visions he had as a child. Phyllis dismisses them as mere dreams and Frank responds to her condescension with a note of his own that she is refusing to "acknowledge certain ambiguities in the universe" (412). It is a scene that drives a wedge between Phyllis and Joyce, as Phyllis is uncomfortable with any ambiguity in Frank's photographing women and girls, and with any ambiguity about Joyce's interest in posing for him.

In Phyllis's announcements of the events for WEDNESDAY, she introduces a psychiatrist and sex therapist who will provide a critique of the contemporary wave of feminism in which women are "trying to, um, reassert, or, um, reclaim their self-image and sexual identity" (420)—the "ums" in Phyllis's introduction feeling like her own thinking aloud and worrying about Joyce. As the scene shifts into Phyllis and Jared having a conversation in which he tries to prove to her that he has empathy (and therefore does not have Asperger's), he asks her questions about how hard it must be to be a lesbian, to have people make fun of her, and to not be pretty anymore. Phyllis tells him not to be cruel, but Jared is attempting to show that he sees what's hard about being her. To truly empathize with people, she instructs, "You listen and you try to see things from their perspective"

(424). We see Phyllis struggling with this herself. She has been to Frank's exhibit and was offended by it—but not, she insists, because Frank takes pictures of women; she would feel the same way if men were the subjects. Jared replies that men's bodies are ugly. Phyllis, thinking he's being self-hating, tells him "Penises are beautiful" (428). She means well with this statement but it will return to haunt.

How do we know something is beautiful rather than offensive? Does the intention of the artist matter, or is it solely in the experience of the audience? Joyce revisits Frank in the gallery after his exhibition and shyly flirts with him. She and Phyllis had argued about the nature and quality of Frank's work and now she's questioning her own experience of it. To her it was beautiful but she doesn't want to be wrong. What if it really is offensive, as Phyllis argues? She wants to feel secure that Frank is not a "sleazeball" (433). When Frank asks what would constitute sleazeball-ness, Joyce, embarrassed, ventures "Iguesslikeifyoujerkedofftothem?" Frank is disturbed by her question, not because she thinks it might be in the realm of possibility that he jerks off to his photographs but because Joyce would essentially be saying that "art is all about the intentions of the artist and not the effect the art has on the audience," which is what matters most to Frank (434). What Joyce seems to *really* want in her decision of whether or not to pose for Frank is his *attention*: she wants to know that he *wants* her to pose for him—so much of desire is feeling the other's desire for you—and wants to feel safe and held. (At home, Joyce and Phyllis want to instill these same values in Jared. He is talking about trying to find a girlfriend. Joyce suggests that he seek advice from Frank. Phyllis says that she can give him advice that's just as good, such as: "Ask lots of questions. Pay attention. *Like* yourself," and "Don't have sex just to have sex" [440]. "I want different advice," Jared responds [440]). Joyce decides to pose for Frank, telling Phyllis it will help release her from self-consciousness and discomfort in front of the mirror. But Phyllis sees it as objectifying herself and submitting to the male gaze. "You want some old white guy to take your picture and get a hard-on," she tells Joyce (444). Joyce responds, "The fact that he's white is irrelevant," but Phyllis shoots back, "No. Wrong. It's part of . . . of COURSE he's white. This is about POWER" (444). The argument reaches its height when Phyllis expresses concern that this is all connected to Joyce's father, who did "something really bad" when she was young (we never find out, and it seems that Joyce doesn't really know, or has suppressed the memory) and now to pose nude for Frank would be "compensating for some very, very weird shit!" (445) This leads to a *long, upset silence*.

Botched, Beautiful Attempts at Communication

Joyce hopes that having Frank talk with Jared will give him a man's perspective and help him mature. Frank doesn't think Jared has Asperger's, and at first offers him fatherly advice to help his mother around the house, before they move into discussion of body awareness and dating. It's a scene that's funny and sweet though also, in its frankness, a bit unsettling. Frank encourages Jared to be more aggressive around women: "don't be a creep" (455), he says, but he suggests telling women that he likes them, complimenting them, and inviting them out to dinner—advice that might work well for Frank but feels sadly laughable for Jared. Jared wonders when you know you can have sex with a woman, which leads into Frank encouraging Jared into "eating women out" (repeating it four times within these few lines), sounding both creepy and dangerously inappropriate with what we've seen of Jared. He gets Jared to hand over his self-soothing electric toothbrush because "It's not sexy" (456). "I thought men didn't have to be sexy," Jared responds. "No, no. We have to be sexy. You misunderstood me. We don't have to be beautiful" (456), Frank tells him.

Body Awareness Week has not gone as Phyllis hoped. On the last day, FRIDAY, as she stands at the blackboard, Phyllis is visibly shaken. The night before, she and Joyce had fought, once again, about Joyce posing for Frank; Joyce accused Phyllis of feeling like she owns Joyce. Now Phyllis addresses the audience, telling them she hopes the week's activities have helped them feel safer and more conscious—though not *self-conscious*, because "we want to feel *seen* without feeling *judged*" (461). This is a scene that Baker looks back on with self-criticism, saying that it uses what is now her "least favorite device" in theater or film:

> A character is making a speech in front of an audience and then in the middle of the speech the character realizes THAT EVERYTHING THEY'VE THOUGHT UP UNTIL THIS POINT IS TOTALLY WRONG, and s/he starts breaking down and saying things like 'I'm sorry, I can't do this' and then in front of the audience begins to stumblingly articulate his/her new more enlightened vision, which is also the vision of the author of the movie or play.[18]

Joyce had promised to be in the first row, supporting Phyllis, but she isn't. Phyllis is thinking aloud, making discoveries, thinking about Joyce's accusation. Is gazing always a matter of trying to own? If you're looking at something, are you necessarily "*possessing* it in some way" (462)? Returning to the prescriptivist-descriptivist debate from earlier in the play, Phyllis asks, "how do we remain neutral?" (462) Throughout the speech, her composure drains away as she contemplates the idea that the male gaze might not be a mere "evil, moving spotlight" but instead "our solar system" controlling all. Her certainty is shattered as she admits, "I want so badly for there to be a right answer" because "if there's no right answer . . . Why does the dictionary even exist?" (462).

The scene shifts to Joyce posing for Frank. Very slowly she takes off a few items of clothing, unlacing a shoe, deciding whether or not to keep her socks on, slowly unbuttoning her cardigan. She is uncomfortable and the audience is probably uncomfortable with her. We tend to be uncomfortable with disrobing in a play: are we watching the *character's* discomfort or the *actor's* discomfort with taking their clothes off? Right as she rips her sweater off and is onstage in her bra, Jared runs in, soaking wet and shivering. Her attention goes to him, caring for him, drying him with her sweater, holding him, while Frank watches. "I did something wrong," Jared tells her. As the scene shifts again, the time continues almost immediately; Frank is gone and Phyllis has returned home. Jared is wrapped in a towel and Phyllis is microwaving blintzes and questioning him about what happened and how old the girl was. We learn that Jared went to the mall and to the pond, where kids would hang out, because he wanted to talk to a girl. "How bad is it to show someone your penis?" he asks Phyllis and Joyce (471). Jared explains that he did not touch the girl but just exposed himself "literally for like a second" (471) because "I was trying to be sexy," heeding Frank's advice (472). The play shows us a bit of growth in Jared; he wants to admit his wrongdoing, displaying empathy as he imagines himself in the girl's position, wanting the other to acknowledge what he did. We are reminded of whatever happened with Joyce's father, which, it's implied, the father did not admit to.

Body Awareness ends with a charmingly imperfect reprisal of the Shabbas ritual, making do with what they have. Phyllis, handing out blintzes, remembers it's Friday and suggests they do the ritual. Joyce doesn't know the Hebrew prayers, so Phyllis pulls out a different Scripture: *Women's Bodies, Women's Wisdom*. Phyllis suggests that Joyce read a passage; "Pretend it's a prayer" (477). Baker shows through this ritual that anything we read can be a prayer—that prayers are found all around us in the everyday wisdom of life. Joyce reads a section titled "*Understanding the Bodymind*" about how the mind is not located in the brain but is distributed through all of the cells of the body. The end of the passage asks if we are prepared to listen to our minds speaking to us through our bodies. Jared quietly responds, "Yes"

(480) and waves his hands over the candle, imitating Joyce's action from the earlier ritual. It gives him a sense of nobility. What part of Jared's bodymind has been speaking to him, we wonder. What kind of awareness might he build in the future?

During this ritual, Frank has silently walked onstage. The other characters don't see him. Earlier in the play Joyce had asked him if he would consider taking a family portrait of her and Phyllis and Jared, but Frank had cut her off, saying it's not the kind of photography he does. The play closes with a "*blinding flash of white light*" (480), Frank taking the family's picture—what Joyce longed for—capturing them at a connected, intimate moment. Or is this a moment in which the male gaze is shown to be always present? Its ambiguity unsettles the Phyllises among us.

Today, looking back, Baker is very critical of *Body Awareness*. In its initial run in 2008, Charles Isherwood called it "not exactly a dazzler"; the description from Chris Jones of the *Chicago Tribune* was "solid but less than scintillating freshman work."[19] As a playwright she has developed beyond it, but it is finding new audiences and renewed appreciation, not simply as Baker has become more famous but also as interest grows in mind-body connections, revisiting the white male gaze, and especially neurodiversity. Not surprisingly, it has been a popular discussion-generating play in university theater department schedules. More recent reviews have centered on the character of Jared and actors' portrayal of a person on the autism spectrum—as voiced in a review of a 2019 revival in Vancouver, "Perhaps as *Body Awareness* shines a light on society's misplaced preoccupation with the perfect body, there is also a growing societal awareness that human neuro/psychological development manifests a range of diversity."[20]

Nocturama

Nocturama was written right around the time of *Body Awareness* and shares a lot with it—it feels as though Baker is thinking through the same issues and questions and creating another version of the same earth-mother and wayward, depressed son characters, here named Judy and Skaggs. Contextualizing *Nocturama* in relation to *Body Awareness*, Baker notes,

> That play ALSO followed ANOTHER period of crippling self-hatred and depression, and I had just become interested in how, even if you're a really well-intentioned depressed person, you can still really

screw up the lives of everyone around you just through the things that being depressed can make you say. I was also interested in what we all mean when we say "depressed."[21]

In an interview with Playwrights Horizons' Adam Greenfield, Baker notes, "*Nocturama* was a lot of fun to write, so of course it's the play that no one will ever produce."[22] This play in two acts (eight scenes in the first, five in the second) and four characters (Skaggs, Judy, Gary, and Amanda) is the only one of the Vermont Plays that has not yet had a full production. It was developed in the Soho Rep Writer/Director Lab, had a 2008 staged reading workshop at the Cape Cod Theatre Project, and a 2010 staged reading (directed by Sam Gold) at the Manhattan Theatre Club. An excerpt was published in the 2009 issue of *Vice* magazine and the entire script is included in Theatre Communications Group's publication of *The Vermont Plays* (2012).

The immediate advancement in Baker's playwriting between her first two works is in her use of space. *Nocturama* takes place in two spaces, which, the playwright tells us, would ideally overlap physically with one another on the stage, rather than be presented side by side or as two wholly different sets. These spaces are two houses: one is old, the house of nineteenth-century poet Elizabeth Collins, which is now a tourist attraction in the town of Shirley. The other is new and currently lived in by Judy and Gary (though it has a nineteenth-century history of its own, as it was the house of Winnie Rosebath, who had an affair with Elizabeth Collins's husband). When the audience enters the theater, Amanda is already onstage, in the older house, reading *Harry Potter and the Order of the Phoenix* (the fifth book in the series, when Harry is fifteen, a sullen and confused teenager transitioning into adulthood; although this is never mentioned in the play, presumably it was a deliberate choice). Amanda, perhaps in period costume since she works as a tour guide, could give the audience the impression of a time traveler—nineteenth-century clothing, reading a contemporary book. Or perhaps she would make the audience think they're seeing a ghost.

As *Nocturama* opens, Amanda leaves the stage and Judy and Skaggs enter, carrying duffel bags full of Skaggs's stuff. Twenty-six years old, he has had a breakdown after a bad breakup with his girlfriend and is moving back home. Not to the home he grew up in, however; he is moving back in with his mother, but she now lives with her partner, Gary, in Gary's house.

The scenes of the play move back and forth between the houses. In Amanda's scenes, she is speaking to the audience, who are imagined as the audiences for her tours through Elizabeth Collins's house. Often the scenes take place in the same rooms, with a character from one scene disappearing during blackout and lights coming up on another character in the same room, which is now, simply by virtue of a different character standing in it, a different room. For instance, Skaggs is sitting in the spare bedroom of Gary's house. Lights blackout on him, then come up on Amanda standing in that room, telling her tour participants that they are in the spare bedroom where Vermont's "beloved poet" Elizabeth Collins composed her work and, Amanda adds, "where she, um, ended her life."[23] Because it is mentioned several times that Elizabeth Collins took her own life and Judy is fearful that Skaggs will commit suicide, to which he frequently responds, unreassuringly, "I'm probably not going to kill myself" (225), the play hints that we may see Skaggs follow this path. He doesn't, however, and arguably Amanda is closer to a kind of death, a death-in-life.

A feeling of dread permeates *Nocturama*. It is thematically addressed through varieties of addiction. Skaggs is depressed and smokes a lot of weed. Judy's partner Gary plays a video game (called Nocturama, which gives the play its name[24]) late into the night, binge-eats, and formerly struggled with infidelity. Judy insists she's not addicted, but her highly-disciplined life and tightly-controlling personality (she's always trying to fix the others, labels the food in the house to keep Gary from eating hers, and admits to obsessive thoughts) suggests a kind of addictive behavior, albeit with healthier habits. She is a "shell-hammerer"; Baker's brother, writer Benjamin Nugent, used this word to describe Baker as a teenager, trying to deal with the depression in their household after their parents' divorce: "I think her impulse was to try to hammer at our shells, to get us to be depressed more openly. I still see that shell-hammerer in Annie's work."[25] Throughout the play, interlaced with the threads of addiction, is a hope for redemption through forgiveness.

Baker is interested in exploring what dread does to us. She will pick it up again in *John*, investigating the sense of holy dread. Here in *Nocturama* she parallels Skaggs's feelings of failure and heartache with the "Puritan Drama of the Soul": the intensive introspection and "compulsive self-analysis" practiced by the Puritans in preparation for the day of reckoning (233). The scene moves from Skaggs to Amanda, who is telling a tour group about the tendency in poet Elizabeth Collins's family to worry constantly, which can be seen as "a sort of *dying Puritanism*" (233) and that Collins (like Judy) is always seeking redemption but it is never enough. Collins's dread and worry can be seen in her poems, Amanda says, which "aren't so much spiritual quests, as endless, um, *disputations*" (233), an observation that echoes what we see in Judy and, metatheatrically, perhaps reflects on Baker's feeling about her own work. Does she initially think of her plays as spiritual quests but fears that they end up as disputations? (She has said in an interview that all her plays have their beginnings in spiritual longings.)

The main thread of the play feels like a dramatization of the Forgiveness Ritual led by Judy's spiritual teacher, Sumi. Much like in the "Puritan Drama of the Soul," in the Forgiveness Ritual, participants visualize that they are in a courtroom wearing a black robe and realize that they are a judge, and everyone in their lives is in the courtroom asking for their forgiveness. The participant can see how vulnerable and scared these people are, and the ritual has the participant (as judge) say, "I release and forgive you, because when I look into your heart I see that you are innocent" (231). "What if they're not innocent?" Skaggs asks. "Everyone is innocent," Judy responds (231). Skaggs is full of anxiety and anger; Gary furtively plays video games each night; Judy is judgmental. She does not want to shame the others, yet does. Of Gary's habit of playing video games until four in the morning she acknowledges it as a dimension of his addiction but also thinks "He should just try to change" (236). Skaggs, feeling the weight of dread of himself, asks Judy if she ever feels like she "might morally be like a really bad person?" (239) Judy's answer: ". . . No" (239). The ellipses show the slightest pause.

In Scene 5 of Act One, the worlds collide: Skaggs enters Amanda's space, walking into the historical house, to get out of the rain and out of Judy's house. Like Jared in *Body Awareness*, at first he struggles to see Amanda as a full human being who has a life outside of the historical home. He envisions her like a doll with the script of the tour wound up inside her, just waiting for customers to arrive "so you can make it come out of your mouth" (245). Though he refers to Amanda's life as "tragic," he soon reveals to her that he's in town because he had a nervous breakdown and called his mother to come get him, and then had his drum kit stolen. So he's back in his home town, "convalescing," but trying to be "open" about it, echoing Judy's language and the Puritan mode of confession (247).

In contrast to Skaggs's struggles with empathy or ability to imagine someone else's life, it appears that Amanda is hyperempathetic. Her eyes tear up in response to his words, though she says that she feels no emotion in connection with the tears. As we will watch Amanda stand apart from and not participate in actions throughout the play, it seems like this moment is introducing a significant disconnect between body and soul, that her body is experiencing something she is not acknowledging: heartache. In her first tour-lecture to the audience about Elizabeth Collins, Amanda tells us that Collins would scribble Latin phrases in her notebooks and even on the walls and in the floorboards. One of her most common phrases was "Cadere Animis," which means, "to lose heart" (223), which describes what we see happen to Amanda over the course of the play.

When she gives Skaggs the official tour, he is most fascinated with the story of Elizabeth Collins's suicide. Was she depressed, he wonders. Depression wasn't the word they used in those days, Amanda replies; Elizabeth had a "melancholy temperament" and was "obsessed" with her father, who died when she was nine (251). (Which seems to mirror Skaggs's obsession with his father, who we learn almost nothing about except that he is the first person Skaggs thinks of needing forgiveness in the Forgiveness Ritual. Amanda, too, has a difficult relationship with her father, who is both physically absent and, through frequent emails, emotionally needy.) Elizabeth Collins also thought that the inanimate objects in her house were alive and trying to hurt her, noting in her diary her fears that "the rocking horse" and the "heliotrope in the garden" are "crushing me'" (252). This is something that Baker has described about her own childhood and that will show up again in *John*.

Skaggs, when describing the tour to Gary and Judy later, is most eager to tell them that Amanda is black. He tells them:

The, uh . . . the girl who gave the tour?
She was black.
Which is kind of interesting. (253)

There's no mention of anyone's race in the list of characters at the beginning of the script, so for readers this is our first awareness of Amanda's race. (Audience members in the theater would, of course, see this immediately.) She is the only character among those in the Vermont plays who is explicitly described as black. Although it could be that James in *Circle Mirror Transformation*, who teaches economics at Shirley State, is black; when Skaggs says he was surprised by Amanda because there are no black people in Shirley, Gary jumps in to correct him, saying "There's a black guy in the economics department. James. His office is across the hall from mine" (254). Baker has said that in *Nocturama* she was interested in "the way liberal-seeming white people talk about black people when they're not around."[26] The white characters in the Vermont plays tend to think of themselves as enlightened and progressive in terms of race, but we see them get uncomfortable and stumble over their language when they're talking about black people. Judy says she saw a woman

31

at The Green Sheep coffee shop who was black. Gary disagrees with her, the woman wasn't black, which causes Judy to ask, "Then what was she?" (254), wanting to get her racially pinned down. When she meets Amanda later, she describes her as "*so* beautiful. I could look at her . . . I mean, she's really gorgeous. In this very interesting way" (317). Skaggs responds, "You always say black people are beautiful" (317).

As in *Body Awareness,* the scene shifts in *Nocturama* resonate with one another. Skaggs feels like he's not really living, describing himself and humans in general as "walking corpses" (259). Judy offers wisdom from her teacher Sumi that will echo the wisdom from KJ's mother in *The Aliens*: "Abandon Hope" (260). Then the scene shifts to Amanda giving a tour. She is in the space of Judy and Gary's bedroom, where Judy, Gary, and Skaggs were just having their conversation. She opens what we've seen as Judy's sock drawer but is now a drawer in Elizabeth Collins's home that held a box with her poems, most of which were about death. Amanda and Skaggs are both feeling a death-in-life. The scene shifts back to Gary, late at night, playing the video game Nocturama on his laptop. Skaggs arrives and argues with him about his lack of motivation to get a job and move on. Skaggs is terrified of failure. At the same time, he's filled with self-aggrandizement, that "the veil has been, um, pulled aside, and I'm seeing the world for what it is, and it's pathetic" (268). Everyone is pathetic except geniuses, such as "that Elizabeth Collins woman" (268), Picasso, and Elliot Smith. When Gary doesn't know who Elliot Smith is, Skaggs gets wound up and grabs his CDs, wanting to play him the perfect song. Gary is concerned that Skaggs is trying too hard to prove that he's cool, which ignites Skaggs's anger and inspires him to put on Elliot Smith's "Roman Candle," a song about Smith's abusive stepfather, which has an agitated tone and a chorus of "I want to hurt him / I want to give him pain," and sends the passive-aggressive message to Gary.[27]

Act One ends with a long scene in which Skaggs has asked Amanda to come over for dinner. The lights come up on Judy preaching to Amanda about her spiritual teacher Sumi's wisdom and it just gets more awkward from there, with everyone bumbling around, uncomfortable and quarreling, and Amanda unable to eat the dinner because Skaggs failed to tell Gary and Judy that she's vegetarian. (Judy pulls out some leftover takeout that is vegetarian.) Amanda is fascinated to be there, though, because Gary's house was Winnie Rosebath's house and Amanda wanted to see its interior. At one point she asks if she can look around, and we see her *"furtively"* open a drawer and impulsively take a *"tiny marble bust of a woman sitting on a shelf"* (282), which we will later learn is a figure of Sumi.

During dinner, the electricity goes out, and the rest of the scene transpires in just candlelight, a nightlight on the wall, and later, the blue light from a laptop. Using a candle, Judy demonstrates for Amanda her current training in EMDR, Eye Movement Desensitization and Reprocessing, essentially leading the audience in this ritual stress-reduction exercise. She holds the candle up, moves it back and forth, and instructs Amanda to follow the light back and forth with her eyes. You state a positive belief, relive a difficult memory, and reprocess it. They're all quiet, watching the candle flame. It's a calming moment for the audience as well. Gary and Judy go to bed. Skaggs and Amanda huddle over Skaggs's laptop, reading intimate emails to one another. Amanda's is from her father; he expresses being lonely and tries to make amends, though we never learn what happened. They read aloud a series of IM (instant messaging) notes between Skaggs and his ex-girlfriend in which they're having "IM sex" (306), which turns them on. Closing the laptop, they sit for a while in an *"excruciating pause"* then start making out (310). Amanda blows out the candle and they continue in the darkness. Suddenly, the electricity returns; all the lights in the house come back on and we see that Gary is standing there watching them. Although Amanda and Skaggs don't see him, the audience does, which would be a really startling end to the act.

Act Two opens the next morning. Amanda has spent the night, but Skaggs coldly ignores her until she leaves. His depression and disagreeableness is ramped up excessively and he fights with everyone. Gary tells him that he has to learn to be nicer to people and he shoots back that Gary is just "like a strange man who is living with my mother" (323). "You're a parasite," Gary responds (325), which is probably how the audience is feeling as well. Baker effectively makes us sit with Skaggs, a depressed, self-loathing, lashing-out young man, for far longer than we would like. She doesn't compress the scene to give the audience just a floating impression of what Skaggs is like; instead, the scene stretches on and gets uncomfortable. In what feels like the climax point of the play, Gary tells Skaggs, "you're not an artist" because Skaggs doesn't practice his drumming and doesn't even try to get new drums. Gary identifies that Skaggs is frightened: he isn't sure what he wants to do, doesn't know how to work hard, and has "no idea how to change" (326). It is catalytic for Skaggs. He goes to see Amanda at the historical house but is rude to her and suddenly gets sick—having a physical manifestation of his spiritual sickness?—vomits in a bag, then leaves the house.

Back at home, Skaggs gets an email from a friend who's just gotten a job as a production assistant on a reality TV show and is moving to Los

Angeles. This moment in the play feels a bit forced: an external plot point to get Skaggs moving. It's also when Gary, playing the Nocturama video game on his laptop, describes it in a way that sounds a bit too conveniently like a metaphor for Skaggs's life. In Nocturama you're stuck in an "underground world" (340) absent of light, but when you kill the sorceress, she turns into a little boy, who you pick up and cradle and "absorb his curse so he can live again" (343). Skaggs seems to be maturing; when Judy gets angry at Gary for eating her secret stash of chocolate, Skaggs pretends that he ate it. He opens up about missing his past life with his ex-girlfriend Meghan. Judy wants to process his feelings with EMDR. She dims the lights, waves a little green EMDR light, and instructs Skaggs to tell them about a happy memory. He then decides to call his friend and take the job in LA.

While Skaggs appears to be moving on, if not growing up, the scene shifts to Amanda, who is losing heart. She is giving a tour and narrating how Elizabeth Collins felt like "she didn't *belong*" (355) anywhere. Her description of Elizabeth sounds just like Amanda herself: "she spent her whole life watching everything without participating . . . seeing everything with this painful, um, clearness . . . and knowing that no one was really seeing *her* at all" (355). She reads a letter from Elizabeth about being at a party where people were dancing and how she just stood aside, watching, and suddenly smashed one of the jasmine flowerpots in the window. Yet "*no one took notice at all*" (356). This scene is visually echoed at the end of the play. Skaggs has left and Judy and Gary are visibly relieved. Gary and Judy have missed their ritual of dancing together; they had refrained while Skaggs was there for fear he would make fun of them. So they put on a *Spirit of South Africa* CD and dance to "Djembe Ni Bara," a heavily percussive piece. The dancing is odd and idiosyncratic and beautifully reconnects them as Judy "uses Gary's negative space" (361) to bring her body closer to his. It feels like the play is coming to a comforting close. Then Amanda knocks on their door to return the bust she took (which is when we find out it is a bust of Sumi), apologizing that she thought it was an antique and has been mortified about stealing it. Judy and Gary are unbothered. Gary, hearing that Amanda is interested in antiques, pulls out a little framed picture of "this very beautiful woman" (364) that they found while cleaning out the basement of the house. "It's a daguerreotype," Amanda says, "*her hands trembling*" (364). We can probably assume that it's a picture of Winnie Rosebath, who was said to be very beautiful, but it's never explained. Amanda stares at the picture, "*bereft*" (365), but the play never explains why she has this response. What is she mourning? Is she empathizing with the lovelorn Elizabeth Collins, who lost her husband to this beautiful woman? Does actually seeing Winnie Rosebath leave her feeling that a long and pleasurable search has ended? We don't know, but Baker's stage direction at that moment opens a space for the actor playing Amanda to find her own meaning.

Gary and Judy invite Amanda to stay and dance with them. Gary puts on "Welcome Children" by African Vibes and he and Judy dance. Paralleling the letter from Elizabeth Collins about being at a party in this very house, Winnie Rosebath's house, Amanda stands aside, watching, in front of the bay window. She *"glances over at the jasmine flowerpots sitting on the windowsill"* and touches one of them, then *"quickly takes her hand away"* (366). Is she afraid she'll smash them, like Elizabeth Collins did? While Judy and Gary continue to dance, getting *"more and more uninhibited and joyful"* (366), Amanda just watches, not participating, while the sun sets and the room gets darker and darker and then goes black.

How are we to take this final scene? I have wondered if it is a staging of the Forgiveness Ritual, with Amanda in the Sumi role, observing how vulnerable and scared Judy and Gary are, how they seek redemption from her. In Chapter 5, Harrison Schmidt offers the interpretation that Amanda is quietly resisting them. He writes, "Gary and Judy are oblivious to Amanda's isolation, and they cannot comprehend why their invitation to Amanda to dance with them offers her no solace. But Amanda neither smashes the flowerpot in resistance to Gary and Judy's white oblivion nor acquiesces to the invitation to dance with them, but instead forges a third path of quiet non-participation"; Schmidt defines "quiet" as Kevin Quashie does in *The Sovereignty of Quiet*, as "a metaphor for the full range of one's inner life—one's desires, ambitions, hungers, vulnerabilities."[28] Baker leaves the audience with a scene of tension, then, rather than the release that originally seemed forthcoming. Amanda, standing watching this white couple dance to African music, calls our attention to the awkwardness of their appropriation of it and their lack of awareness of how this might make Amanda feel. She stays on the outside, still not belonging—here in this home or, it may be implied, in the town of Shirley.

Circle Mirror Transformation

Circle Mirror Transformation was the play that put Annie Baker, and the town of Shirley, Vermont, on the map. Its initial run at Playwrights

Horizons in New York was extended twice, it won several Obie Awards (Best New American Play, Best Director, and Best Ensemble for the cast), was voted one of the top 10 plays of 2009 by the *New York Times, Time Out,* and *The New Yorker,* and enjoyed the distinction of being the second-most-frequently produced play in the United States in the 2010–11 theater season. This was the first play she worked on with director Sam Gold, who would go on to become her most regular collaborator. The way they tell the story is that they were looking for a project to take to the Sundance Institute. Baker had "45 pages of a play she was going to scrap," and wanted Gold to read them.[29] That was the genesis of *Circle Mirror Transformation.* She has described the play as "just me being like, Okay, what if I just write, not worrying about marketability or wondering if people will like this or pay attention to it? What if I write something that I, alone in a theater, would enjoy watching?"[30]

It was the play that introduced me to Annie Baker as well, and I like to think of it as the play that shows why everyone should study theater. As Jennifer Cayer writes, "Performing, as a primary technique of the self emerges in Baker's work as a redemptive means for humans to situate themselves as subjects and give shape to new worlds."[31] Baker is "explicit about the transformative promise of acting, as a profession and as a daily practice of willful unhinging from one's repeated self-performances in order to risk entry into a new identity, relationship, or affiliation."[32] While many of the reviews refer to the setting as a "drama therapy" class, my reading of the play is that the Creative Drama class the participants have signed up for is something more akin to "introduction to acting." That is what the character Lauren is expecting, and the others, too, seem to be interested in exploring dramatic expression and might be fearful of a group therapy session. The beauty of this setup, though—as anyone who's ever taken an intro to acting class can tell you—is that studying acting is studying how to breathe, how to be present, how to connect with your own body and relate to others' bodies. It is emotionally challenging, vulnerable work. The characters in this play "are not fools," Baker writes in her author's note; "They are noble everyday people who took this class because they wanted to add a little meaning to their lives."[33] She shares with those reading and planning to produce her script, "I am very attached to these characters, and I hope that you will portray them with compassion."[34]

One of the ways to portray that compassion is to heed all of the pauses and silences in the play. "Without its silences, this play is a satire," Baker writes; but with its silences it is, "hopefully, a strange little naturalistic meditation on theatre and life and death and the passing of time."[35] *Circle Mirror Transformation* creates compassion so intimately and effectively, Alan Berks observes, because it is a play written "in the first person," meaning not that it is autobiographical or that it has a narrator, but that

> everyone involved in the production is working from the inside of the story, seeing the characters as themselves first and the story as their own first, and telling the story from a limited and flawed and compassionate place with all the world's limitations in place and no judgment, a story-telling style that is more true to most people's actual experience of their own lives. One that embraces humanity and all its flaws and doesn't insist on "saying" something to the audience.[36]

Circle Mirror Transformation is set in a community center. The stage is spare: we're looking at a windowless dance studio with a wall of mirrors and a "big blue yoga ball."[37] (There were originally scenes outside of this classroom, but Baker eventually realized that "the fun of the play is the fact that it's confined to this dull, windowless little space."[38]) It takes place over six weeks, with the time marked by indications of Week One, Week Two, and so forth. Each of the six weeks is divided into several smaller scenes (mostly five smaller scenes, though Week Four has six scenes and Week Five has four), separated by blackouts.

The play begins in silence. Lights come up on the dance studio, with the five characters lying on the floor. At least fifteen seconds of silence pass before the first character, Theresa, speaks: "One" (89). This is followed by "*A long silence*" (89). (There are eight stage directions of "silence" in the first scene.) There is no explanation given at this point, but everyone who has taken an acting class knows immediately what they're doing: learning to listen to one another and to sense when it's their turn to contribute to the counting up to ten. These scenes of counting are used to punctuate and shape *Circle Mirror Transformation*; Baker returns to them four times. In response to the premiere production at Playwrights Horizons in New York, audiences said the counting felt very organic; in order to give that impression, Gold had choreographed it very tightly, arranging a series of colored lights that flashed on the ceiling to give the actors their cue to speak their number.[39] Similarly, in other exercises, although the characters appear to be randomly participating in theater games, moving about the room, Baker has the scenes precisely timed and frequently inserts stage directions such as "This should last at least thirty seconds" (94) or "About twenty seconds pass" (95).

In the character list, we get nothing but these people's ages: Marty (55), James (60), Theresa (35), Schultz (48), and Lauren (16). Everything else gets revealed through the dialogue—more precisely, through a series of acting exercises. In composing *Circle Mirror Transformation*, Baker said, "I knew I wanted the audience to learn about the characters through formal theater exercises" and for "information about these people to come out in the strangest places," and for us

> to know them all intimately by the end of the play, but without having heard any lines of dialogue like: "Hey, Marty. Remember when we fell in love 20 years ago in Eureka, California?" I also wanted to show how beautiful (and noble!) it is when people throw themselves earnestly and unselfconsciously into something, even if it's a therapeutic reenactment.[40]

In rehearsal for the premiere production, Gold had the actors play the theater games for real; "seeing all the strange and beautiful stuff that the actors came up with was incredibly inspirational," Baker said.[41] Some of their material found its way into the play, and she decided to have the actors actually improvise the title game Circle Mirror Transformation for each performance.

Baker's exposition is "feather-light,"[42] as each scene slowly unfolds the characters through the theater exercises. One such exercise is the act of delivering a monologue as another person, introducing that person with information learned, and observed, and intuited, by interviewing them earlier. Inevitably, these introductions reveal a great deal about the teller, not just the subject. Throughout *Circle Mirror Transformation*, much of the exposition about the characters is conveyed through these monologues. They follow a similar pattern of moving from surface observations to unspoken desires or pains: we learn that Marty hopes to leave the town of Shirley one day and move to the Southwest; that Schultz is still acclimating to being divorced; that Theresa doesn't want her parents to die; that James fears becoming his father; and that Lauren would like to stop putting so much pressure on herself. Stated so matter-of-factly, the desires and fears sound quotidian, even banal, and that's the point; Baker wants us to take the time to notice ordinary people in ordinary pain.

Although the exposition unfolds slowly over the course of the play, the character development and relationships—much like in such drama classes—happens very quickly. All five of the characters are on the brink of life transitions. Schultz, recently divorced, and Theresa, recently escaped from a bad love affair, newly relocated to Shirley, and in the midst of shifting professions (from acting to the healing arts) become attracted to one another. In Week One, Schultz tells her, "you have very alive *eyes*" (101). Theresa has a hula hoop, which serves as a conversation piece among the characters and as a focusing mechanism for the audience. When Schultz expresses interest in it, she raises the hoop and begins hooping. This goes on for a while, with all the characters watching and getting *"a little hypnotized"* (106). It is a moment always singled out by audiences, suggesting that they get a little hypnotized as well.

To take the character development deeper, Baker has them tell one another stories from their lives, listening for significant details in order to re-tell the stories later. Marty begins with a sweet tale of meeting James many years ago at a hippie wedding in Eureka, California. He had been the kind of guy whom all the women flocked to but he had chosen Marty. Theresa follows this with an odd, cliche-ridden story of being on the New York subway and overhearing a stereotypically Jewish old man surprisingly spouting anti-Semitic conspiracies. The class falls into awkward silence, not knowing how to respond. Although Marty had told them the class was a safe space for everyone to be open about sharing anything, the reaction to this non-PC story indicates that, like in the household of Joyce and Phyllis and other politically correct denizens of Shirley, there are stories that are not appropriate to tell.

An allure of a community acting class is that it allows socially-sanctioned touching. The others can guide you and move your body around when doing the exercise of Imaging, where one person creates a scene from their life using the others as set and props and characters. And in Week Two's game of Explosion Tag, Schultz, when tagged by Theresa, *"is thrilled to be touched by her"* (113) and we see how it opens him physically to flirt and show off: *"Schultz explodes: silently, beautifully, atomically"* (114). Lauren, however, the youngest of the group, is awkward and doesn't participate fully, though she watches everyone carefully. This class isn't what she thought it would be, and her question to Marty may be what some of the audience members are asking themselves: "Are we going to be doing any real acting?" (134) by which she means creating a play. Marty tells her that they *are* acting. When Lauren's dissatisfaction continues and she raises the question again later, Marty explains that they are doing the exercises to learn how to "be totally present. To not get in your head and second-guess yourself. Or the people around you." Lauren responds, "I want to know how to become a good actress." Marty assures her that this is what good actors do. This is the process.

The relationship between Schultz and Theresa gets complicated, offstage, between the third and fourth scenes of Week Three. In Week Three, scene I, before class starts, we see them kiss in the classroom. (Unnoticed by them, Lauren walks in, sees them, freezes up, and walks out.) Later in that scene, Schultz introduces Theresa via monologue, looking *"tenderly in Theresa's direction"* (125) as he speaks as her; in scene III, they are kissing and holding hands. However, in the following scene, Week Three, scene IV, there's suddenly a distance between them and a new attraction growing between Theresa and James, who are doing an exercise in which they repeat one word, trying to make themselves understood via tone alone. The gibberish language, untethered from logic, allows them to say what they're really feeling—to be emotionally vulnerable without fully revealing themselves. After at first repeating their nonsense words—Theresa repeats "goulash" and James "ak mak"—and giggling at how silly it sounds, Theresa's tone shifts into seriousness, with her subtext saying *"I feel incredibly lonely. . . . I lie in bed staring at the ceiling, and I think about couples and families, like you and Marty"* (137). James, because he is giving Theresa his full attention to figure out how to respond to her repetitions of "goulash, goulash," which have suddenly become serious, moves from thinking that he doesn't understand her to being pulled toward her. After *"A long silence"* both express the same thing:

> THERESA: *(I feel like you understand me)*
>   Goulash goulash.
> JAMES: *(I feel like you actually understand me)*
>   Ak mak ak mak.
> *They gaze at each other.*

When the class is asked what Theresa and James were communicating, Schultz responds hesitantly, with concern, ". . . They seemed very connected" (138). Lauren is definite: "They were in love" (138). This is met with silence—no one wants to affirm it, not Schultz or Marty, not James or Theresa—and the intensity of this moment causes Theresa to excuse herself and leave the room. Marty follows her.

This, so far, at the halfway point, has been the most emotionally powerful and revelatory scene of the play. Baker wisely follows it with a physical one, which allows the actors to process and discharge the emotional energy and invites the audience into an energetic mirroring of that release. They do the title exercise, Circle Mirror Transformation. As the lights come up on the scene, Theresa is swinging her arms back and forth and making a sound, "WOOP" (140). The others mirror it back to her. Then Marty calls out to Lauren to transform it; Lauren takes the gesture and sound and transforms it into a different gesture and sound, which the others mirror back to her. Baker notes, *"This is the only improvised part of the play"* (140), though she instructs that it end with Schultz taking someone else's gesture and transforming it into *"a form of solemn and silent davening"*; everyone, mirroring it, *"silently davens on their knees for a while"* (140). This prayerful rocking back and forth, involving the whole selves of both actors and characters, helps the actors metabolize the emotional intensity of the scene. It is essentially a form of movement meditation for everyone in the theater. Baker gives no indication of an intermission in her script, but if a production chose to have one, it would be at this point.

Week Four beautifully follows the intensity that can develop over a short period of time—and the cool-off just as quickly, while one still has three more weeks of class to endure the discomfort of seeing one another. As Week Four opens, we see Schultz arrive first; he turns on the lights and assesses himself in the mirror, then starts doing calisthenics, a sign of his self-consciousness and desire for self-improvement. Theresa arrives. After a brief, uncomfortable exchange of greetings there is *"A long, terrible silence"* (141). We learn that Theresa hadn't been calling him back. Schultz insists he's not angry but is just disappointed and needs someone he can depend on. When Theresa apologizes, *"Schultz convulses in horrible, strained, silent laughter"* (144). Theresa suggests that they take a break of seeing each other. Outside of class, that is. But they still have three weeks of class together.

As we can see in the scene which immediately follows, Theresa has become enamored with James. She is now presenting the introduction-via-monologue, enjoying "being" James, showing him that she knows him and admires him. (As Schultz had done earlier in his introductory monologue as her.) She tells the story of James heroically walking away from his bar exam, deciding he didn't want to participate in the flawed legal system. Becoming self-conscious of gushing too much about Marty's husband, Theresa shifts into introducing James's daughter, Erin, and his wonderful wife Marty. As the monologue unfolds, Baker shows us how studying acting helps us observe closely and listen for what is not said. Theresa shares that James has come from a family of alcoholics—then, showing James that she understands him and has insight into him, she says, as James, "I mean, I haven't said this," but he fears that he will become his father.

In Week Four, scene III, Lauren is in charge of directing the Imaging exercise, and in choosing James and Marty to play her parents, she ends up revealing the recent strains in their marriage. Lauren, not being experienced at how to do this exercise fully, gives Marty and James very little information to go on. James, as Lauren's father, is simply told to act like he's reading a newspaper. Marty, attempting to demonstrate to the class how you can take whatever is given, even if it's very little, and create a scene, tries to start a conversation with James-as-Lauren's-father, but the scene morphs into one about Marty and James. She tries to get his focus, asking him directly to pay attention to her, telling him that she's lonely. They get into a squabble, and she asks him why he doesn't just leave. "I'm stuck," James says. "Well, I'm stuck, too," Marty responds. The stage directions tell us James *"is in pain"* (151). The scene has crept into the reality of their lives. Is James trying to express that he's stuck in the scene, unable to improvise dialogue comfortably? Is he expressing that he's stuck in his relationship with Marty? The discomfort builds into a barely veiled discussion of James's shame over being estranged from his own daughter, Erin. Marty tells James that his daughter—Lauren in the scene, Erin in real life—needs his attention, that's all. James nods, and *"he and Marty look at each other sadly"* (153). When Marty turns to ask Lauren how they did with the scene, Lauren pauses for a long time and then says just "That was pretty good" (153). The deflation is lightly comic and relieving for the audience, who have just watched an intense scene. Lauren seems to remain in the world of that improvisation, though, as in the following scene, she listens to James telling Theresa more about Erin, watching him carefully, chewing her sandwich, while James reveals that he was unfaithful to Erin's mother and that Marty had inadvertently revealed this to Erin, who has stopped talking to him. We get the sense that that may be uncannily close to what happened to Lauren's own parents.

The play is well crafted to follow one or a pair of characters, then another: first Theresa and Schultz, now Lauren. After getting to know a bit about her stresses with her parents, and watching her gaze coolly at James, it is now her turn to be introduced in the monologue exercise, by Marty. Each of the characters has begun their monologue by saying something pointedly kind about the person they're introducing. Marty, expressing that Lauren can't wait to get to college and to explore theater and dance, or veterinary school, states as Lauren but editorializes as Marty that she is overwhelmed with feeling that she has to make all the big decisions now, though in actuality she has plenty of time.

As we watch the characters engage in the theater exercises, the timeless question is suggested: how much does art imitate life or life imitate art? In Week Five, Theresa and Schultz are paired up in the exercise of creating a story out of just two repeated lines: Theresa is to say "I want it" and Schultz is supposed to reply "You can't have it," then switch to the phrases "I want to go" (Theresa) and "I need you to stay" (Schultz). Does saying "I want to go" and "I need you to stay" *express* the feelings they are already having or does it *create* those feelings? When Lauren is in a role-playing scene with James in which she is Theresa and James is Theresa's ex-boyfriend, Mark, she is affected by James-as-Mark's abusive comments and tells Marty that she was really starting to feel bad—revealing, although she's not fully aware of it, that she was finally present in the scene rather than self-conscious and mentally standing aside. Throughout Week Five, Marty has had a tiny Band-Aid on her forehead; in scene IV we learn that she had fallen out of bed. Schultz diagnoses "night terrors," which can give a person mini-seizures, and wonders if Marty had been abused as a child because night terrors are a common symptom for people who've experienced abuse. In the moment it just strikes us as possibly intrusive and perhaps revealing something about Schultz's own childhood, but it is interrupted by James swooping in, exhilarated that he has hooped for over a minute, which signals to both Schultz and Marty that he was just spending time with Theresa, and that his exhilaration can be contributed at least as much to that as to his physical exertion. This makes both Marty and Schultz uncomfortable, which is only amplified when James unexpectedly swoops in on Marty to give her a passionate kiss.

The tension and pain between Theresa and Schultz culminates during the game "When I go to India I'm going to bring ___" in which everyone has to remember and repeat back what everyone else has said. When they get to Schultz, he rattles off the list but leaves off the item Theresa put on it, "a tiny velvet cape" (177). Lauren points out that he forgot it. "Did he?" Marty asks; "Who remembers?" Lauren insists he forgot, and neither James nor Marty noticed, which leaves Theresa to make the decisive observation that Schultz did indeed forget the cape, which will eliminate him from the game and banish him from their circle. He is so viscerally affected—unsteady on his feet, staring at himself in the mirror—that Marty decides to end the game. She has to quickly improvise a new game, which leads them into the most revealing trust exercise of all: their deepest secrets. Marty gives each person a scrap of paper and instructs them to write a secret that "you've never, ever told *anyone*" (181). For almost a minute the space is silent as each scoots away from the others and writes, then folds up and hands their paper to Marty. She explains that each will pick one of the pieces of paper and will stand in front of the group, read the secret silently to themselves, then read it aloud to the others. If they should happen to pick their own secret, they read it anyway; Marty assures them that no one will know. This sets up a scenario in which we in the audience as well as the characters are trying to guess which secret is connected to which person. The brilliance of Baker's writing here is that it's not entirely clear; the exercise serves to intertwine the characters and their stories and more deeply engage us in feeling for them and wanting to know more about them.

A couple of the secrets do seem to clearly connect to one character or another: James's reading of "I have a problempossibleaddiction / *(he looks up)* / . . . that's written as one word . . . / . . . with internet pornography" (185) seems to point directly to Schultz (and we might wonder, was *this* what caused the rift between him and Theresa?). Lauren's reading of "I think I might be in love with Theresa" feels as though it must be James—and the *"very long silence"* that follows it indicates that all the others feel that as well (185). But others are more ambiguous. Schultz is the first to read one, and says, "My father may have molested me" to which the group responds with *"A slightly shocked silence"* (184). Because Schultz just introduced that idea to Marty in the previous scene, we are likely to think that that is Marty's secret, that it awakened some new awareness in her. (Although it could be Schultz's own, or Lauren's, which might explain why she eyes James so warily after he plays her father.) Yet the one that Marty reads aloud also feels like it could be hers: "Sometimes I think that everything I do is propelled by my fear of being alone" (186). Although a match-up of the secrets and characters would tell us it's probably Theresa's, because Marty responds so tangibly to it—her voice shaky, her eyes glued to the paper, refusing to make eye contact with the others—it really feels like it's her own secret, and that she's revealing to herself how lonely she's been and that she's been staying, in her marriage, in the town of Shirley, just because she doesn't want to be alone. Yet the same could be said of all of them. Once again, Baker allows the actors and the audience to clear the tension of that scene by following it with a scene of release: they finally count to ten without interrupting one another. They were all present and connected.

As Week Six opens, we can sense immediately from body language and behavior that James and Marty have separated. Marty enters the room first, turns on the lights, stands around listlessly, then sits down on the yoga ball and bounces "*sadly*" (188). Then James comes in and they look at one another silently. He asks her how Phyllis is, which suggests that Marty has moved out of their home (and may make us wonder if she is staying with Phyllis from *Body Awareness*). Schultz arrives for the final week of class with a present for Marty, a Native American dreamcatcher for her night terrors. Later we see Schultz attempting to patch things up between Marty and James. He has been tasked with re-telling the story that Marty told at the beginning, about how she met James at the hippie wedding. Schultz recreates most of the story as Marty told it, then adds that James made her feel seen, and she knew they'd be together forever. Marty, feeling exposed and uncomfortable, tries to cut off Schultz's romantic ending. Theresa affirms it, though, by telling him it was "beautiful" (200). "*Schultz can't quite bear to look at Theresa, but he nods*" (200). He has grown bolder, more able to reach out and be vulnerable. They all have; that is what can be so remarkable about something as simple as a community drama class.

In the last exercise of the class, Schultz and Lauren are role-playing that they have met up again ten years from now and have to project what their lives are like. Both begin by projecting positive visions in which their dreams have come true. Schultz is happily remarried. Lauren has become a veterinarian and runs a clinic with her veterinarian-boyfriend. Schultz wonders what happened to her dream of acting, and Lauren starts to tell a story of acting in college, but can no longer see this clearly enough to articulate a vision of it. Instead, what seems clear for her in that moment is that her future lies in becoming a vet (204). Schultz asks if she's heard from any of the other classmates, and specifically if she knows what happened to Theresa. Lauren, aware of Theresa in the room and the awkwardness between Schultz and Theresa, provides positive visions: Theresa has become a massage therapist and married a good-looking and somewhat famous actor. Schultz responds that he's happy for Theresa; "She really screwed with my head. [....] But ah ... I don't really think about her that much anymore" (205). How do we take this moment? Is Schultz conscious of standing in the classroom right then or is he lost in the scene and truly looking forward? Is his response a way of getting back at Theresa or of forgiving her? It's beautifully uncertain.

As Schultz turns to Lauren to ask her what happened to Marty and James, the space and characters undergo a subtle transformation. The stage directions tell us: "*Over the next minute, the lights fade so that Marty, James and Theresa eventually disappear, and only Lauren and Schultz remain, in a spotlight*" (205). The scene shifts from being in the present in the classroom to a real-life future encounter; it seems as though we are now watching future-Schultz and future-Lauren. Lauren, possibly recalling James's detail from the first week that Marty loves the Southwest and has long wanted to live there, says that Marty moved to New Mexico. (Jennifer Cayer reads this scene as a "bold and loving" move by Lauren to imagine a future for Marty and push her toward it.[43]) Lauren also emphasizes Marty's care: that when Lauren played the role of Anita in her high school production of *West Side Story*, Marty came to see the show. Schultz then names what everyone is thinking, that Marty and James are no longer together. Lauren wonders, "This is kind of a weird—but do you ever wonder how many times your life is gonna end?" (207). That is, how many times you'll experience a full transformation in which it feels that a whole life has ended and a new life has begun, and the previous life doesn't feel like it was really real. Schultz isn't quite sure how to answer it but Lauren's questions are good ones about theater as well as life. As Cayer puts it, for Lauren, "the shifting reals across a lifetime are inevitable, everyday"; life itself, "akin to theatre games, is a series of changing roles, sets, and casts of characters."[44] And because Baker ends the play with Schultz and Lauren in this spotlight and never returns us to the dance studio, it makes us wonder about what is really real here at the end with the characters' lives. In fact, she increases the sense that what we've just been watching may have been Schultz and Lauren meeting again in the future because she suggests in the stage directions that "*perhaps, very very faintly, we hear the sounds of a street in Burlington: people talking, a car honking, plates clinking at an outdoor restaurant*" before the spotlight goes out and the play ends (208). As Matt Trueman writes, "Baker ends with a *coup de théâtre* of breathtaking simplicity: a drama exercise imagining a possible future cross-fades into a hopeful reality."[45] In this play, the town of Shirley "becomes a laboratory for life transformations, an imagined yet vivid place that prompts the characters, and potentially the audience forward into the larger world with an enlivened sense of the communal aspects of creative agency."[46]

It is on this note where Baker most diverges from Chekhov: her ending leaves us with a tempered hope for the characters' futures. Schultz and Lauren are projecting a rosy future for everyone in the class, beyond the pains they've all witnessed one another experiencing over the previous six weeks. Though this might be a kind of double-voicing, a speaking aloud to convince yourself of the truth of your hopes, unlike Sonya's soaring projection in *Uncle Vanya*, Lauren's and Schultz's stories of their own and the others' futures are modestly optimistic.

In its New York premiere at Playwrights Horizons, Charles Isherwood wrote that *Circle Mirror Transformation* "is the kind of unheralded gem that sends people into the streets babbling and bright-eyed with the desire to spread the word"; when he saw it, he "emerged with the same giddy sense of discovery, the same almost proprietary need to ensure that this small, quirky, immensely lovable new play does not go unnoticed by theatergoers in perennial search of fresh voices and boundary-bending experiments."[47]

In London it premiered at the Royal Court in 2013, directed by James Macdonald, and was the first play under artistic director Vicky Featherstone's leadership, with Imelda Staunton as Marty and Toby Jones playing Schultz. It wasn't produced at the Royal Court's usual space in tony Sloane Square, Chelsea but instead, as part of its "theatre local" project, at the Rose Lipman building in Haggerston, north London, an actual community center. "First impressions are not encouraging," Aleks Sierz wrote, describing the space as having "duck-egg blue walls, dirty windows, faded carpet squares, discoloured ceiling tiles, encrusted neon strips, cluttered notice boards." He added, "Don't go if you feel depressed."[48] But, as the play begins, "you soon realise that this community centre is a perfect setting"; *Circle Mirror Transformation* is "deliberately small scale and often consciously undramatic," but "still lingers long in the mind."[49]

One general difference between British and American appraisals of this play might be summarized in Michael Billington's observation that "I found myself admiring Baker's sensitivity while hungering for a bit more theatrical attack."[50] He lamented that while it is a "quietly perceptive" play, it is "an inward-looking play about inward-looking people" and that "while Baker tells us a lot about her characters, we learn little about Vermont," and contrasted *Circle Mirror Transformation* with Louise Monagahan's *Pack*, "which used a series of community centre bridge lessons to explore race and class."[51] Clare Brennan's review of the 2018 revival at Manchester's HOME theatre similarly critiqued that the play conformed to naturalism's "slice of life" but lacked its "examination of the social, economic and political forces that shape people alongside the emotional and psychological ones," and therefore the characters seemed "thinly drawn and two-dimensional"; what's more, "the focus on emotional entanglements explored through game-playing has a 60s-70s feel (RD Laing-lite)."[52] Matt Trueman, however, reviewing the Royal Court's production, concludes that *Circle Mirror Transformation* is "a play that leaves you determined to care more and to care better; to check your ego and donate your time and energy to others. Because, for all that Marty and the others mess up, time and again, they mean well and they keep trying. Kind hearts win out in the long run." [53]

It is easy to feel empathy for people who seem to be trying to offer something to the world but are stymied in their attempts, whether because they are awkward, or funny-looking, or uneducated—people who have little power to move in the world, people who don't attract the attention of others. The characters of *Circle Mirror Transformation* are endearing and moving. But it's much harder to feel empathy when people are irritating, even more so when they seem to pose a threat to others. In *Body Awareness* and *Nocturama*, Jared and Skaggs are unpromising young men who seem to have little to offer the world or their families, and don't appear to be moving on into successful adulthood. These figures are often the objects of laughter in popular culture, for instance, on *Saturday Night Live*'s sketch, "Old Enough! Long-Term Boyfriends!" about adult men learning to do things on their own, or in the *Clerks* films of Kevin Smith. Jared and Skaggs aren't played for laughs. Baker makes them real enough to be embarrassing in their everydayness, not over the top or silly. It is easy to recoil from them, but Baker gives them dignity by giving them attention, without sentimentalizing them or turning them into sudden heroes.

When I first read *Body Awareness* and *Nocturama*, I was distinctly put off by Jared and Skaggs. But as a result of rereading and writing about the plays, I stopped recoiling from these characters and started developing a patience with them, which eventually softened into, if not fully affection, compassion. (By the time I read *The Aliens*, I found KJ and Jasper both moving and funny.) It made me wonder, how much of empathy is a form of patience with people? An ability and willingness to give them time and space? At its etymological root (as Jared could tell us), patience is connected with suffering, a willingness to suppress our restlessness or annoyance when confronted with delay. What happens when audience members leave a performance feeling the accomplishment of having been patient? It takes working through the restlessness and the anger and the slog of boredom (i.e., when you are aware that you are enduring something and you've made a decision to do so) and only then a clearing where you no longer feel angry or annoyed, but you're not indifferent. You feel an equanimity that is pleasurable. You can let the other person be themselves without worrying about yourself. You feel open enough to let them have that space. You feel *curious* but with a neutral calm, like Phyllis's note about the neutral observer. Part of the pleasure experienced is having attained a spiritual accomplishment, as in a contemplative practice. In the plays which follow these, Baker ramps up the challenge for audiences to sit in contemplation of—and with—characters who don't seem to be doing much of anything, as we'll see in the next chapter on Baker's final Vermont Play, *The Aliens*, and her Pulitzer Prize–winning follow-up, *The Flick*.

CHAPTER 3
THE PRESENCE OF SILENCE
THE ALIENS AND *THE FLICK*

After reviving naturalism in the first three Vermont Plays and *Uncle Vanya*, Baker ventured further into exploring what is *inside* the moments—not just observing but dwelling with her characters, listening for "the presence of everything."[1] She followed her affection for Thomas Mann's statement in his preface to *The Magic Mountain* that we take the time to tell the whole story and be "unafraid of the odium of appearing too meticulous," for "only thoroughness can be truly entertaining."[2] *The Aliens* (the fourth of the Vermont Plays) and *The Flick* give meticulous attention to what, to many audiences, felt like nothing: the everyday conversation and not-conversation between unemployed men hanging out behind a coffee shop and low-wage employees cleaning a movie theater. The plays received a lot of notoriety for their frequent, and long, silences, though in Baker's mind, "there's actually very little ACTUAL silence" in her work; there are "a lot of moments of not-talking," she concedes—and these tend to be her favorite moments—but if we listen we'll realize "there's a whole symphony happening" onstage.[3] (Her use of the word "symphony," and her score-like writing, attentive to each moment onstage, calls to mind John Cage's famous composition "4'33", three movements of different lengths, which sounded to its first audiences like nothing. As Arthur C. Danto puts it, "it's often been proposed that Cage was teaching his audience to listen to silence," but he was actually trying to get them to "listen to the sounds of life."[4])

The silence in Baker's plays isn't a "portentous, Pinter-esque silence," laden with subtext ("although that can be great too," she says), but just "the absence of talk."[5] Nor is she conceptually exploring stage silence in an avant-garde fashion. Instead, she's attuning herself, and the audience, to "the things we do when we're not talking. Someone jiggling their knee. Someone staring into the sun for a full minute and humming. Someone flossing alone at night in their bathroom."[6] She laments that playwrights spend little time exploring these actions onstage "because people are so freaked out about holding the attention of an audience who would rather be at home watching action movies and sitcoms. But as an audience member, there's something really exciting to me about watching someone scratch their elbow onstage and not say anything. Partly because a lot of audience members get weirdly uncomfortable and tense when that happens. I had no idea you could alienate people so much just by being quiet. Some audience members really start to freak out. And then other people love it. That's really interesting to me—when half the audience is going crazy and half the audience is enthralled."[7]

Audiences to both *The Aliens* and *The Flick* come around, again and again, to the plays' strains on our attention; these are long, challenging plays that demand the audience's sustained attention. In her fans, this attention inspires a kind of devotion, in the sense that people are devoted to them, enthusiastic about them, but also in the sense that the plays are a devotional *practice*. It reminds me of Simone Weil's famous insight: "Attention, taken to its highest degree, is the same thing as prayer. It presupposes faith and love"—"Absolutely unmixed attention is prayer."[8] Tim Sanford, artistic director of Playwrights Horizons, described audiences of *The Flick* "imbued with rapture for a theater experience unlike any they had experienced and for a production that stayed with them for days, even weeks afterwards."[9] Baker's plays, filled with the sounds of everyday life, challenge assumptions about what is important to listen to. The slackers sitting behind the coffee shop and low-level employees of a movie theater sweeping up popcorn are easily overlooked and disregarded. But if you listen carefully, you may find yourself "watching the loneliness puddle around you like a pleated skirt, the prolonged silences stretching before you with no actor or playwright prompted to fill them or distract you from that emptiness of sound and motion. We bear the characters' isolation and our own—like mirror images this aloneness reflects back and forth between actors and audience."[10] It may seem like little is going on in *The Aliens* and *The Flick,* but if you're attentive, you'll notice how Baker entices viewers into practicing the prayerful art of listening to the presence of everything.

The Aliens

New York Times critic Charles Isherwood, naming *The Aliens* his "Play of the Year" for 2010 because of its moving portrait of friendship, noted that her "theatrical metabolism will strike theatergoers attuned to the Martin McDonagh school of snappy sensation as virtually moribund. The scenes in her plays move at the loping pace of real life, not the choppy, artificial speed we're used to seeing presented as entertainment."[11] *The Aliens* premiered in 2010 at Rattlestick Playwrights Theater in New York, with Sam Gold again directing. It won the 2010 Obie Award for Best New Play (alongside *Circle Mirror Transformation*). It was also the first of Baker's plays to be produced in the UK; its London premiere was later that same year, in September 2010, at the Bush Theatre, directed by Peter Gill. Seen from across the Atlantic, *The Aliens* looked like a commentary on the United States. The Bush Theatre's promotional materials described the play as putting "modern day America under the microscope to ask what happened to the generation who never grew up."[12] In 2011 *The Aliens* played in Russia, in Moscow, Omsk, and St. Petersburg, and was roundly praised, with Annie Baker called "the American Chekhov" for her portrait of ordinary unremarkable people.[13]

This two-act play takes place on a very spare set: the back patio of The Green Sheep coffee house in Shirley, Vermont, where we see just a few plastic chairs, a picnic table, and recycling and trash bins. It's a small cast of three characters: Jasper, aged thirty-one, "simmers with quiet rage"; KJ, aged thirty, sports a beard and man bun and drinks mushroom tea; and Evan, aged seventeen, is in a "constant state of humiliation."[14] Baker invites her audience to sit with these young men and watch the time pass along with them. "At least a third—if not half—of this play is silence," she notes, and adds that "pauses" should be "at least three seconds long" while "silences" should last "from five to ten seconds" (3). Charles Kruger calls it an "extraordinary risk" that Baker writes these "intensive silences" into the play—and the effect is "amazing. We seem to be experiencing KJ and Jasper's relationship in real time, not theatrical time at all."[15] Martha Schabas observes that "Baker's writing may give the illusion of coasting on its long mumbling tangents; in fact, it's asking that the actors be so specific in their interpretations, and so emotionally tuned in, that volumes are spoken when nothing is said."[16] The play opens with *"A long silence"* (3) during which Jasper and KJ are sitting at the picnic table, Jasper smoking, KJ drinking a to-go cup of tea. KJ and Jasper are men who haven't made anything of themselves. They are who, parents fear, Skaggs of *Nocturama* and Jared of *Body Awareness* will become. KJ describes having studied philosophy and math at the University of Vermont, but dropped out. Jasper never finished high school but is writing a novel. These are men Baker has known; she's mentioned having spent a lot of time during her high school years hanging out at just such a coffee shop in Amherst, drinking tea and listening, and Christopher Soden notes how Baker has closely observed "certain aspects of male culture, the sparse verbal exchanges, the intense demand for respect, the absence of extravagant feeling."[17]

After the long silence at the beginning of the play, KJ begins singing to himself, a composition of his own about burning out rather than fading away, which finishes with "TRIPLE DIMENSIONAL SUPERSTAR" (5). The dialogue initially sounds very insubstantial as KJ asks Jasper about a mutual friend, Orion, who lives on a wind farm, but throughout this exchange KJ is observant and alert to Jasper's mood, and asks him if he wants to talk about it. Jasper's responses come slowly, separated by pauses: "Andrea?" "Not really." [. . . .] "It's sad. I mean, it's really fucking sad" (8). Jasper's girlfriend has evidently broken up with him but KJ doesn't try to pry or fix it. "She was into Power," Jasper tells him; "her thing was like [. . . .] that she'd like 'lost her personality.' In the shadow of my . . ." (9). KJ quietly nods and then looks at the sun, trying to sneeze, and the two sit in silence. The energy shifts when *"Jasper suddenly kicks a chair over. It makes a terrible noise"* (10). "Whoa," KJ responds, but doesn't criticize him or comment on it or mock or tease him for his outburst. The door opens and Evan comes out. He has been sent to tell the guys that they are not allowed to sit out back. They ignore him, saying that they know the manager and can sit there. It's Evan's second day at work and he's afraid of getting into trouble, but he finally goes back inside. Jasper puts the chair he kicked back in its place, and sits down. And that's the action of the first scene.

The second scene opens in a similar way: KJ is sitting on the patio, concocting his mushroom tea. Evan brings the garbage out and dumps it in the bin. KJ encourages him to take a sip of the tea, which Evan—trusting, and not knowing what it is—does. KJ calls Jasper on his cell phone, wondering where he is. Listening to him on the other end, he responds, "You are on fire, my friend" (16). In response to Jasper's manic energy, to his creative juices flowing? We start to hear Jasper from offstage, getting closer to the patio, talking on his own phone, then he arrives, still telling KJ about his new development in his novel in which his protagonist goes to California and meets Henry Miller, who will now be a character in it. We continue to get signs of Jasper's simmering rage, as the stage directions indicate that he's wired, smoking *"agitatedly"* (17). Yesterday Jasper had not wanted to talk about his girlfriend; today it comes pouring out that she called him last night to tell him she's been dating someone else. Then he tells KJ that he remembered something that KJ's mother, Sandy Jano (Kevin is Kevin Jano), once told him. Jasper had been sleeping on floors, and she told him that his "in-between state" could be powerful. She said, "the state of just having lost something is like the most enlightened state in the world" (21). (Readers will recall Judy in *Nocturama* talking about the importance of being able to Abandon Hope.) After his breakup phone call Jasper felt both "stabbed" and "*euphoric*" (21), and it inspired him to move his novel's protagonist from Iowa City to California. Jasper feels this as momentous but KJ seems unfazed, disappointing him. Evan comes out with a final bag of trash to deposit on his way out of work. Jasper offers him a cigarette, and their friendship begins.

KJ and Jasper used to have a band. Jasper wanted to name it The Aliens, "After the Bukowski poem" (29), he tells Evan. Baker said that at one point she contemplated including the poem in the play; its speaker sounds very much like Jasper and KJ. The voice is at first cavalier, saying, "You may not believe it / but there are people / who go through life with / very little / friction or / distress," and only later reveals the despair beneath his cool exterior: "but I am not one of / them."[18] Leaving the poem out of the play, however, has us discover this for ourselves.

The following day will be the Fourth of July. Even though Evan doesn't have any plans, noting "Sometimes the Fourth, like, depresses me" (30), he responds favorably to Jasper and KJ's invitation to join them for their gathering—until he discovers that it will be held right there, on the back patio. Evan nervously tries to enforce the no-loitering rule; it competes with his gratitude at being included in the older guys' plans and his desire to hang out with them, and finally the tension is too much and he exits.

KJ and Jasper are highly attuned to one another's moods and psychic states. Jasper, watching KJ lying on his back humming, asks him if he's "freaking out" and urges him to tell Jasper if he starts "feeling weird again" (33). KJ, thinking that it is Jasper who's feeling weird, tells him he's "projecting" (33). At this, Jasper "*nods bleakly*" (33). There are small hints like this one that both Jasper and KJ have pasts of substance abuse and possibly depression or other mental illness. KJ watches Jasper's chain-smoking, and Jasper monitors KJ's substance use, pouring out his psilocybin tea and confiscating the peppermint Schnapps that Evan brings to the Fourth of July party, explaining that they can't have KJ drinking, for the last time he did so, he zapped people. Demonstrating this, Jasper "*makes a little beak with his fingers and zaps Evan with it on his arm*" saying "Zhoop. Zhoop. Zhoop. Zhoop" (43). It makes KJ angry but we can also see his awareness that Jasper is caring for him.

Act One ends with the Fourth of July gathering. During the scene, the sky turns dark, moving into night. When the scene opens, Jasper is reading from his novel, while KJ listens, fully engrossed. The novel is sensually detailed and erotic in the vein of Jasper's heroes, Henry Miller and Charles Bukowski. Though his prose sounds derivative of those authors, Jasper is earnest and the writing is good enough for the audience to take it, and him, seriously. He reads a couple of long passages, and it makes a reader of the script realize that there is a lot of listening in this play. Of course an audience is always listening, but Baker has us pay attention to how the characters listen to one another, even when neither is talking, and the audience is implicitly asked to pay quiet attention to them in silence and to listen to Jasper's novel. Evan arrives in the middle of Jasper's reading and he too quietly listens, standing near the edge of the patio. In this section of the novel, Jasper's protagonist has set off on the road and as he passes farms and cornfields and truck stops and crosses state line after state line, he has a realization that "most of America looked like . . . most of America" (37). This makes "his dream of California" begin to fade away. He starts to doubt the country as a place of dreams, and starts to doubt what he's always been told about himself, that he's a "*Genius*" (38). Being considered a genius has put an unbearable weight on him, burdening him with the loneliness of carrying expectations. Jasper's novel ends with an image of God waiting on him "impatiently," asking:

> *When's the new painting gonna be finished, son?*
> *When you gonna stop fucking around?* (38)

KJ and Evan sit very still. Then KJ jumps up and "*does a little prayer jog around the recycling bin*" while Jasper "*tries not to beam*" (38–39).

Like Uncle Vanya in his cry that he could have been a Schopenhauer or a Dostoevsky had he had the time and resources, Jasper and KJ express a mix of self-aggrandizement and self-loathing that they are geniuses who haven't lived up to their potential. The play shows us that Jasper is talented and KJ is intelligent and that, in other circumstances, they might have been conventionally successful men. Yet there's also a sense that, in their minds, if they can't be geniuses, they can't be anything. There's no place for them in the middle of ordinary life.

Evan has brought sparklers for the party. "SHPAHKLAHS!" Jasper responds, then apologizes if it sounds like he's doing imitations of Jewish people, assuring Evan, "I have no problems with Jews" (44). Jasper explains that KJ's mother once had a theory that KJ might have Jewish ancestry, though she was wrong, and that he, Jasper, is "one-sixteenth Cherokee"

(44). The real revelation is that "KJ here has dreams that he's black" (45), that he hangs out with black people and feels "really, um, accepted—" (45). This makes KJ smile, despite himself. Jasper continues that in the dream KJ realizes that not only do they all "really like" him but he himself is black: "I was one of them" (45). "And I was really happy," KJ adds (45). Both KJ and Jasper giggle at this. Evan finds it weird. Desires of this sort are threaded through the Vermont Plays, where we see white people wanting to be comfortable around black people and to be accepted by them. Yet, from what we can tell from Amanda in *Nocturama*, Shirley would be an uncomfortable place for a black person to live.

KJ and Jasper sing a song from their previous band days. (The songs for the script were written by the actors who originated the roles of KJ and Jasper, Michael Chernus and Erin Gann, along with Patch Darragh, who played Jasper in the first staged reading of *The Aliens*.) As the sky darkens, fireworks go off in the distance, KJ dances with a sparkler, and for a moment, this odd space behind the coffee shop feels magical, and Evan feels like he belongs.

The most dramatic piece of action in this play happens offstage, between the acts. When Act Two opens a week later, Jasper has died, but Baker withholds this information for eighteen pages of the script, until Act Two, scene 3, when it is revealed that Jasper died of a heroin overdose. (KJ says it was an accident; it's never made entirely clear whether that is true.) What we see at the top of Act Two is KJ sitting by himself, drinking tea and thinking. Baker gives this time onstage—*"at least twenty seconds"* (51)—and then we hear KJ thinking aloud, "If P then Q" (51), before another stretch of silence as he continues thinking. (Baker had been reading Wittgenstein with Mac Wellman, which inspired the character of KJ: "The line between a really rigorous tractatus and a freshman in college going, 'What if *your* red isn't my red?'—it reminded me of all these townies with shrooms I had known," she says.[19]) Evan enters, excited to tell the guys that he met a girl at music camp and experienced his first kiss. He is curious to know about KJ's "first . . . whatever? Kiss. Or—" (53). KJ tells him two stories: one about an older girl trying to give him a blowjob at an Allman Brothers concert, and another about having sex with a younger girl in high school, then cheating on her and, when he told her, watching her as she "crumpled" to the ground (54). Hearing this, Evan wonders when KJ's first *serious* girlfriend was; after two separate stage directions for *"weird pause,"* we get the impression that KJ has never had a serious girlfriend and that the friendship with Jasper has been the most substantial and important relationship of his life.

Scene 3 is the scene of revelation. We get a hint that something is amiss because KJ is now lying across two plastic chairs that have empty mini liquor bottles under them. When Evan comes out, heading home for the evening, he wakes KJ up and KJ asks him, "Do you like Jasper more than me?" (64). He is still speaking of Jasper in the present tense, not the past. KJ still tells Evan, when asked where Jasper is, that he's sick, but now adds, "I wanna kill myself" (64). This gets Evan to change plans: to call his mother and tell her he'll be late for dinner, and to stay with KJ. He's irritated with his mother's overbearing care when she asks him what he wants for dinner but then tells him why they can't have that item. This leads KJ to share an intimate story of when he was about five years old and was obsessed with a word, constantly repeating it: *"Ladder. Ladder. Ladder"* (66). His mother, Sandy Jano, didn't get upset with him; she understood his need to say it, that there was something he was trying to express through it, so one night, as he was whispering it to himself, she sat in bed with him and told him to just say that word as long as he wanted and she would sit with him throughout. KJ begins repeating the word, "Ladder," over and over, 127 times. It is mesmerizing, like a chant. About two-thirds of the way through, he begins to cry. Then, after *"A long pause,"* he tells Evan that Jasper died a week ago. Evan, in disbelief, anger and frustration, pushes the recycling bin until it topples over. It is *"very, very heavy"* and takes him a long time. KJ (and the audience) watch and wait. After Evan goes home, KJ puts the recycling bin back up, which likewise takes a long time. These long stretches also wisely give the audience time to process this new information and loss. The long silences give Jasper's death dignity.

We see Jasper's effect on Evan in the next scene, which opens upon Evan furtively smoking a cigarette on the patio, taking some pleasure in having learned how to smoke. He calls the girl he met at music camp to tell her about Jasper, referring to him as "a genius" and "a novelist" and "like one of my best friends" (71). This shifts our perspective of Jasper slightly; we are now seeing him through Evan's admiring eyes. KJ doesn't appear in this scene but walks in for the next, carrying Jasper's guitar case. If Baker's audience has been nodding to themselves about how *Waiting for Godot*-like this play is, she seems to nod back when KJ, like Estragon, *"bends down and unlaces his shoe. He turns his shoe upside down. / A pebble falls out onto the ground"* (72). Evan has been visibly shaken by Jasper's death; he feels, though he can't quite articulate it, transformed, like one life has ended and a new one is beginning (75). (This echoes the feelings of Lauren at the end of *Circle Mirror Transformation*.) KJ has him kneel for a blessing;

he touches Evan's cheek with a quiet "Zhoop" (76). KJ is thinking about moving away from Shirley. He gives Jasper's guitar to Evan and tells him to play something. Evan is concerned that he doesn't know any originals, that he, unlike KJ and Jasper, hasn't written any songs of his own. KJ responds, "*I'm* a genius. *Jasper* was a genius" and "Maybe you're a genius too!" (82). The play ends with Evan "*haltingly*" but increasingly confidently playing "If I Had a Hammer." When he's done, KJ encourages him: "You're gonna go far" (84). The final stage direction is *"Evan tries not to smile. But then he does"* (84).

The Aliens has been widely produced; its intimacy and moving portrait of friendship and spare production elements have made it a popular choice. In 2017, reviewing the production at Toronto's Coal Mine Theatre, Carly Maga wrote that "A play that revolves around the existential pain of three white men in America may not feel like the most politically relevant story that could be told today," but *The Aliens* "certainly paints a moving portrait of codependency, insecurity and toxic masculinity in a late capitalist society that praises productivity and wealth."[20] While that's true, Baker's portrait is more timeless and more affectionate. KJ and Jasper are creative and caring; the friendship among the three men changes all of their lives. Erin Keane captures this well in her description that *The Aliens* is "a love letter to the fragility of chosen families and the gentle geniuses our fast-paced society quietly leaves behind."[21] Aleks Sierz identifies the subtleties, the "surprisingly tricky" nature of *The Aliens*, which

> sometimes treads very near the edge of making a statement far larger than its characters are able to think of, but then steps back and contents itself with, well, being itself. Just like its characters. So while we sometimes expect an explosion of feeling, and have to endure an unnecessary interval, what we are left with is a gentle ache—and a sense of compassion for life's losers, its incapables and its hurting souls.[22]

The Flick

Jean-Paul Sartre writes that the greatest art is watching the passing of time. While this could be said of any of Baker's plays, it feels particularly apt for *The Flick*, in which Baker investigates contrasts of felt experience of time between film and theater, where "time is passing at the same rate for the actors on stage as it is for the audience," and between celluloid and digital ("time works differently with celluloid than it does with the digital image").[23] We might say she's engaging the audience in an exploration of Bergsonian sense of time and duration. "We normally place ourselves in spatialized time," that is, "clock time," which is "uniformly calibrated," philosopher Henri Bergson wrote; "We have no interest in listening to the uninterrupted humming of life's depth. And yet, that is where the real duration abides."[24] Immersing ourselves in art is a nourishing exercise in duration—releasing ourselves from the tick-tock of clock time that dominates our lives and listening to "continuous," "indivisible" time, that uninterrupted humming.[25] Though some, it is true, argue that this immersion in duration is merely an exercise in endurance. *The Flick*'s durational experience has inspired frustration and walking out among some; for others, euphoria.

The play marked an acceleration point in Baker's career, winning the Susan Smith Blackburn Prize, an Obie Award for playwriting, and the 2014 Pulitzer Prize for Drama. It was a divisive Pulitzer choice, though Charles Isherwood applauded this "rare case of the award's going to a play that truly nudges the art form in new directions."[26] Baker shies away from labels such as "experimental," arguing, "I think of my work as very accessible, if not too accessible. I beat myself up in private over being overly accessible and conventional, so I'm always surprised when people say stuff like 'cutting edge' or 'divisive.' I think of myself as a panderer."[27] In its original production at Playwrights Horizons (February–April 2013), directed, once again, by Sam Gold, audiences needed some time to get acclimated to this innovative new work. After 10 percent of the audience walked out at intermission, artistic director Tim Sanford wrote a letter to the theater's 3,000 subscribers. In it, he acknowledges "initial concern about walkouts," but how he also "began to pay attention to the other voices, the voices that urged Annie and Sam not to cut a second" because they had had an experience of "rapture."[28] After it won the Pulitzer Prize, producer Scott Rudin brought Gold and the original cast back for a revival at Barrow Street Theatre in May 2015, which ran for nearly eight months, a commercial and critical success. By the time it premiered at Steppenwolf Theatre in Chicago two years later, audiences were raving about the ecstatic experiences it induced.

The Flick was Baker's first play to be produced at London's National Theatre, where its run sold out almost immediately.[29] Michael Billington wrote, "This is like no other play in London. It moves at its own unhurried pace and magically exposes the souls of lonely people in danger of being left behind in our new, digitised age."[30] British audiences may have also appreciated its implicit class critique as *The Flick* shows the ways class puts constraints on the mobility and dreams of its characters. In a conversation with Marc Maron for his *WTF?* podcast, Baker emphasized, when Maron suggested that the character Sam couldn't "actualize his dreams," that this wasn't so much a matter of Sam's ambition as it was "well, *class*."[31] When audience members walked out of the initial production at Playwrights Horizons, it was a clear signal that many of the standard theater subscribers (wealthy, white, older) did not think it was worth their time to sit patiently and watch working-class people cleaning for three hours.

The Flick is a tribute to Baker's love affairs with film and theater, letting each know how it is unique. It takes place in a "falling-apart movie theater" in Worcester County, Massachusetts. The set is the movie theater auditorium, with the audience in the place of the screen. That is, onstage we see the seats of the movie theater facing us; on the upstage wall is a window into the projection booth and a door leading into the lobby. "We, the theater audience, are the movie screen. The beam of light from the projector radiates out over our heads."[32] The space represents a "face-off" between theater and film, and Baker has said that she wanted to evoke the feeling when you're snapped out of film reverie and brought into the liveness of where you are, which is what theater does. The idea came to her one day when she was watching a movie all the way to the end of the credits, and then, while she was still in the dreamy movie-mode, the overhead lights snapped on and the theater employees came in, "shit-talking" while they started to clean.[33]

The Flick has three main characters: Sam, who is white, thirty-five years old, wears a beat-up Red Sox cap and "used to be very into Heavy Metal" (4). He belongs to the working class, has a brother who is developmentally disabled and was institutionalized for most of his life, and still lives with his parents. He is in love with Rose. Avery, who is black, is twenty years old and is taking a break from college; he has recently experienced a breakdown and suicide attempt when his mother left the family. He wears "red slightly European-looking sneakers" and is a serious film nerd (4). Rose is white, twenty-four years old, and has the coveted job as projectionist in the theater. She is described as "sexually magnetic, despite the fact that (or partly because?) her clothes are baggy, she never wears makeup and her hair is dyed forest-green" (4). (There's also a fourth actor who plays two small roles, A Dreaming Man who falls asleep in the theater, and Skylar, a new employee.) Their costumes are the typical movie theater uniforms of polo shirts embroidered with "The Flick" (the name of the movie theater) on the chest pocket. Baker described the characters as they "started emerging from the movie theater set in my mind": Rose, the "'unattainable' girl up there in the shadows who was dying for someone to get to know her 'for real'"; Sam, who worries he'll be "working there for life"; and Avery, the "young film buff who came from both a different race and class background than the other characters in the play."[34] Although they are often described in reviews as "misfits" or "loners," Baker insists that they're not. ("I'm much more of a loner than they are," she says.[35]) They are, however, outsiders: "Three of the great 'Others' of American cinema": "a black guy, a woman, and a Jew (although I no longer make Sam's Jewishness obvious)" who are "quietly (maybe even unconsciously) fighting against their respective pigeonholes."[36] Baker explains that she

> grew up knowing lower-middle-class Jews, hyper-educated black people, and women who wear baggy clothes and no makeup, and yet it is so rare to encounter any of those people in plays and movies. It feels like those people are like forced to wander outside of and on the periphery of plays and movies. So I literalized that—they're like cleaning up everyone else's crap AFTER the movie is over.[37]

At the top of the play, a pre-show scene puts us into that familiar, pleasurable sensation of being in a movie-watching trance. We hear Bernard Herrmann's Prelude to *The Naked and the Dead* playing and, for two minutes (the length of the piece of music), the audience sees just the light from the projector beaming over their heads, and "*abstracted dancing images shooting out*" of it (7). At the end, "*there is a bright flash of green, and then white*" (7) which will be the signal throughout the play that a movie has ended. At this point, onstage, the movie theater overhead lights flicker on. The play is beginning. The movie trance is over, and now that the stage lights come up, we can see that we are facing the dingy seats of a rundown movie theater. The magic is over. And yet the magic is beginning. We move from the magic of film—the trance—to the magic of theater—the liveness.

The door at the back of the theater opens and Sam and Avery come in carrying push brooms and dust pans. "We call this the walkthrough" (9) is the first line of the play. Sam is showing Avery how to clean the movie theater. Much of the play takes place while Sam and Avery are sweeping up popcorn, throwing away discarded cups, and mopping the floor. While this looks random it is highly choreographed. Apparently the runtime of the show can vary depending on the size of the set; some smaller theaters have experienced shorter runtimes. Yet the timing may be a matter of direction more than space. Gold describes the second production of *The Flick*, with the same cast, at the Barrow Street Theatre, a different house, with a different size set, and yet their choreography of the movement and silences was so precise that the running time was the same.[38]

On his second day, Avery is late for work, and when he arrives and grabs his broom to join Sam in the sweeping, we see their awkwardnesses and insecurities, the power struggles, even as we see the first inklings of what might become friendship. Sam, feeling abandoned by Avery when he doesn't show up for work, is fearful that Avery will get promoted to projectionist before him. The work they do is humiliating—not just sweeping up the usual concession stand items but the weird things people sneak in, like chocolate-tapioca pudding, which is smeared on the floor and causes Avery to gross out because of what the pudding looks like, confessing to Sam that he's "shit-phobic" (18). They laugh about a website that rates pictures of people's shit, which creates "*A happy pause in which they realize they've broken the tension, and then awkward pause following that happy pause*" as they go back to sweeping (19). A minute later, a person appears in the window of the projection booth, which signals to the audience that that space will also be a playing space of the play and not mere set dressing. It is Rose, setting up the next movie. Sam yells up to her, and watches the window for her, but she doesn't respond.

François Truffaut's *Jules and Jim*, a favorite film of Baker's, serves as a structuring motif in *The Flick*. In the film, Jules (like Avery) is introspective and insecure, Jim (like Sam) is extroverted; they develop an unlikely friendship that thrives because of their differences. The free-spirited Catherine (like Rose), always wanting to be truly seen and known for herself, not just as a desirable object for the men, forms the third of the triangle. In *The Flick*, the two men, Avery and Sam, have a developing camaraderie that is always held in tension by their class differences and ambitions, and at least from Sam's perspective, Rose's attention. At several points in the play, *Jules and Jim*'s signature song "Le Tourbillon" ("The Whirlwind") is heard (once whistled by Avery, once sung by Jeanne Moreau in a clip from the film), and as *The Flick* closes, the orchestral theme "Vacances" is playing. Although we don't hear this in English, lyrics from "Le Tourbillon" such as "We met, we knew, we lost each other from view" and "each blown their way by the whirlwind of life" resonate with the play. Rose lightly flirts with both guys, bringing an "Astrology and your Love Life" book into the theater and speculating about their signs' compatibilities. She first sets her sights on Avery, trying to get him to notice her by drawing him in sexually. Sam declares his love for her, and at the end of the play it appears they have become, at least for now, a couple.

Rose and Sam introduce Avery to Dinner Money, a petty scam they've devised to resell 10 percent of the night's tickets and take 10 percent of the cash for the evening. They are essentially creating their own internal economy. Rose defends this practice, arguing that they are "vastly underpaid" and their manager "Steve is a total douchebag," plus "it's like a like a like an employee tradition" (34) at the theater. Avery is uncomfortable and doesn't want to participate. He assures them he won't tell Steve, but is aware that he will be the one blamed if the scheme is ever discovered (and it is, and he is). Rose and Sam insist that no one has ever been caught before. Baker follows this with a long, silent stretch in which a lot is happening nonverbally, Avery taking off his glasses and wiping them on his shirt, putting his head into his hands, Sam and Rose mouthing questions and concerns to one another in "*mutual gestures of panic*" (37). Avery finally succumbs to the pressure and agrees to go along. "Richard Pryor and Angelina Jolie," Sam calls out, to break the tension (38).

Sam and Avery's relationship develops through such movie-talk. Avery takes the stance that there has been no great American movie in the previous ten years—since Quentin Tarantino's *Pulp Fiction* (1994). Sam is constantly throwing out film titles to challenge that assertion (*Avatar*, *Titanic*), to Avery's scorn. Or we come upon them in the middle of riffing on the Six Degrees of Kevin Bacon game of connecting two actors who would seem to inhabit entirely different spheres by linking them, step by step, through other actors they have been in movies with. None of this is explained to the audience; it is assumed we know this game. Avery is a whiz at it. After he successfully works through the challenging connection of Michael J. Fox and Britney Spears, Sam expresses awe: "You have like a ... that's like almost like a *disability*" (26). "It's actually like the opposite of a disability," Avery responds (27). To break through moments of tension and attempt to reach out to Avery, Sam will toss out two actors' names.

Venturing away from the safe subject of movie games and great-film debates risks illuminating the class differences between the guys. Avery asks Sam the seemingly innocuous question of what he wants to be when he grows up, assuming that cleaning the movie theater is not Sam's lifetime career. This is followed by a pause, and Sam saying, "... I am grown up," then "That's like the most depressing thing anyone's ever said to me" (42). But then, after we've watched them finish sweeping, emptying their dust pans, and are on the way out the door, the scene ends with Sam's "A chef" (42). It's a strong punctuation for the end of the scene—and suggests that we don't know Sam.

Baker set the play in the summer of 2012 because that was when the movie theater industry was just beginning to seriously turn digital. Avery has chosen to work at The Flick because it's one of the only theaters left in the county that has held onto a 35-millimeter projector. *The Flick* was in part inspired by an experience Baker had watching one of her favorite films, Bergman's *Fanny and Alexander*, wondering why she was not enjoying it, and suddenly realizing that it was because the theater was projecting the film digitally. In *The Flick*, Baker puts these convictions into the character of Avery, who argues that it is immoral to project a movie made on film through a digital projector. Later he will write a letter to the new owner of the theater imploring him to retain the 35-millimeter projector: "Film can express things that computers never will. Film is a series of photographs separated by split seconds of darkness. Film is light and shadow and it is the light and shadow that were there on the day you shot the film" (140). Avery's description sounds, of course, like the play we are watching—a play made up of many short scenes separated by moments of darkness (i.e., blackouts). In a series-preview essay written for Playwrights Horizons, Tim Sanford says thus about *The Flick*:

> Film takes the platonic allegory of the cave to its furthest extent, fancifying shadows into dazzling illusions that distract us from the originating strong moral forms Plato espoused that no one today believes in anymore. So what's the difference if we cut out the shadows altogether and replace them with pixels? Well, in Annie Baker's world, that substitution would be tragic because the interplay of light and shadow in a way replicates the real life struggle between her characters and their inner lives.[39]

Rose counters Avery's passionate argument with a practical one that all theaters will be digital and The Flick will have to go along to stay in business. She and Sam are indifferent to Avery's ardent expressions of love for film. Rose states flatly, "I'm kind of over movies" (88). When Avery reads his impassioned letter to Sam and asks if it has convinced him of the necessity of keeping the 35-millimeter projector, Sam replies, not unkindly, that he doesn't really care. But to Avery, films are "like my life" (89).

Avery is a lonely soul, longing to make friends but not knowing how. We see him alone in the theater, talking on the phone with his therapist, stopping himself mid-story, fearful that he is boring even the person he pays to listen to him. As a playwriting strategy, this wisely breaks up the story and calls the audience's attention to the most important part which is immediately to come. Avery recounts a terrible dream in which he's just died and is in a Purgatory-type space where people are waiting to move on. A person arrives with an "ISBN-type scanner thing" (64) and Avery is surrounded by shelves of all the movies he has ever watched. He is given the scanner. He discovers that the way they decide whether you'll get into heaven is by scanning your history—the movies you've watched and books you've read to see if there is one that "you truly truly loved," the movie that "like symbolizes your entire life" (64). Avery takes the scanner and runs it over his cinephile collection—Japanese Yakuza films and Truffaut and *Barry Lyndon* but nothing's happening. Even when he runs it over *Fanny and Alexander*: nothing. He fears he's "going to hell," that he hasn't "truly like, loved or whatever in the right way" (65). The film for which the scanner beeps and beeps? *Honeymoon in Vegas*. Avery had been obsessed with it when he was four. He's initially upset that *this* film exemplifies his life. But then he realizes he's going to heaven, and it releases him.

(Baker actually had the same kind of dream experience, though it was about books. She assumed "her beloved Beckett or Thomas Mann would set the scanner off" but when she ran it over the bookshelf, "it went 'boop-boop-boop'" over the collected works of Jane Austen, which embarrassed her "because it's so girly and so trendy to love Jane Austen."[40] Reflecting on that dream, she thinks it was "more about femininity and being a woman" because for a long time she "was in denial about talking about being a woman"; it was her way of pushing back against "being raised by hippie feminists in a hippie town, with a lot of identity politics woven into education. As little girls, we were supposed to talk about a woman who'd inspired us and I wouldn't. I was like 'François Truffaut!' I wouldn't name a woman and it was really important to me that I didn't have to."[41])

Avery fears that his life will never change, that maybe he is just destined to stay that "weird depressed guy" (66) and there's nothing to be done. He tries to build a friendship with Sam by suggesting that they stay late one night and watch one of the old 35-millimeter films that are in the projection booth. Sam, cagey at first about his weekend plans, finally reveals that he has a brother who is developmentally disabled—"Retarded" he says, "Like in the actual definition of the word" (74–75)—and is getting married that weekend. Rose offers to watch the movie with Avery, which devastates Sam; he turns away from them, sits down, and faces the movie screen *"beseechingly"* (76).

Act One closes with this scene in which Avery and Rose stay after closing to watch a film. It opens with the flash of green and then white that indicates the end of a movie, then with Avery mopping and Rose working in the projection booth. Suddenly a dance tune blasts and Rose kicks through the door and dances up to Avery. Baker's stage directions encourage the actor to improvise and make it different for each performance; maybe Rose *"incorporates a couple moves from bhangra and/or hip-hop and/or West African dance classes from her past"* (81). The heart of the scene is a long, carefully choreographed section with no dialogue. In the script, it runs just over a page of stage directions. Rose and Avery leave the movie theater and go into the projection booth. The main part of the stage is empty, then, and the audience sees the characters from afar, through the projection booth window. They are threading the projector, Rose teaching Avery how to do it. Then a movie begins: the *"six-minute-long opening-credit-sequence music from The Wild Bunch"* (90). Avery and Rose return to the movie theater and, as they watch the movie, Rose initiates sexual play with Avery, kissing his neck, contemplating, then deciding against, nibbling his ear, then stroking his neck and shirt with her index finger, and finally unzipping his pants and touching him (out of view of the audience). During this entire time, Avery remains frozen and unresponsive, looking ahead at the screen. Eventually, Rose stops, embarrassed, then leaves the theater and goes upstairs to turn the movie off. When it clicks off and the theater lights come back up, Avery is *"as if released from a spell,"* and doubles over in shame. Long, awkward silences follow. Avery reveals that something like this has happened to him before and that he struggles with intimacy and often would rather just watch a movie. His vulnerability inspires Rose to share her own embarrassed feelings of isolation and sexual weirdness, which brings them into a comfortable shared silence and allows Avery to open up and tell Rose that today is the one-year anniversary of the day he tried to kill himself, and that he continues to be depressed—he reveals that he almost missed his second day of work at The Flick because he couldn't get out of bed and that he lied to Sam about why he was late. (Which causes us to recall we saw this in scene 2.) The advice everyone gives is always "Be Yourself, but I have no idea what that fucking means" (99). He's always faking it, Avery says, and it looks like everyone else is too. At the end of the scene, which closes Act One, they sit quietly together in the movie theater looking up at the blank screen, while "Le Tourbillon" from *Jules and Jim* plays.

Act Two opens three days later, when Sam is back from his brother's wedding. Avery is careful to reconnect with him. Sam tells a long and winding story about having seen a movie with his family and having brought tamales into the movie theater, even though he hates when people do this to him. (Baker has singled out this detail as one of her favorites precisely because it is "non-illustrative" and doesn't matter to the progression of the play.) The story was intended to have a point but Avery doesn't get it, nor does the audience. We get the sense that Sam saved this up, wanting to share it with Avery, wanting to return with a big story for him that they could analyze and discuss. And that Sam is avoiding what is really on his mind: what happened between Rose and Avery while he was gone. Avery responds that they just talked—but when Rose enters and asks Avery to cover for her on the projector, thus revealing that while Sam was gone she showed Avery how to work the projector, Sam picks up a bag of popcorn from the floor and *"flings it gloriously into Avery's area, popcorn showering everywhere"* (116). The following scene is later that night, where we watch Avery and Sam *"mop in terrible silence together"* (117), the only sound for quite some time the mops being wrung out and then slapping on the floor. When Rose comes in to distribute the Dinner Money, Sam, with his eyes glued to his mop, asks her quietly why she showed Avery how to work the projector. It is humiliating for him to watch younger, newer employees rising past him in the ranks, especially when he wants to impress Rose and get close to her. Facing the screen (i.e., facing the audience), and away from Rose, he finally bursts out that he loves her. He tries to tell how this is more than a crush, that he dreams about her all the time, but it comes out wrong. Rose feels like his declaration is more about him than about her. Recalling her earlier conversation with Avery about inauthenticity, she sighs and says, "It's like you're performing or something" (124).

At this enormously painful moment for Sam, and empathetic moment for the audience, Avery suddenly bursts back in and the mood turns to the comic. Avery announces that someone defecated on the men's bathroom floor and spread it on the walls. What's more, Avery confesses, he just added to the mess by puking on the bathroom floor. This scene gives Sam the opportunity to be heroic. He takes charge, instructing Avery to sit down and breathe, and for Rose to get Avery water, while he heads up the aisle and *"stoically thrusts the mop up into the air like a sword"* (128). When he's gone, Rose says to Avery, "Sometimes I worry that there's something really,

really wrong with me. / But that I'll never know exactly what it is" (130). (This is echoed in the male characters in the Vermont Plays, but especially in "A Short History of Weird Girls," the episode of the television show *I Love Dick* that Baker co-writes. Baker is really attuned to feelings of shame and how they manifest and fester.)

As the play winds down, the digital threat has indeed materialized. Avery's letter is disregarded by the new owner, who switches the theater to digital and changes its name to The Venue. The employees get new uniforms—though they're just like the old uniforms with new colors and branding. The new owner discovers the Dinner Money scheme and blames Avery. Avery wants Rose and Sam to admit their parts, which causes a class and friendship rift. Rose doesn't want to confess to it for fear they will all be fired. She points out that Avery does not actually need this job; he can borrow money from his father and go back to college, whereas Rose is $20,000 in debt for student loans and Sam can't afford to move out of his parents' house. When Avery mentions that the new owner is also getting rid of the old projector, Sam ventures that maybe Avery wouldn't have wanted to stay, anyway. At this, Avery walks up the aisle to the door, then turns and delivers the Ezekiel 25:17 speech from *Pulp Fiction* (which Sam has been begging him to do throughout the play): "THE PATH OF THE RIGHTEOUS MAN IS BESET ON ALL SIDES BY THE INEQUITIES OF THE SELFISH AND THE TYRANNY OF EVIL MEN" (159).

The next scene has us watching from far away. Most of the stage is empty. Sam and Rose are up in the projection booth, disassembling the film projector. This takes a while; Baker gives this ritual the time it needs. Then they install the digital projector, which takes no time at all, and feels illustrative of the cold efficiency of the digital world. It appears that the play is starting all over again. When the digital projection is over (its light is harsher, more blue, than the warmer film projector's light had been), the house lights in the movie theater come up and Sam trains a new employee, Skylar, who has worked at movie theaters before and is faster at cleaning than Sam is. While he's waiting for Sam to finish, Skylar walks up to the movie screen and *"lightly touches"* it (166). Sam yells out to him and asks him why he did that. Skylar responds, he always has an "urge to like . . . / I always just kind of want to touch it. / Don't you?" (166). Critic Tyler Coates observed that when you read this scene on the page it looks like merely a "little observed moment" but when he watched Sam Gold's production at the Barrow Street Theater, it was much more substantial, like "coming up to a membrane between worlds."[42] It's not a breaking of the fourth wall, but it's a gentle reminder to the audience that they are watching a play and "we're all a part of this communal experience."[43]

In the final scene, Avery returns to pick up the projector, which Sam has saved for him after he and Rose disassembled it. Sam appears contented, for the first time in the play; he and Rose appear to have become a romantic couple. Avery, however, has lost in faith in people since the Dinner Money discovery and Rose and Sam's refusal to admit their part in it. Wanting to hurt Sam, Avery tells him that one day he'll come back to town and Sam will still be working at the movie theater, while Avery will be "living in Paris or something" (173). He recalls the ending of Woody Allen's *Manhattan* when Mariel Hemingway's character is leaving for London and tells Allen's character, "You gotta have a little faith in people" while the music swells up (174). "This is like the opposite of that ending," he says (174). As Avery walks toward the door, Sam tries for one last moment of connection through a Six Degrees game: "Macaulay Culkin to Michael Caine" (175). Avery shakes his head and walks out. Yet this ritual is strong enough to eventually pull him back. Sam stands in the aisle and stares at the door. Baker's stage direction reads, "*A very very long amount of time passes*" (176). Sam waits. Finally, Avery returns, but while he recites the connections, showing off his extensive knowledge of the most arcane and hard-to-reach connections, he is unsmiling, and remains unsmiling even as Sam "*bursts into a beatific grin*" and continues to smile to himself as Avery leaves and "Vacances" from *Jules and Jim* swells up (176).

James Wolcott, reviewing the Barrow Street revival of *The Flick*, writes, "I feel no kinship with those who ejected/bailed/fled like thieves in the night at intermission during the original production. They missed out big-time, depriving themselves of a slow-brew, absorbent experience so seldom offered in the hyperspace of attention-deficit culture where all phasers are on stun." He describes that play as requiring "an orientation period of adjustment as one black-out scene of popcorn sweeping succeeds another—the lack of visual and aural stimuli re-tuning one's receptors," but once his "attention passed a certain threshold, any grip of boredom receded and I found myself in the sort of rapt fascination that is like a holiday mood."[44] Jesse Green concurred, writing that "rarely has so much feeling been mined from so little content"; he acknowledges that many audience members will find the duration and silence a burden, but he found that "the silence, like a halo, makes everything it surrounds more beautiful." Ironically, since it's a play about love of the movies, *The Flick* "may be the best argument anyone has yet made for the continued necessity, and profound uniqueness, of theater."[45] Scholar David T. Johnson compares the pace of *The Flick* to slow cinema, which does "real work for the viewer in a fundamentally positive sense" and ties the viewer to the space of the movie theater, "because it is in the theatre where such slowness, working against the temporalities of conventional cinema, has the least possibility for interruption—and where, too, one might experience that slowness with others."[46] Sarah Crompton, reviewing the National Theatre of London's production, writes that *The Flick*'s "quiet unfolding makes you watch and listen"; like film, which the play celebrates, Baker and Gold conjure "a stillness that is almost like a painting, rewarding patience, forcing you to pay attention."[47]

Why do some find the demands of attention unbearable, while others relish, even crave them? Why would some people prefer to give themselves an electric shock than to sit quietly with their own thoughts for fifteen minutes?[48] While some audiences complained of being bored by the slow pace and quiet stretches of *The Aliens* and *The Flick*, Baker counters that she feels "over-stimulated and bored by a lot of the theater" she sees "because of the breakneck speed at which it's performed. There's this obsession with 'pace,' and I think it's because we're terrified of boring audiences that are used to looking at the internet while watching TV while talking on their iPhone."[49] As a result, theater keeps chasing digital media instead of embracing its uniqueness as a live artform, its ability to exist in real time with its audience. *More* boredom, not less; *slower* theater, not faster, might be wisdom for the future. Playwright Paula Vogel is optimistic that "the theater is actually going to grow in the twenty-first century, because it forces us to slow down. The circadian rhythms are being lost, technology is speeding up, so we have to go somewhere and literally have a one-to-one relationship with the tick-tock of the clock."[50] I hope she's right. John Cage is quoted as saying, "If something is boring after two minutes, try it for four. If still boring, then eight. Then sixteen. Then thirty-two. Eventually one discovers that it is not boring at all." We need to "recultivate our relationship with boredom," Tracy Bersley writes; when we do so, it will reshape our "relationship with empty space and time," and we will "regain something monumental. We regain the ability to have an engaged imagination."[51]

In *The Aliens* and *The Flick*, Baker achieved with composition, pacing, and use of time what she had long admired in a favorite film, Chantal Akerman's *Jeanne Dielman, 23, quai de commerce, 1080 Bruxelles* (1975), also often discussed in terms of its long length (3 hours, 21 minutes) and slow tempo. Giving your attention to three days in the life of a middle-aged woman through the repetition of everyday details (boiling potatoes, washing dishes, tending to an afternoon prostitution client) turns out to be deeply absorbing, even hypnotic. Some viewers of *Jeanne Dielman*—imbued with rapture, like some audiences of *The Flick*—find themselves going about their own daily rituals with heightened awareness and fascination. And Baker just keeps getting more creative with staging time and harnessing audience attention, as we will see in the next chapter's discussion of *John* and *The Antipodes* and the TV episode of *I Love Dick*, where she also now explores the sacred and subversive power of desire.

CHAPTER 4
STORIES OF COMPLICATED DESIRE
JOHN, I LOVE DICK, AND *THE ANTIPODES*

When she won a MacArthur Fellowship in 2017, Baker characterized her work in this way: "With every play I write, I am trying to reassess what it means to watch a play."[1] The walkouts of *The Flick* didn't quash her; nor did the Pulitzer Prize rein her into creating more of the same in the hope of more acclaim. Instead, she pushed the boundaries of theater even further. As Tyler Coates wrote for *Slate*, Baker was inspired to "produce a follow-up that was even longer, more aggressively subtle and quiet, and larger in philosophical scope. In doing so, *John* surpasses its predecessor and becomes Baker's true masterpiece: an examination of the murkiness of human relationships in which one of those relationships is the one between an audience and a playwright."[2] (In Chapter 5 of this book, Thomas Butler explores this idea further, arguing that Baker is making an ethical demand on the audience, that "the plays lead us to recognize the insistent realness of the lives of others.")

Baker's plays post-*The Flick* have become stranger, weirder, more surrealistic, as she continues innovating with time and space. Baker's Vermont plays, her adaptation of Chekhov's *Uncle Vanya*, and *The Flick* were written in a recognizably naturalistic form. In *John*, Baker presses naturalism's fealty to time and the presentation of life as it is by inviting the audience to *listen* to the sounds of the world onstage perhaps even more than to *watch* them. This subtly sensory play was dubbed by Toronto critic J. Kelly Nestruck "numinous naturalism" and responded to with a kind of religious fervor: "Annie Baker is a playwright who can make you believe in God."[3] *The Antipodes* unfolds into a kind of sacred rite and inspired comparisons to the Symbolist work of Maeterlinck and Strindberg. In between these plays, Baker co-wrote an episode of the television show *I Love Dick*, which blended naturalistic observation with surrealistic representations of inner life.

John, *I Love Dick*, and *The Antipodes*: all of these scripts dramatize stories of complicated desire. What we also see in these three works is Baker's exploration of women's desire, which until this point in her career was largely left unaddressed.

John

John (2015) was the first of three plays to premiere at the Signature Theatre in New York as part of Baker's position as Signature Theatre Residency Five Playwright. It was directed by Sam Gold. When asked by the London *Evening Standard*, "Why did you write *John*?" Baker replied, "I wrote it because everything that happens in that play relates to something I was grappling with, personally, philosophically, politically, at the time I wrote it."[4] Baker has long been a prodigious reader, steeping herself in philosophy and psychology in preparation for writing a play, and for *John* she wrote "66 pages of notes," which range from "the tourism industry in Gettysburg, Pennsylvania, and the eerie world of American bed and breakfasts" to "notes on William James's *The Varieties of Religious Experience*" and "first-hand accounts of madness in the nineteenth century," as well as "a lot of people," such as Rilke and Kleist, "writing about the power that dolls and inanimate objects hold over us."[5] Pulling it all together, she says:

> all of that relates to the theme of religious dread and responsibility, and how people in secular culture become obsessed with the supernatural as a way of stimulating an old-school kind of religious dread. I also wanted to upend the genre of the relationship drama. So I wanted to write a play about a young couple breaking up that also related to ideas about selfhood and autonomy and American history and God.[6]

The result is a layered, enigmatic play in which all that research has been absorbed into the pores of the story. Its title, *John*, might evoke all the Johns of holy dread, such as the Gospel of John and St. John of the Cross, and also calls to mind Jean Cocteau's *The Holy Terrors* (*Les Enfants Terrible*): a tale of a brother and sister orphaned, who tell each other stories and build a private world out of their fantasies, which we see the characters Elias and Jenny do.

Baker prefaces the play with an epigraph from Heinrich von Kleist's "On the Marionette Theatre," a work as enigmatic as her play: a philosophical, theological, psychological, speculative essay-story. Kleist's narrator encounters a dancer friend who laments that marionette puppets are superior to human performers because they have no human volition and therefore can never be guilty of affectation. Paradoxically, they have more grace: "Grace appears most purely in that human form which either has no consciousness or an infinite consciousness. That is, in the puppet or in the god." According to Kleist, humans are self-conscious, "in-between" creatures, between the puppet and the god, who painfully struggle to attain grace. In *John*, we see a young couple, Jenny and Elias, who are painfully struggling with self-consciousness and affectation, always worried about how others see them. And we see an aged woman, Mertis, who is puppet-like in being completely free of affectation, and god-like, in her ability to read minds and her attunement to all the animate power of the universe. Baker wrote the play for and around the actor Georgia Engel, who played Mertis in the Signature Theatre production and looked a bit like a marionette puppet: she "has the mechanical carriage of a wind-up doll. Her face is plastered with the painted grin of a marionette—charming, but it won't go away."[7] She also has the sweetness and grace—both a gracefulness and ease in relationships and a religious sense of gracing others by caring for them—that Elias and Jenny lack and that are hard to come by in everyday human life.

The epigraph and Baker's research notes signal that *John* is exploring territory shared by theater and theology: presence. It is a play about watching, being watched, and being watched over. As Paul Woodruff writes in *The Necessity of Theater*, "If we are unwatched we diminish, and we cannot be entirely as we wish to be" but "if we never stop to watch, we will know only how it feels to be us, never how it might feel to be another," and thus in "watching well, together, and being watched well, together, with limits on both sides, we grow, and grow together."[8] As Thomas Butler writes in his essay in Chapter 5, "adequately attending to the specific reality of other people" is both "the burden central to Baker's dramatic world" and "an ethical demand" she has her audience face. Throughout the play, Mertis asks others if they've ever felt watched. In the character descriptions, each is introduced in terms of their vision: Elias, we're told, wears glasses; Jenny and Mertis don't wear glasses; the fourth character, Mertis's friend Genevieve, is blind. In its exploration of watching and being watched, *John* feels like a metatheatrical commentary on "the weird power of theater," as Baker says of *Fanny and Alexander*.[9] She was drawn to the way that Bergman shoots the inanimate objects ("the statues and the toy angels and the clocks and the puppets and the lamps"[10]) as though they are always watching Alexander, and envisioned a stage full of dolls and miniature figures looking at the characters and audience. Chloe Lamford's set design for London's National

Theatre production had "Upwards of a thousand eyes stare out at us in the form of dolls, figurines, ceramic angels, cherubs and a glass menagerie. This is a play about seeing and unseeing eyes."[11]

Mertis, in her own all-seeing way, stage-manages the space, calling the audience's attention to the fact that they are watching a piece of theater, but also seeming to create a theater within the theater. In each scene, she changes the music on an onstage jukebox that plays different Bach melodies. The play is almost entirely scored with Bach underneath the scenes, adding to the aura of religious dread. (Alex Ross alerts us to listen to Bach's "curious variations" and "strange tones," his "art of holy dread," his "devotional intensity" that is "alien to most modern listeners" but is perfectly suited to Mertis.[12]) More mysteriously, Mertis also changes the hands on the onstage grandfather clock to move the time forward to the next scene. (In the Signature Theatre premiere, Georgia Engel carefully removed a key from her blouse to unlock the clock, and as she moved the hands to change time, the stage lighting shifted to indicate the new time of day—reinforcing the magical feeling that Mertis is controlling the time.) At the opening and closing of each act, Mertis comes out and pulls open or closes a theater curtain. So when she asks the others if they ever feel watched, the audience watching them might murmur in self-conscious laughter as we are brought to attention of the strangeness of the live theater situation in which some people sit and watch other people pretend to live.

At the same time, all this talk of watching and being watched seems to transcend that reality to evoke a spiritual realm. When Mertis asks Jenny if she ever feels watched, she explains that she means this not in an everyday social media-surveillance way but by "a larger presence" that sees you (68). Baker has said she had this experience when she was young, of always feeling watched. She describes herself as "a really weird, sort of supernaturally-obsessed kid" who felt her stuffed animals were watching her; while her parents were atheists, she felt that there was "definitely someone up there controlling it," she built religious shrines in her bedroom, and her mother told her, "You would be a religious fanatic if we'd let you."[13] *John* becomes an imaginative space to explore this. Mertis creates a sacred space in her bed-and-breakfast, where angels whirl in the candlelight, and Baker creates a sacred space for the audience to come and sit and contemplate their own place in this cosmos.

The critics' responses show their reaching for words to describe the mystical quality and effect of this play: Jeanmarie Higgins, in her essay in Chapter 5, calls it "uncanny"; Charles Isherwood, "supernatural naturalism";[14] Andrzej Lukowski, "on the cusp of magical realism";[15] and J. Kelly Nestruck, "deeply moving and nourishing in a way others find religion at this time when many of us are giving up on one another."[16] Hilton Als writes, "By not rushing things—by letting the characters develop as gradually and inevitably as rain or snowfall—Baker returns us to the naturalistic but soulful theatre that many of her contemporaries and near-contemporaries have disavowed in their rush to be 'postmodern.'"[17] *Time Out* listed *John* as #42 among a list of 50 "Best Plays Ever Written."[18] (I should note that it wasn't universally praised. A dismissive review from *The Spectator*: "The plot of a play usually starts within ten minutes but not here: nothing happens. That's the point."[19])

On its surface, *John* looks like an old-fashioned naturalistic drama. It unfolds in three acts, with two intermissions. In a visual departure from Baker's earlier plays, which were staged in fairly spare spaces, *John* appears to have a traditional fourth-wall house set, the living room of an inn, which is stuffed with matter: a Christmas tree, a player piano, and many, many knick-knacks and miniatures. The play takes place in a bed-and-breakfast in Gettysburg, Pennsylvania, a town haunted by having been the site of the American Civil War's bloodiest battle, where one can still visit a historical house, the Dobbin House, with what Mertis calls a "slave diorama," mannequins crafted to look like enslaved persons hiding in the floorboards on their journey through the Underground Railroad.[20] (As with many of Baker's plays, the setting imbues the play with a racialized undertow.) And it is a fitting locale for a tale of a young couple who are on the last battleground of their relationship.

The thematic elements of being watched and watched over are dramatized using many of the conventions of a Gothic ghost story: two travelers arrive late at night to a country inn, where they are the only guests; the objects in the inn—a painting on the wall, a doll on the stairway—seem to be alive and to be watching their movements; the proprietor of the inn tends to someone in the back room who may or may not actually be there. But Baker elevates *John* above the typical Gothic story by infusing it with a sense of the numinous, from theologian Rudolf Otto in *The Idea of the Holy* (1917), which describes the feelings of awe and spiritual elevation we associate with the presence of divinity. Although the play's skeleton follows a traditional "relationship play" dramatic arc—insecure couple arrives at inn, fights, breaks up—the play unfolds associatively and, as Baker notes, the "somewhat young and immature central relationship" is part of a "larger, more expansive musing on madness, and intimacy, and the numinous."[21]

Influenced by Victoria Nelson's argument in *The Secret Life of Puppets* that post–Enlightenment Western society has repressed religious impulses and driven the transcendental underground, only to seek for it in art and literature, particularly tales of horror, Baker's seemingly naturalistic play is teeming with spiritual life. As Charles Kruger puts it, "Baker constructs her reality with a series of themes, feelings, abstract sensations, mysterious connections" that works like a "tarot reading or other kind of divination."[22] "It's like a suspense thriller in slow motion," observed Craig Baldwin, who directed the premiere of *John* in Sydney; "I think Annie is purposely using a horror movie setup and those tropes but rather than going for the cheap pay-off, she suspends you in a place of creepiness and horror. You get all the chills but you also experience a real richness as you watch these people respond to this very strange environment."[23]

From the beginning *John* establishes a tension between what is seen and what is heard. One of Baker's innovative strategies is to have much of the opening scene take place offstage; the audience is put in the position of having to listen to rather than see most of the action. When the play begins, the house set is empty. (The Signature Theatre production kept the production so dimly lighted that the stage was often shrouded in half-darkness and actors' faces were occluded.) The onstage jukebox radio is playing Bach's "St. Matthew Passion, Aria No. 20." The audience sees the effect of car lights pulling up to the inn and hears the engine turning off, car doors slamming, and the doorbell ringing. A full ten seconds pass before Mertis comes downstairs and goes out to greet the guests. The first few lines of the play are spoken offstage; we hear Jenny's and Elias's voices saying hello, we hear their bags thumping, and then finally they enter the set. When they are initially shown up to their room, Baker's stage directions note, "*This next section is heard faintly. We shouldn't catch all of it*" (13). (Tyler Coates writes that he overheard an audience member whispering, "Are we *supposed* to hear them?"[24]) The audience hears footsteps and Mertis pointing out things that sound intriguing, though we never get to see them (a dolphin string, a memory wheel ceiling). We hear bags being set down on the floor, Mertis wishing the couple a good night, then the sound of Mertis walking downstairs. She reappears to the audience as she walks around the living room turning off lamps. As one lamp remains on, she hears, faintly, the sound of Jenny and Elias arguing upstairs. Mertis pauses her work to listen, which also calls the audience's attention to them. Faintly from upstairs come the voices of Elias, "I'M TELLING YOU HOW I FEEL," overlapping with Jenny's "Okay, okay, Stop yelling" (15). Because they're offstage, we are *more* aware of overhearing them than we would if they were "characters" on the stage in front of us.

Jenny and Elias have young-people problems. They've been together for three years but the strains and signs of relationship winding-down are evident. Elias feels "trapped" (23). He had been betrayed by Jenny, who had an affair with a man named John. (And may still be involved with him; her phone dings with secret texts throughout the play.) Jenny is irritated with minor things such as how loudly Elias eats; while he crunches cereal, she "*very very subtly puts a finger in her ear*" (27), which arouses Elias's anger at her passive-aggressiveness. Later in the play, Jenny betrays his trust when she tells Mertis about a traumatic event from Elias's childhood, when his parents allowed a man, a stranger sitting in a hot tub with them, to kiss Elias on the mouth. After she reveals this, there is "*A long silence*" and Jenny is described as both "*gleeful*" and "*terrified*" at having told his secret (92). Elias responds, "At times like this the fact that you tell me you don't have very very deep wells of rage towards me is so obviously um laid bare as a huge whopping lie" (92). Describing their relationship, Jesse Green writes,

> I'm not sure I've ever seen a couple's blowout arguments rendered as accurately as Baker renders them here: unfair, nonsequential, compulsive, zingerless. This is not *Who's Afraid of Virginia Woolf?* with its polished knives. Still, the Albee play is the only comparison I can find for Baker's dramatization of the way such arguments eat up and eventually become the relationship. Neurotic Elias and passive-aggressive Jenny, with their interlocking injuries, are only "happy" rubbing their sores.[25]

The most intimate moments of Elias and Jenny's relationship are when he responds to her request for a scary story—when he is conjuring up a chill of old-school religious dread to pull them closer. He begins to tell her an urban legend type of tale of a man and woman driving late at night on a cold rainy highway and pulling into a mysterious motel, where they see a face at the window—but he disappoints Jenny by breaking off at the revelation point. He can "only do build-up to scary. / Not scary itself," he explains [25].

As in many Gothic horror tales, the house itself feels alive and Baker deepens this trope by raising philosophical questions about the life of *things*. In the inn, Jenny is disturbed by the presence of an American Girl doll, Samantha, who is sitting in a rocking chair on the landing of the stairwell. She had that very same American Girl doll as a child, and feels as though

Samantha has followed her—that she escaped the box in Jenny's parents' basement in Ohio, where she's been stored, and has turned up in Mertis's bed-and-breakfast to reproach Jenny for abandoning her. (In the Signature Theatre production, lighting designer Mark Barton kept Samantha lighted in such a way that it appeared she was always watching the action.) Jenny tells Elias, "I feel like she found me" (19). When Elias wonders whether Samantha is angry that Jenny kept her locked in the basement for so many years, Jenny can't face it. This question is returned to later with Genevieve, who responds, "Of course she was angry. . . . Angry to be a doll! [. . . .] With one expression on your face! Frozen! People manhandling you. And then put in a dress. Put in an itchy little dress!" (68–69) This feels reminiscent of political theorist Jane Bennett's "thing power," an argument for seeing things as having their own kind of energy, indeed, their own kind of consciousness, that humans exist in relation to, rather than over.[26] Genevieve presents us with the contrast, and the ideal, in Mertis, who "takes very good care of her matter" (71).

More disturbingly, Baker also explores men's desire for women who are like dolls, whose bodies and minds can be manipulated by them. Genevieve tells a story of when she went mad. She had left her husband, but realized he was still with her; he had taken possession of her soul, inserting his judgments and thoughts into her. As though she were a doll, Genevieve "felt his fingers opening and closing my lids" (62), dictating when she would wake and sleep. His name was John. (It feels eerily coincidental to the audience, as does the uncanny similarity of the names of Jenny and Genevieve.) Genevieve still feels his presence watching her. Jenny will later say to Elias that her affair with her own John persisted because he had essentially "cast a spell" on her (69). Near the end of the play, when Elias and Jenny return to the inn, exhausted from a day of sightseeing and fighting, Elias puts his arms around Jenny, who is "frozen still" (133), like a statue. He manipulates her limbs, then picks her up and carries her, "*stiffly like a mannequin,*" to the couch and lies down next to her. Elias says to her "*quietly*"—perhaps talking to himself more than to her—"Maybe this is just what it feels like," meaning "True love" (134).

The stage has a peacefulness when Elias is not around. At the top of Act Two, he is out visiting Civil War sites, while Jenny, dealing with painful menstrual cramps, hangs out with Mertis and Genevieve. Genevieve believes that Mertis's house is haunted. Highly sensitive to any noise, she hears rustling sounds, possibly "wings" (73) upstairs, a sound later heard by the audience. The beating of wings calls to mind angels, who are also visually present to us on the set in the form of figurines; Genevieve gently holds and caresses one of them, an angel playing a lute. The sound of wings also recalls birds. Elias is deathly afraid of them but Mertis adores birds and has memorized all the different names given to groups of them. She recites these for Jenny, ending with her favorite, "An exaltation of larks" (83–84).

As part of their unfolding conversation about being watched, Jenny shares a mystical experience she had in New Mexico when one night she and a friend got high and lay out on the deck looking up at the stars and she "felt like the universe was having sex with me" (75). It made her feel "held" (76) and was a profound experience that she struggles to articulate, finally settling on "Less alone in my alone-ness" (76). Earlier, in Act One, Mertis had gotten a phone call from Genevieve in which, in response to an unrevealed question, she quoted a Latin phrase from John Henry Newman (quoting Cicero), "Numquam minus solus quam cum solus" (38). In that moment, the phrase—"never less alone than when alone"—doesn't get translated or commented on. Now, though, in Act Three, it returns. Mertis recalls a phrase she heard somewhere, "Deep Calling Unto Deep," which she, Jenny, and Genevieve repeat five times, making it feel like an incantation. It isn't cited in the play but comes from William James's *The Varieties of Religious Experience* (which has influenced Baker's plays "more than any other book" except perhaps Mann's *The Magic Mountain*[27]), in which he quotes a clergyman writing, "the deep that my own struggle had opened up within being answered by the unfathomable deep without, reaching beyond the stars,"[28] an echo of Jenny's mystical experience.

At the end of Act Two, Elias returns from his haunted house tour, upsetting the peaceful evening. (Jeanmarie Higgins, in her essay in Chapter 5, explores the warmth of Mertis's feminine space and the women's cozy relationships when Elias is out of the house.) The act closes with two painful, claustrophobic scenes of Elias and Jenny fighting, but if audiences feel tempted to leave the theater as the house lights come up for the second intermission, Baker ropes them back in. As people are beginning to stand and move toward the doors of the theater, Genevieve gropes her way out of the red curtain and stops them. "Stay five more minutes," she says. She has a story to tell them. She instructs someone in the audience to time her so that she stays under five minutes, and then launches into a tale of the seven stages of her madness. She felt scorpions inside her brain; at another point "two hundred Benedictine monks entered my right ear, took a tour of my head, and then exited out the left" (110). She felt connections to every soul—not just persons but the souls of objects—and felt that "God was doing some kind of experiment on me" (110) but then realized it was all the work of her ex-husband John, who had battled with God and won. "I was now in a godless world. John's world" (111). On the night of her fifty-seventh birthday, Genevieve went blind, and ends her tale by asking the audience to imagine themselves in the condition she found herself: "Sitting in the center of your own life with no thoughts at all about what other people are thinking" (111). Then she disappears again behind the curtain. If audiences had been thinking of leaving, they probably come back for Act Three.

Act Three, after that startling fourth-wall breakthrough, opens quietly. There is no music playing. Elias is sitting alone at the breakfast table. Mertis, because of the late night previous, did not have a chance to do her stage-managing. She turns on the jukebox to Bach's *Magnificat in D Major* and sets the clock to 9:08 a.m., then gets Elias breakfast. Elias tells Mertis that he and Jenny will be leaving a day early because they're having some problems: they don't know whether to stay together and he is troubled by Jenny's frequent lying. Mertis asks Elias if he's in love with Jenny, a seemingly simple question, but it troubles Elias, who admits he is confused about what it means to love someone versus to be in love with someone. He always feels trapped in relationships, with the women looking to him like insects sitting on his doorscreen.

Is he trying to hold himself back from being known? From being really seen? Mertis asks him her favorite question, whether he felt watched when he was young, which inspires Elias to reveal that the traumatic story Jenny told of his being kissed by an adult stranger, "that hot tub thing" (126), was actually his first memory. And the Watcher saw it: "He was definitely there. Watching that. / Watching over me" (126). Mertis wonders whether the Watcher was caring for Elias; he, puzzled by her question, wonders if she's a Christian. "I'm a Neoplatonist," she answers (128). This is a laugh line because it's unexpected, and it punctuates the end of this section (the doorbell rings, announcing Genevieve's arrival) yet it also synthesizes Mertis's views and those of the play, with Neoplatonism's view that all descends from a world soul, a One watching all.

Act Three, scene 2, calls us into the Deep. There is no stage action, no dialogue. Instead, we are read to. Onstage Mertis reads to Genevieve from H. P. Lovecraft's "The Call of Cthulhu" while the audience listens and watches the lighting change to indicate the transformation from day to sunset to night. Mertis changes the time on the clock, clears the dishes from the table, but does not return. The stage is quiet. Baker juxtaposes these very quiet scenes with claustrophobic ones, alternating calming the audience's nervous system with revving it up again. Throughout the following scene, while Jenny and Elias return for their final battle, Genevieve remains onstage, but in the dark, unseen by them. Elias demands to see Jenny's phone to read the texts that he assumes are from John, threatening to hurt the Samantha doll, to "set her on fire" (143), if Jenny refuses. Jenny throws her phone at him, grabs Samantha, breaks up with Elias and goes upstairs. It is the last we see of Jenny in the play.

Mertis comes in and turns on the light, revealing Genevieve, the blind Watcher, startling Elias, and possibly the audience as well—or have we noticed her watching the entire scene? Mertis suddenly remembers that it's the first weekend after Thanksgiving, which means it's time to light her angel chimes. She pulls out Swedish angel chimes from a cupboard, puts candles on them and lights them. This scene, the last one of the play, is, like the first scene, filled with quiet stretches in which the characters, and therefore the audience, simply sit, watch, and listen. They *"watch the angels fly in circles"* (151) and *"listen to the existence or nonexistence of the sound"* of rustling or wings that Genevieve hears (152).

John winds down with a quiet, beautiful speech about love and reminds us that this is ultimately a play about love. Elias and Jenny are struggling but we hope that they will one day be able to find a love like Mertis has with her husband George, who she met later in life, after a long and unhappy first marriage, and who, throughout the play, she tends in the back room because he is ill. She tells Elias the story of meeting George—a story that is a tribute to Baker's own husband, Nico Baumbach; *John*'s dedication page reads "The last page of this play is dedicated to Nico." Meeting George, Mertis says, was like "walking out of a dark wood," like "emerging from the cold and into the sun," and made her think that "anything is possible" (154). Mertis lets Genevieve and Elias—and the audience—sit with that loveliness for a while, then suggests they listen to music and turns on "Les oiseaux dans la charmille" from Offenbach's *Tales of Hoffmann*. They, and we, listen to the music and watch the Swedish angel chimes fly. It feels like the play is going to end on this settled, contented note. (Or it *seems* like a contented note, though the lyrics of the song are about a mechanical doll whom Hoffmann thinks is real and has fallen in love with.) Halfway through the song, Jenny's cell phone, which Elias has been carrying in his pocket, dings with a text message. Elias puts the phone on the table. Mertis looks at it and, in the last line of the play, asks, "Who's John?" So, Elias was right, Jenny was still in contact with her former lover, John; or, perhaps, Genevieve's ex-husband John is haunting the premises. Either way, the energy has suddenly shifted to end *John* on an ambiguous note.

There is something in *John* that is "not susceptible to rational analysis and that only adds to its teasing fascination," Michael Billington wrote of the London production, calling it "a piece of American gothic" in which "what Baker does, remarkably, is use the trappings of a spooky thriller to explore universal emotions: above all the need to escape the sense of solitary confinement inside our own skins. It's less a play of ideas than of atmosphere and one that works through a masterly accumulation of detail."[29] Jill Dolan suggests that the ambiguity of the final moment "gestures out toward all that remains ineffable, unknowable, and undecidable, all experienced in the temporary but comfortable companionship of those who might not be watching over, but are there to witness with."[30] Hilton Als declared in his *New Yorker* review of *John* that it's a big shift for her "on a political level," that "she has declared her ambition. The truth is that it's still an anomaly for women artists to claim this kind of space for themselves and their work"; in the past, he argues, Baker "distanced herself from that particular problem by writing about boys—mostly white boys," but in *John* "it's the women who quickly take and then hold the stage."[31]

I Love Dick

In 2017, Baker co-wrote (with playwright and actor Heidi Schreck, who had originated the role of Theresa in *Circle Mirror Transformation*) the most talked-about episode of the television show *I Love Dick*, based on Chris Kraus's 1997 cult novel. It wasn't the first time Baker had worked in a writers' room for TV or film, but it appears to have been the most positive experience. *I Love Dick* creator Jill (now Joey) Soloway hired exclusively women and gender non-conforming writers for the show; following Kraus's own autofictional approach, for the episode the writers shared stories of their own sexual experiences. (Soloway notes that "We were trying to get really granular, naming our moments of witnessing our younger selves and how we came into contact with the idea of sexual shame. And I think that in a room with all women, we felt compelled to tell the whole truth, and nothing but the truth. Because we weren't just trying to do that extra bit of shading that you start to do when there's a cis man around."[32]) Schreck gives Baker credit for the conception of the episode.[33] They took the stories shared in the room and melded them with images from films by female experimental filmmakers. The result, "A Short History of Weird Girls," was described by Alexis Soloski as "the best twenty minutes of television I've seen in years," indeed "revolutionary" in its insistence that "sexual identity is crucial to a broader sense of identity, of a piece with emotional and intellectual development"; it "takes women's desires seriously in all their convolution and excitement and shame."[34]

I Love Dick is a story of complicated desire. At one point in the novel, Kraus says, "I've set myself the job of solving heterosexuality (i.e. finishing this writing project) before turning 40."[35] Baker, who loved the book, responded that it "really does feel like an attempt to figure out and describe the bonkers algebraic equation of being a heterosexual woman."[36] In the television adaptation, experimental filmmaker Chris and her scholar husband Sylvère go to an artist colony in Marfa, Texas, where Chris falls in love with—it might be more accurate to say becomes obsessed with—the director of the colony, sculptor Dick. (In the novel, Dick is a media theorist and the setting is Los Angeles.) She expresses her obsession through love letters, which she turns into an art project. Her desire is personal and erotic and public and ambitious; it reawakens her artistic imagination and reignites her sexual relationship with Sylvère. The TV adaptation opens the view beyond the (white, straight) triangle of Chris, Sylvère, and Dick to consider the histories of other women's desires and how they've been shaped by Dick. In the "A Short History of Weird Girls" episode, we see three women (Chris; Paula, the curator of Dick's gallery; and Toby, a performance artist at the colony) and one sexually fluid person (Devon, an aspiring playwright who grew up in Marfa) write letters to Dick telling stories of the awakening of their sexuality, which are also awakenings of sexual shame. ("Weird girls" is Kraus's own term for anyone bravely exploring sexual desire.) They deliver these letters as monologues to the camera, while behind them, younger versions of themselves are enacted.

As soon as Soloway read the script, she wanted to direct it: "I love this script. I love weird girls. I am a weird girl. I've always been a weird girl. OK, yeah, less so now that I identify as nonbinary, but whatever."[37] "The script became an idea for me," Soloway wrote, "like an entering-into-evidence in the court of public opinion, like testimonies" because "in a way, all of us are on trial for being weird."[38] In the episode, as each of the characters is saying "This is where my shame comes from," Soloway wanted to "obliquely treat each image as if it were a photograph dropping onto another photograph in a courtroom, maybe a courtroom of the world."[39] Directing the episode felt like "the making of a document, with a sort of weaponizing feel, something zealous meant to raise hackles," it felt like an "argument," in that it was "doing all of the things with TV that you aren't supposed to do. Propagandize. Teach. Be didactic. Sedition."[40]

Kraus described her new genre creation of fiction/autobiography/critical theory as "Lonely Girl Phenomenology"[41] and Baker and Schreck theatricalize that, creating a phenomenological style to the episode that is visually and emotionally different from the more straightforward realism of the other episodes in the series. They pick up on an image from one of the letters in the novel, in which Kraus discovers that "through writing it's also possible to re-visit a ghost of your past self, as if at least the shell of who you were fifteen years ago can somehow be re-called."[42] In each of the monologues, we not only see the younger selves in the background, but at a crucial awakening moment of desire, we see the character's body get temporarily animated as though they are shimmering ghosts of themselves. To use Soloski's description, they are overtaken by a "glowing blur."[43] Soloski, however, finds the significance of this somewhat confusing and wonders whether it is intended to represent "sexual desire or a more comprehensive sense of identity."[44] Emily Nussbaum describes the episode as "nearly musical," as we watch the sexual backstories of the characters, "pinpointing the origins of their sexual feelings and their creative drive, which is to say, their relationship to Dick."[45]

The episode opens with scenes from Naomi Uman's 1999 experimental short film *Removed*, in which she excerpted scenes from a 1970s German soft-core porn film and, using a bleaching chemical process on the film stock, "erased" the body of the woman the men are looking at; it creates the sense that the woman's body is animated—flickering, pulsing—and ghostly, with blurred borders, and by making it stand out from the rest of the film, it materializes and foregrounds her desire.[46] "Dear Dick," we hear Chris say, as she does at the beginning of each episode, "I've been horny since I was six."[47] She narrates scenes from her childhood and adolescence of sexual desire blended with shame—and also with *art*, as these desires are bound up with her aesthetic awakening. In one of them, she and a childhood friend want to have sex with a rock star as though they are Louise Bourgeois's sculpture, "The Couple"; they wanted to "act out the Cyborgian split projected onto every woman in this culture." The rock star's response: "You're weird. Weird girls." We see her meet Sylvère, who gets aroused when she pleasures herself, a scene straight out of *Removed*. When he touches her with his foot, we see the animated glowing blur on her body. She wonders about other women's desires and poses the question, "What if we all started writing you letters?"

We then see the histories of Devon, Paula, and Toby. Each of them addresses the viewer as though we are Dick, so we also see the manner in which they interact with Dick: Devon envying, Paula negotiating, Toby competing. Devon grew up on a ranch owned by Dick's family; he often came into her house and she watched his swagger, his easy way with women, how he could sidle up next to one and put his hand on her waist. He became the ego ideal of her own masculinity: she wanted to *be* Dick—to be "the hand, not the waist." We see Devon's glowing blur when she taps his shoulder as though she's cutting in for a dance and substitutes herself for Dick, putting her hand on his woman's waist. Named Delores at birth, Devon shakes off that feminine name as well as female gender conventions. In college, Devon falls in love but gets heartbroken when her girlfriend leaves for a boy. Devon flunks out and moves back home to Texas "to figure out who the hell I should become." Paula grew up with a feminist activist mother; to rebel, she developed a crush on Michael J. Fox's character from *Family Ties*, Alex P. Keaton, who was a political conservative. (This is a detail from Baker's own life.) As a young girl, she worshipped her mother, and we see her curator's aesthetic eye already at work in the way the camera shows us young Paula admiring the shape of her mother's ears, neck, and hands. The discovery of her mother's menstruating, the realization that she is a woman, not just a beautiful mother-art object, alienates Paula. She takes refuge in reading; touching herself while she reads arouses desire and comfort, and it is at this point that we see her own glowing blur. When she learned that this was called masturbation, she turned against it. This, she says, is what she admires about Dick: "You refuse to give anything a name." When she is hired as curator, she proposes a list of female artists, but he is dismissive of them all, refusing to say yes to anything. Toby's story is the most confrontational. She starts her letter as the others do, "Dear Dick," but then adds, with a note of scorn, "or should I say, Dear Great Man, Genius, Loner, Cowboy." She lists his accomplishments, which she is already piling up alongside his, with an aim to surpass him. We learn in her backstory that Toby was sexually abused by her father; as a young adolescent, she is shown internet porn by her cousin and it's something she can't get out of her head. Young Toby's glowing blur overtakes her as she watches her cousin watching the porn, puzzling at the cousin's laughter. Toby will go on to examine the formal properties (the shapes and colors) of hardcore pornography in her doctoral studies. Her dissertation advisor, appalled, asks, "Have you thought about switching to Gender Studies?" Toby answers, "I'm an art historian. I have no interest in gender studies." Addressing Dick, wondering why he gets to make whatever he wants in the desert, she says, "we should be able to study beauty, too. We shouldn't have to be gender studies majors." The episode ends by telling Dick, "Your time is running out," for "We are not far from your doorstep."

In 2016, Soloway delivered a keynote address for the Toronto International Film Festival (TIFF) on "The Female Gaze."[48] The female gaze does not just turn the tables on the male gaze, Soloway argues; it isn't a reversal of power dynamics in which, instead of men seeing and women being looked at, female creators objectify men. Instead, it is a gaze that is aware of how it feels to be looked at and can empathize with the subject. It also gazes back. In "A Short History of Weird Girls," Dick is presented as an object (at one point posed on a couch, naked, draped in a Navajo blanket). Chris addresses the-camera-as-Dick, "I don't care how you see me. I don't care if you want me. It's better that you don't. It's enough that I want you." As Ruth Curry puts it, Dick is "not the sexy cowboy played by Kevin Bacon, but just a guy. Dick is no one special. Dick is a play on words. Dick is a metonym. Dick is shorthand for any standard-model man anywhere—his only power comes from the imaginative energy these women, these artists, invest in him."[49]

I Love Dick began streaming on Amazon in 2017. Though it is "just a show," "it is as close to redemption as we can get in 2017," Rebecca Pitts writes, "the salve to our collective metaphorical pussy-grab."[50] The weird girl is a kind of monster. That capacious, and capricious, sense of monstrousness, and Baker's experiences in writers' rooms, both generative and abusive, surface again in her next play, *The Antipodes*.

The Antipodes

A steady reader of Baker's plays will notice several new and unusual things upon opening the script of *The Antipodes*. First, its larger cast of nine characters: six hired writers (Eleanor, Adam, Danny M1, Danny M2, Josh, and Dave); their boss, a veteran writer, Sandy; his production assistant, Brian; and his administrative assistant, Sarah. (Previously, *Circle Mirror Transformation*'s five was Baker's largest cast size.) Second, the pace: "*a fairly fast clip.*"[51] *The Antipodes* is an intermissionless, one-act play with few silences and no blackouts.[52] What has stayed consistent with Baker's other plays is that her conception started with a stage picture ("a conference table surrounded by chairs"[53]) and it stays in this space: a windowless conference room that serves as some sort of writers' room. There's nothing in the room except a conference table and chairs and a giant stack of boxes filled with cans of seltzer water. In its premiere at Signature Theatre, designed by Laura Jellinek, the table, "with exits on either side, sits at the center of the theatre, with the audience observing the actors in banks of seats—like facing down to an operating table—from either side."[54] In Chloe Lamford's set for London's National Theatre, over the conference table a "bright, cylindrical light hangs oppressively low."[55] At Signature Theatre, the bright shades of different-flavored La Croix boxes were the only pops of color onstage; at the National Theatre, the unvarying greenness of the enormous stack of Perrier boxes added to the pale sickliness of the room.

The most significant innovation in *The Antipodes*, however, is what Baker does with *time*. We learn from the dialogue that four months pass over the course of the play. The writers never leave the room; only Sandy and Sarah come and go. Sarah is the only character with costume changes that indicate the passing of days; in the National Theatre production, her outfits were drastically different each time she entered, to call attention to this, and to the radical sameness of the others and our questions of whether they *ever* get to leave. Eleanor, who knits during the meeting, has a sweater by the end. To show time passing, Baker does not use blackouts or other distinct scene-markers; instead, she inserts an asterisk ("*") in the script. This indicates *"a leap forward in time,"* which should be indicated by *"subtle shifts in actor behavior and movement and without lights or sound"* (6). At Toronto's Coal Mine Theatre, the actors "just pause and move onto another scene with a completely different energy."[56] Reviewing the production at Red Stitch Actors' Theatre in Melbourne, Robert Reid observed that "It creates a sense of discontinuity to their conversation, highlighting the social, ambitious and strategic absurdity of creative humans."[57] In the National Theatre production, "When the notion that time might actually move in different dimensions is called into question, Sarah enters the room at an eerily slower speed to the conversation taking place around her."[58] These are cinematic techniques that we take for granted in the movies but don't see onstage. They were also inspired by Baker's favorite book, *The Magic Mountain*, in which Mann slows time to spend an entire chapter on one moment but speeds through World War I in a single paragraph.

Halfway through the play, Sandy asks the existential question that lies under the play and haunts it: "What if we could tell the story that's the only story we all need to know?" (65).

Yes, *The Antipodes* is about stories, and the importance of stories, but, as Andrzej Lukowski writes for London's *Time Out,* "beneath its laconic surface, *The Antipodes* is endlessly shifting and complex, and it's about an enormous number of things. It's about the way men behave in packs in the workplace, to coerce and isolate women," as well as "the strangeness of the world that exists beyond our ability to describe it, the horror of the inexplicable (the title, never spoken, is clearly not a reference to Australia but to the world beyond our knowledge)."[59]

Its opening is unusual. There's no stretch of silence. No music or sound. No lighting cues. Just a mysterious opening line to get us situated in this world: "No dwarves or elves or trolls" (7). The writers are brainstorming a story about monsters—though nothing overdone like vampires or werewolves; they're searching for something out of the ordinary, like a manticore or a gorgon. Unlike Soloway's writers' room in which Baker created the *I Love Dick* episode, this one is painfully like the majority of such rooms: All are white except for Adam. All the writers are male except for Eleanor. *"I worked off the assumption that both Eleanor and Adam were hired due to pressure from HR,"* Baker notes after her character list (3). I take this as a subtle critique of the whiteness and maleness of most writers' rooms; Marie-Helene Bertino counters, "We must contend with the fact that holding the places of six undifferentiated white men onstage was more important than casting diversely. If this was exactly the point, the play should have made it. I left craving innovation."[60] (For the National Theatre production, the writers were a mix of British and American, and Sarah was Irish.)

It is Baker's most abstract play to date, with little plot (or, as Ben Brantley quipped, "it's nothing but plot. Or rather plots, of every conceivable stripe, which bubble and spurt from the mouths of everyone onstage)."[61] The plot, such as it is, is like one long brainstorming session. We never learn precisely *what* they are working on, though it seems to be a TV series or film or video game; keeping it unexplained makes us wonder if it's something more futuristic, or more primitive. We learn very little about the writers except what they disclose through their storytelling. (Curiously, Baker also knows little about them. She varied her usual composition method for this play and did not create detailed biographies for the characters. "What you learn about their lives is what they perform for their coworkers," she has said.[62]) Who are they as human beings? What kind of life do they have outside of the writers' room? What are their ambitions as individual writers? Are they, as Tim Teeman asks, merely "content generators" who are "exploited in the name of art"?[63] Throughout, the play explores "Who owns stories, what are they, what service do they provide, what use are they," and "who are they for."[64]

When the play opens, it's the first day for this particular group of writers working together, and Sandy gives them his opening-day "schpiel" (16). What they are there to do sounds both clichéd and sincere: "tell a really good story" (17). Sandy likes to wax philosophical and ambitious in motivating them: "The rest of the world might be going to hell, but stories are better than ever," "Let's fuck with everyone's heads and shift their relationship to space and time," "Let's make something wild and crazy but so fucking truthful that it gives everyone a new sense of empathy and commonality" (18). Josh deflates this soaring rhetoric with the question, "But it's about monsters, right?" (19). The power dynamics are immediately clear: Everyone needs to please Sandy. They need to follow his rules. They need to create something brilliant.

As Holly O'Mahony writes,

> Fittingly for a play named after the "antipode" – a point on the earth that's opposite another – the play sees Sandy give his team a set of rules then do the opposite himself: no phones are allowed in the boardroom, yet he's consistently texting; the office is a safe space where workers are encouraged to be honest and transparent, yet on opening up, one is ousted; and the only two women in the office are either ogled, patronised or professionally jeopardised by having their ideas stolen.[65]

The first of the time leaps occurs after Sandy has just instructed them to tell stories of not necessarily literal monsters but "something monstrous" (19). After the time leap, Dave says, "Sure. I'll go first" (19) and starts telling a story about his first sexual experience. This isn't about monsters; the audience realizes they have to catch up with something. It's like we've gotten a little zap, like we've suddenly awoken and missed something. Most of the men's experiences are cliches we've seen over and over in movies: thinking about baseball to last longer during sex; engaging in a threesome. Eleanor is uncomfortable in the room. Prodded by the others, she tells a story of losing her virginity that feels real and truthful; it has freshness and specificity and is a tale of female sexual pleasure. But at the end of it, Sandy's phone beeps and he gets up and leaves. Eleanor wonders if that means it was a bad story. Has she bored everyone with the truth of a woman's experience?

This impression gets reinforced after Danny M1 tells a long and graphic tale of infidelity and fear of having contracting a painful STD, which ends in a lurid scene of masturbating in the shower. Sandy's response: "That's a good story" (30).

Josh is always pitching ideas about time. He throws out, "What if time had two axes" (31) and asks the others how they see it—horizontally, vertically, as a spiral. Are we always going forward? Can we never go back? Later Adam will bring up the Hindu notion of time as cyclical, moving through eras called the Yugas (we are currently in the Kali Yuga, "the most demonic fucked-up age" [55]). Is time monstrous? These time questions keep us thinking about time, both in the abstract and in trying to figure out what is happening in the real time of the play. While they are brainstorming story ideas, mysterious things happen outside the conference room. Sandy starts leaving more frequently, then stays away for a while—his wife is ill, his kids have a birthday party—and some kind of storm rages outside.

Sandy is full of the mythologies of show business. He regales them with his description of Jerry Madigan, the kind of old-school writer who had a system, who taught Sandy everything he knows about "journeys and exploits" (36) and "hunches and gut reactions" (36) and "rundown and condensation" (37)—a long speech about nothing, his repeated clauses ending with a lot of "airy power words."[66]

The play deepens, and we start to differentiate the characters more, when Sandy has them tell stories of the worst thing that's ever happened to them. Dave jumps in, a bit too eagerly, to tell a violent story about his father shooting himself in the face to spite his mother, who finds his body, is traumatized by it, and checks herself into an institution. Although in real life it would be a horribly painful experience to live through, the way Dave tells it feels a bit too pat and Hollywood-ready. He's clearly told it a lot and sees it as the story that defines him: "It made me who I am" and "made me want to tell stories" (48), he concludes. This is followed by a "biggest regret" (49) story by Danny M2, an odd and sincerely reflective tale about one summer when he lived on a farm and had the task of securing the chickens in their coop at night so that the foxes didn't get them. He was too scared to pick them up even though he deeply desired to; "there was something about their chests, those fluffy alive chicken breasts, and I loved the idea of holding them firmly but lovingly in my hands" (50) but he was also afraid of hurting them, so he didn't pick them up and would just trust that they would get into the coop by themselves by nightfall—thus risking that a fox could come along in the meantime. His real regret is not that a fox ate a chicken—no chickens died under his watch, luckily—but that he didn't take a risk and explore a desire. He tells them he thinks the story is really about a fear of having missed out on some "specific kind of joy" that would have transformed his life if he had just picked the chickens up that summer (51). It's a tale that feels startlingly true (and reminiscent of Vanya and of Avery in *The Flick*) but, as with Eleanor's story, there's no response from the group. Even though the story was real, telling it makes it feel false to Danny M2. Unlike Dave, who has capitalized on his horrific life experience, Danny M2 confesses that he would prefer to keep his personal life private and not make it into a story for others' consumption. This is met with *"Silence"* (52), the first and one of the very few stage directions of silence in this play. He has broken a silent, unwritten taboo. When the characters are most vulnerable, we see Sandy on his phone. While at first *"it seems like Sandy might say something,"* he starts texting, then dials a number, then leaves the room. A few minutes later, Sarah comes to summon Danny M2, who exits and never comes back.

As the time leaps forward, the play shifts into a more surrealistic mode and the stories told get stranger. Sarah is instructed by Sandy to tell a story which begins in a realistic fashion (dealing with a new stepmother) but veers into fairy tale territory (with a talking doll, reminiscent of *John*) and visiting an old woman who lives in a little blue house that has fenceposts topped with human skulls. This Hansel and Gretel story morphs into a Rumpelstiltskin one in which Sarah is locked in the house and given the impossible task of separating moldy from good kernels in an enormous vat of corn—which the doll does for her while she sleeps—and at the end taking one of the old woman's skulls home, where its eyes burn her evil stepmother and stepsister and turn them to ash. This story is met simply with *"Pause"* (61). Then Sarah takes everyone's lunch orders and exits.

Recalling the *Wizard of Oz*, when the writers hold a conference call with Max, the head honcho, they don some kind of virtual-reality-type goggles and all face an empty chair at the head of the table. This is where Sandy usually sits, so it indicates the shift in power to have Max there and Sandy among the others. We don't see a projection of Max; we just hear his voice, which is a "posh British accent" (61). Max's voice gets garbled in a bad internet connection and crucial points get dropped or blipped, but no one, not even Sandy, will stop Max to fix it. Brian and Sarah scramble around in the background but are unable to clear it up. Sandy, trying to impress Max, launches first, into a lowering of expectations (it's been "only" five or six weeks since they started, he says—calling our attention to how long it's been), then a big philosophical pitch for asking questions such as "What would communication look like without time?" (64), culminating in wondering if we could go back to the beginning of storytelling, "Could we remake our collective unconscious?" (65) Now it's Sandy's turn to receive the silence from a listener. What Max wants is not the "heady stuff" (66) but for them to "just tell a really simple *(garbled)*, to reel people in and make them *(garbled, garbled)*" (67). To tell a simple story that will move audiences and make a lot of money for the studio. When they sign off and take off their goggles, everyone starts speculating about whether Max has had plastic surgery, but Sandy is clearly worried, and will soon start spending less and less time in the room with them.

The next time leap takes them to discussion of Alejandra, a writer who gets mentioned very early in the play as someone who was difficult to work with because she made everyone feel self-conscious and judged—"Everything offended her" (70); the men who worked with her agree. But their descriptions of her also make her seem more serious than the rest of them; she wanted to talk about the war, or a solar eclipse—substantial matters. Sandy tells a story of hearing from HR that someone has reported a "Hostile Work Environment" (71), and he immediately suspects Alejandra. He presents himself as the creator of an open, comfortable work environment, but by this time in the play we have seen how he pointedly ignores Eleanor's and Sarah's stories and presumably sent DannyM2 away. After Sandy confronted the writers to talk about the hostile work environment, Alejandra never returned to work—and disappeared altogether, lost to her family as well. (Later, when things get crazy and the lights flicker on and off, Eleanor will whisper, "Alejandra?" [94].) Sandy takes this story as an opportunity to rant about HR diversity policies and why they shouldn't force him to "hire a woman or a... or a Chinese person or whatever" unless he wants to (76).

As they are getting exhausted and not progressing on the project (whatever the project is), Adam proposes that it would be a relief if storytelling were made fully scientific—if you could just attach electrodes to people's heads and make them feel all the things that stories make us feel. "But the whole thing where we have to make up some fictional world or some fictional series of events or narrative concepts would be over" (78). In a way, it's all scientific already, he concludes: "We all pretend there's something magic about it but actually it's just algorithms" (78).

Sandy stops coming in for a while. There's a funny stretch of short time leaps in which Sarah keeps coming to give his excuse for that day: his wife isn't feeling well, it's the kids' birthday party, his therapist died. The writers get worried that Sandy is going to pull the plug on the project, even though (or because) he keeps sending empty notes of encouragement via Sarah: "you guys are geniuses" (82). And then suddenly he's back, giving them a pep talk about how "stories are a little bit of light that we can cup in our palms like votive candles to show us the way out of the forest" (83). When he leaves, he tells them to be careful in "this crazy weather" (84), our first clue that *something* is going on outside the conference room. We never see them leave, but we keep hearing details that they have left to prepare for some kind of what seems to be a worldwide climate emergency. Adam: "I filled my bathtub" (86). Josh: "I bought five flashlights" (86).

Suddenly the play shifts into faster, more frequent time leaps (even as the time is stretching longer outside). Each new scene opens with another writer announcing that there are a certain number of stories in the world ("seven," thirty-six," "ten") and categorizing them. In a shift that feels like *a lot* of time has passed and that they've run out of steam, Brian, the assistant, steps forward and becomes the leader. He teaches them how to make a sigil, a practice from chaos magic in which they write out their intention ("To come up with the right story" [91]) and then remove and rearrange letters to make it a whole other, unrecognizable phrase that contains the intention but moves it to the subconscious mind ("AWW PUUTEM RAD TROTS" [92]), which they recite like a mantra. While the others sleep (the storm has begun outside, and they are holed up inside to finish the project), Brian engages in a ritual of some sort. He takes *"an animal skin"* out of his bag and puts it over his head, takes out a *"small thurible of red liquid"* and mixes one of Eleanor's probiotics into it, then draws blood from his shoulder with a dagger and adds that as well. Dipping his finger in the red mixture, he draws symbols on his chest, performs dance-like *"prayer gestures"* (93), and announces that there are "eighteen" kinds of stories in the world, which he lists.

Near the end they are feeling completely drained and hopeless—though Dave tells them this is a good sign, that Sandy has always maintained "this horrible hopeless feeling is the feeling you get right before it happens" (95). (Which recalls the advice from Judy in *Nocturama* and Sandy Jano in *The Aliens*.) After a *"very very long silence"* (95) Adam begins telling a story, in a flat affectless tone, of the beginning of the world. It is long and fantastical and feels like the Ur-story of all mythologies, elements of Sumerian and Greek and Hebrew creation stories, starting with a "great father alone" in the void who is lonely and produces another being out of his head, and then a sacred cow to feed the new being, and then many other beings who procreate with one another and violently overthrow and kill one another, all the way down to a woman in a garden with a serpent, and that, Adam concludes, "was the first story ever told" (99). It's a tour de force monologue onstage, running three pages in the script. But in the writers' room no one wrote down Adam's story. Brian wasn't taking notes; he never does when Eleanor or Adam speak. Brian is nauseated; he coughs up blood and a small creature (a *"jellyfish"* or *"seahorse"* or *"anemone"* [100]), then leaves. With Brian gone, Sarah gets to step up and become the production assistant who takes notes.

The final leap of time takes place after everyone has gone home to check on their homes after the storm. Eleanor is wearing the sweater she's been knitting throughout the play. She rescued some childhood objects from her mother's basement: a troll doll, her secret diary, and the first stories she ever wrote. Sandy returns; he's experienced an existential crisis and thinks "maybe there are no more stories" (108). He puts them all on hiatus and says that he and his family are heading up to their cabin near "the border" (109). The writers don't leave. Instead, Baker gives the play an optimistic ending. Maybe the stories are all over for the Sandys and Maxes and their ilk. But Eleanor restarts the storytelling—in a sense, restarts the world—with the tales she wrote as a child. There will be new stories.

The Antipodes marked a new story for Baker herself. For the New York premiere she worked with a new director, Lila Neugebauer, instead of her usual collaborator Sam Gold. In London, she co-directed the National Theatre production with designer Chloe Lamford, who created the much-raved-about set for *John*; *Time Out* praised their collaboration, noting that "Baker and Lamford direct beautifully, creating a sort of dreamy deadpan or strangely filtered reality."[67] Of all her plays to date, *The Antipodes* has received the most mixed response among professional critics. While she's always drawn a self-selecting audience, and has alienated other audiences, she has been critically acclaimed. Ben Brantley continues the accolades, writing that *The Antipodes* "leaves you glowing with a wondering satisfaction. I mean the happy satiety that comes from being in the hands of a real right-brain/left-brain author who channels her ineffable instincts with a master artisan's practical skills."[68] Marie-Helene Bertino, however, writing for *BOMB*, thought that the style shift didn't quite work: "Surrealists must achieve an uncanny calibration of the supernatural, information dispersal, and novel concept that gives concreteness a poetic intangibility, and vice versa. Withholding specifics works if while familiar elements retract, something else advances. In *The Antipodes,* nothing did."[69] Marilyn Stasio sees it as a good writer's bad play about being unable to write; Stasio seems to take seriously the inanity of many of the writers in the room, rather than seeing the inanity as a critique of such writers' rooms.[70] Robert Reid from Melbourne: "*The Antipodes* is a strange ritual made of variety clippings and DVD directors commentaries." Where it goes wrong, Michael Billington argues, is in its surprisingly general exploration of creation stories; to him, it "feels like a thesis-drama, created to prove a point rather than, as in Baker's best work, a play that allows ideas to emerge from the interaction of people."[71] Yet by 2022, when it was playing in Toronto, critics were calling it "an absorbing and mysterious meditation on the power and importance of stories and storytelling" and "the play we all need to see right now."[72] Oscar Wilde famously wrote that "when the critics disagree, the artist is in accordance with himself."[73] The mixed response may indicate a discomfort with a new mode of storytelling from her; or a sharp observation of the strange messiness of this particular play.

These three scripts—the plays *John* and *The Antipodes,* the TV episode "A Short History of Weird Girls"—are all formally inventive in how they open time to the viewer, and through time, desire. In *John,* Baker pulls audiences into a house that feels both layered in time, rooted in its haunted Civil War history, and eerily out of time; while Mertis's world opened into new possibilities with love of George, Genevieve cannot fully escape from John's story, forever narrated by John. In *I Love Dick*, Chris, Devon, Paula, and Toby are able to stand outside of and witness their past selves, though all are living in a Dick-shaped artistic and erotic world. In *The Antipodes,* time flashes before our eyes, but realistically, with no pyrotechnics; as in life, we're just suddenly aware of having moved on. Its ending gives us a glimmer of possible radical hope that Eleanor's stories will begin a new era, will break through time to create a new epoch. Muriel Rukeyser famously stated (in 1968), "if one woman told the truth about her life" that "the world would split open." Watching the caring friendship of Mertis and Genevieve, hearing the characters in *I Love Dick* confess their complex truths, and applauding Eleanor's rise from the conference table to begin storytelling anew, I wonder if we will be seeing new stories, new truths, and new conceptions of time from Annie Baker as well.

CHAPTER 5
CRITICAL PERSPECTIVES

CARING ABOUT THE MATTER IN ANNIE BAKER'S DRAMA

Thomas Butler

In a 2015 conversation with Marc Maron on his podcast, Annie Baker noted a change in her work over the years:

> I started to realize that my plays were a little too neat, and I felt like they were tying themselves in a little bow at the end. And with this new one [*John*] I want it to be a mess. I'm going to intentionally make this play kind of in the end make no sense and make total sense at the same time.... I really want to stop trying to explain anything to anybody.[1]

She and Maron moved on before she could say which plays she believes have tidy endings. At this point in the conversation, they were talking about *John* (2015), which is surprising given that that play more than any other ends so definitively when Mertis reveals that Jenny received a text message from John, Jenny's sometime sexual partner. It may be too much to say that *John* ties itself into a bow at the end (it's unclear, for example, whether Jenny's dinging phone throughout the play always indicates communication from John), but it doesn't seem to give way to the open-endedness Baker says she now prefers. In other interviews, Baker describes the change in her work by describing the emphasis she puts on the physical aspects of her more recent work. For example, in 2017, she told Greta Gerwig,

> For early plays of mine, I started with character. But I think that's because I hadn't been in theaters; I hadn't worked that much. I'm very interested in character, obviously, but once I started having my plays produced, I became so fascinated by the theatrical experiment and the weirdness of theatrical space, so now all my plays start with space

and stage picture and setting—or container is maybe the better way to put it.²

Here the idea of containing a play is presented less as a formal concern (the little bow at the end) than as a physical element of the performance (the container). In this essay, I will show how Baker's growing interest in the physical aspects of theater reinforces a thematic concern that courses through all of her plays, namely, the demand that her characters and, indeed, her audience exercise care and attention toward others.

"A nomenclature issue"

Baker's first produced play, *Body Awareness* (2008), presents dialogue, humor, and tenderness that are recognizable in all of her plays, but what is striking in view of her later work is the spareness of theatrical space. The play examines how the language of people's political identities in contemporary America (it's set in the fictional town Shirley, Vermont, in 2005) can put them at a distance from their lived experience. In short, the play traces how two self-consciously liberal women, a middle-aged couple named Joyce and Phyllis, deal with the confident chauvinism of a houseguest. Phyllis, a psychology professor at Shirley State College, has organized Body Awareness Week on campus, which involves a variety of artistic performances and exhibitions. For this reason, a guest artist, a photographer named Frank Bonitatibus, is staying at the home of Phyllis, Joyce, and Joyce's 21-year-old son Jared. The central tension of the play centers on Phyllis's and Joyce's different responses to both Frank and his art. Frank is fifty-nine years old and quick to share his enthusiasm for, among other things, his eclectic spirituality. He is certainly full of himself, but the real problem comes once he describes the nature of his photography. He photographs naked women. He insists that the women pose voluntarily in order to "reclaim their body image."³ Phyllis is immediately suspicious of Frank's motives and turns entirely against him when she learns that his work includes photographs of "little girls," who have posed, Frank adds, with parental permission (401).

Phyllis and Joyce are both quick to sniff out hints of misogyny and to embrace a self-congratulatory political identity. Baker has admitted that these characters grew out of her observation of hippies and academics in her hometown of Amherst, Massachusetts. Phyllis reveals a lot about herself when she, while lying in bed with Joyce, insists that Joyce's job as a high school teacher does not place her "in academia" (382). And, similarly, Joyce reveals a lot about herself later in the play when she tells Frank that she and Phyllis take pride in being "politically sensitive without being overly PC" (432). Baker leaves it up to the audience to decide whether Joyce is "overly PC" when she praises one of Phyllis's colleagues for being not only fabulous but also African American and part Native American, she asserts without being certain. For both Joyce and Phyllis, their politics are central to their identities, and their politics are entwined with their use of language. The play's title refers to Body Awareness Week, which Phyllis coined in an effort to expand the campus's discussion from what she sees as the too-narrow scope of National Eating Disorder Awareness Week. It is, she says, "just a nomenclature issue" (387).

Much of the play traces the fissures of the nomenclature issue. Jared, Joyce's son, spends his time reading the OED, and Phyllis complains in a disagreement about Frank's photography that Joyce is acting like the language police. Throughout the play, characters are in different ways asking what words mean. Jared, who may or may not have Asperger's Syndrome (there's disagreement among the characters), grows frustrated by the loose way in which people use language. And he is happy to break down OED definitions of common words for anybody who will listen to him. Eager to start dating, he imagines that women will be impressed by how much etymology he knows. Jared's attachment to dictionary definitions adumbrates the rigidity the other characters have regarding concepts and values that no dictionary can adjudicate. For example, the play asks without resolving whether Jared actually has Asperger's. Jared insists that he doesn't, Frank says he doesn't, but Phyllis, the professor of psychology, is sure he does. Joyce, Jared's mother, wants Jared to see a psychologist in the hopes of getting a more definite diagnosis, a suggestion Jared bristles at, insisting that he's not "retarded" (375). How do you cope when definitions or diagnoses of things and people aren't available?

Similarly, the play asks without resolving whether Frank's photography is exploitative. Both Joyce and Phyllis, of course, recoil at the prospect of women being exploited by a male photographer, but it's hard to know if that's what Frank is up to. Joyce tells Phyllis that she found the photographs "actually incredibly moving" (401). By the time Phyllis gets around to seeing them, well after she lambasted Frank's art, she tells Jared that they were "totally offensive and horrible" (427). As the week with Frank in the house goes on, Joyce falls for him, as he reminds her of her ex-husband.

After Frank asks Joyce if she would like to pose for him, she agrees, inciting Phyllis's expected fury. It's hard to conclude that Joyce, a 55-year-old woman, could be thought to be exploited in this case, but her clarity of thought may very well have been compromised by either her attraction to Frank or her annoyance with Phyllis's priggishness. When Joyce hazards that posing would be freeing, Phyllis says she's being an idiot. In the end, Joyce goes ahead with the photo shoot, but as soon as she undresses to her bra, Jared enters in distress, and the shoot ends before it ever begins, never to be mentioned again in the play.

The uncertainty of the nature of Jared's diagnosis and of Frank's art stands in contrast to the certainty of Phyllis's and Joyce's abstract yet definable political identities. Once when Jared is reading the OED, he takes a break to instruct Phyllis on the lexicographic distinction between descriptivism and prescriptivism. Phyllis quickly turns it into a matter of identity by glibly asserting, "I'm anti-ideology" (423). She automatically processes the world into the conceptual schema of her politics. In an argument about whether Joyce should pose for Frank, she deftly identifies the tension at the heart of the play. Phyllis accuses Joyce of joining the "enemy." When Joyce asks who the enemy is, Phyllis offers a list:

PHYLLIS: Um, prejudice? Misogyny? Exploitative . . . exploitativeness?
JOYCE: These are concepts. Not people. You think I've joined those concepts? (459)

In brief, Phyllis's problem is that she is deeply aware of political concepts but is blind to whatever doesn't fit into those concepts. In a moment that Baker later found problematic, Phyllis delivers a speech on the final evening of Body Awareness Week to all attendees. She goes off script, pauses, and reveals something she seems to be working through: "I want . . . I want so badly for there to be a right answer" (462) "*overwhelmed*" at this moment (463), which implies her reckoning with all that doesn't fit into categories, principally, the human beings she loves. We can be as careful as we like with using language properly and endorsing the right political ideas, but, Baker suggests, what really matters happens where there is no right answer, namely, in the messiness of our behavior with other people, each of whom exists in excess of any definition.

In order to present a play that is ultimately about language, Baker limits its non-linguistic elements. In subsequent interviews, Baker admits that this is less a matter of artistic choice than her inexperience as a playwright.

For example, in Nathan Heller's *New Yorker* profile, she says, "*Body Awareness* was written with very little thought about physical space and time and duration and design and all the things I think about now when I sit down to write."[4] Even though she seems critical of her inattention to physical space, the effect supports her thematic concerns. The stage is divided into three parts: Stage left is a kitchen, center stage is a bedroom, and stage right features a blackboard. Props are suggestive of the spaces rather than representative of the spaces. Here, for example, is part of Baker's relatively scant instructions for the set: "Center stage is a queen-sized bed. This is Joyce and Phyllis's bedroom" (369). This description reveals Baker's limited interest in the material things of the play. It's as if she doesn't want the audience to get distracted by the stuff that doesn't really concern her primary interest in the pitfalls of language and definitions. Appropriately, the play ends as Frank surreptitiously snaps a photograph of Joyce, Phyllis, and Jared: "*There is a blinding flash of white light*" (480). The flash severs whatever attachment the audience may have had to the things and people they've been looking at. All of that becomes immaterial.

Baker's preference for a light set continues in her next of her plays set in Shirley, *Circle Mirror Transformation* (2009). All of the play's action takes place in a largely empty community center dance studio where the play's five characters meet weekly for an acting class. The play is divided not into acts but into weeks so that each of the six segments presents the class from each of the six weeks. The *Guardian*'s theater critic Mark Lawson was struck by how each week opens with an empty stage, prompting him to ask Baker whether "the 'everyone out' moments come to her during rehearsal or writing."[5] Baker answered, "Oh – that always emerges at the writing stage. I just really like looking at empty rooms!"[6] Through the play, the room remains empty apart from the five actors, a yoga ball, and, at one point, a hula hoop.

What we're left with are the characters attempting acting exercises with uneven deftness and self-consciousness. Marty, the 55-year-old instructor, has the group, which includes James, her husband, do things like play explosion tag, tell the life story of another student in the character of that student, and lie on their backs and collaboratively count to ten without interrupting one another. By the third week of class, Lauren, a 16-year-old girl eager to become an accomplished actor, impatiently asks Marty if they would ever get around to doing "real acting."[7] Certainly not in Marty's plans, the effect of the students' halting exercises is a series of revelations about the students' lives that lead to meaningful understandings of themselves and of one another. Yet these revelations largely come about through indirection. For example, in the fifth week, Marty plays the part of Lauren and divulges strains in Lauren's parents' marriage and then lands on something Lauren would be unlikely to acknowledge or articulate: "Maybe one day I can stop putting so much pressure on myself" (164). The characters transform by gaining an understanding of themselves through the other characters' playing or mirroring them.

As in *Body Awareness*, the action of the play happens in its language. In one exercise in the third week, Schultz, a 48-year-old carpenter, has the difficult task of recreating his childhood bedroom by using only the bodies of his classmates as props. They oblige and do their best to contort themselves into a bed, a tree, a baseball glove, and a stuffed snake. The scene is a comic failure, capped by Marty imitating a stuffed snake while sitting on James's back, which at this instant is a bed. Schultz dejectedly admits that the contrived scene neither looks nor feels like his bedroom. A more effective way to see and feel one's past comes through conversation, even when it's indirect or oblique. For example, Theresa, one of the students, moved to Shirley five months ago after ending an unhappy relationship with someone named Mark in New York City. In an exercise, Lauren and James perform an imagined argument between Theresa and Mark. The real Theresa can't help herself and takes over Lauren's part and articulates with clarity the fundamental problem in their relationship: "You could never just let me love you and be free. You were so . . . you were so judgmental and moralistic" (170). And she goes on, greeted by her classmates with silence and then hearty congratulations. In the play's final scene, Schultz and Lauren perform an imagined conversation that they have with each other ten years in the future. Importantly, Baker directs that everything and everyone apart from Lauren and Schultz should "*disappear*" presumably to ensure the audience's focus on the spotlit conversation (205). Lauren asks Schultz how many times his life will end. After Lauren rephrases the question, Schultz responds, "Uh . . . I don't know. I guess I feel like my life is pretty real" (208). Real feeling and self-understanding, both of which are in short supply in earlier scenes, come about through dialogue, even when it is, as Beckett has it, just play.

Baker has gained a reputation for her ear for dialogue. Nathan Heller reports that when Baker was seventeen she would tape-record people's conversations and transcribe what they said. "Reading the conversations on paper," Heller writes, "she could see not just how people spoke their minds but how they failed to–all the filler, the obliqueness, and false starts."[8] Coinciding with the opening of *Circle Mirror Transformation* at The Huntington Theatre Company in Boston, she was interviewed by Playwrights Horizons Literary Manager Adam Greenfield, but she asked that they conduct the interview over email rather than as a live conversation because "speaking is a kind of misery."[9] Yet it is also a kind of consolation because everyone finds themselves in the predicament Baker describes. Through Baker's career, moments of solidarity between dissimilar characters have a particular poignancy. For example, at the close of *Circle Mirror Transformation*, when the teenage Lauren and the middle-aged divorcé Schultz conclude their imagined meeting in the future, "*They smile awkwardly at each other and do not move*" (208). The bond is understated and unmistakable, and it anticipates the conclusion of Baker's next Vermont Play, *The Aliens* (2010). Evan, the nervous teenager who works at a coffee shop, befriends two wayward older men who spend their days hanging out by the coffee shop's back door. At the end of the play, after one of the older men dies from a drug overdose, the other, KJ, assures Evan that he's "gonna go far."[10] "*Evan tries not to smile. But then he does. They stand there. Blackout*" (84). There is an affecting solidarity in Baker's Shirley plays, but it emerges not through lofty speeches but rather uhs and yeahs of ordinary, self-conscious, and uncertain talk.

But this takes time. Just about every piece published on Baker's drama comments on how long her plays are and how much silence there is in the dialogue. Sam Kahn begins his laudatory essay "The Triumph of the Quiet Style" by noting how groundbreaking the pauses and silences were in Baker's early work: "Her success is so sweeping that it's almost hard to remember how *weird* her style seemed five or ten years ago, and how much it ran against all the prevailing headwinds of playwriting, which, for decades, had been all about making plays faster, more shocking, *edgier*."[11] Right from the opening of *Circle Mirror Transformation*, audiences know they are in for a new kind of theatrical experience. The five characters are lying on the floor of the dance studio preparing to collaboratively count to ten but not before, Baker notes, "*at least fifteen seconds of silence*" (89). In a note in the first publication of the script, Baker writes, "Without its silences this play is a satire, and with its silences it is, hopefully, a strange little naturalistic meditation on theater and life and death and the passing of time."[12] In the script of *The Aliens*, which premiered six months after *Circle Mirror Transformation*, Baker goes a step further: "At least a third–if not half–of this play is silence" (3).

Baker acknowledges what John Cage revealed long ago in *4'33"*: that silence in performance has less to do with the composition itself than with the audience's experience of the piece. She said in an interview, "I think the one thing left that really makes people uncomfortable is empty space and quiet."[13] Therefore, we need to be particularly attentive when reading pause-filled exchanges, like the one between KJ and Evan in *The Aliens* in which KJ admits that Jasper has died:

> EVAN: Um.
>   *A long pause.*
> KJ: He died.
>   *Evan looks at him uncomprehendingly. Pause.*
> KJ: Jasper died.
>   *Pause.*
> EVAN: . . . No he didn't.
> KJ: He died a week ago.
> *Pause.* (67)

This dialogue certainly conveys important narrative information, but Baker is more interested in how the audience experiences that information in the context of the halting, uncomfortable pauses. In the first scholarly essay on Baker, published in 2011, Jennifer Cayer argues that Baker's "searching language, purposeful, scripted silences–and the deftness with which the actors voice it–become the central and sustaining spectacle."[14] Through the silences, the audience becomes increasingly aware of its own position as spectators. That shift of sensibility is necessary to give life to the notion Cayer finds at the heart of Baker's work, namely, "that we cannot exist, we cannot survive, without someone to see us."[15] The plays then strive to push the audience members to recognize their interdependence both in the immediate sense of being a spectator of a theatrical spectacle and more broadly in the sense of living among other people outside the theater.

Cayer's essay is remarkably prescient, given that it was written when *Circle Mirror Transformation* and *The Aliens* were still in production, well before *The Flick* and *John* were written. It offers a way to understand Baker's distinctive plays as doing something that has ethical import. Cayer argues that both *Circle Mirror Transformation* and *The Aliens* present characters performing for other characters as a way to "get glimpses of a world they haven't yet seen for themselves."[16] The performances, whether the singing of songs in *The Aliens* or the acting exercises in *Circle Mirror Transformation*, illuminate a path of transformation the characters may happily pursue. As the audience becomes aware of itself as spectators while watching these performances of performances, it gains an awareness of its own ability to transform in the world. As Cayer puts it, "Baker's drama . . . delicately oscillates between immersive spectatorship and intervening moments that invite an awareness of the audience's agency and responsibility as watchers."[17] The contention here is that the characters' halting speech and unpracticed performances make the audience members aware of how they relate to others in the world. Cayer doesn't explain the nature of the audience's possible transformation but leaves open the possibility of an ethical effect of the plays in the world.

My argument up to this point is that Baker's early plays, principally *Body Awareness*, *Circle Mirror Transformation*, and *The Aliens*, make use of their scant sets and ample silences to attend to how people use language. In the plays, characters come to recognize the paucity of their understanding of language in relation to the people around them (e.g., Phyllis) or an understanding of themselves when they see their lives performed in language (e.g., Lauren and Theresa). The hopeful pull of these early plays comes largely from the characters' ability to see themselves in new ways and to, in turn, change their lives. This ability is most apparent at the end of *Circle Mirror Transformation* when Lauren and Schultz describe their happy imagined future lives. Baker doesn't show her characters' realized transformations, but she simply leaves the possibility open. The more daunting challenge in Baker's work is to extend that possibility for change into the lives of the audience members, and it is one of her preoccupations in her work after *The Aliens*.

"We're looking at all the matter"

After *The Aliens*, Baker's imaginative world moved from Shirley, Vermont, and arrived, by way of a Russian country estate in her 2012 adaptation of *Uncle Vanya*, at a movie theater called The Flick in Worcester County, Massachusetts. This change of setting may not have covered many miles, but it constituted a significant aesthetic development. First, the set of *The Flick* (2013) is startlingly inventive. It is a movie theater, and we, "the theater audience, are the movie screen" (5). This note in the script suggests Baker's new recognition of the audience's role in her drama. Much of the action of the play entails two of the three principal characters cleaning between the rows of seats, and, in Baker's hands, this, of course, takes time. The play famously runs for over three hours. As subsequent productions in different theater spaces make clear, the number of seats on stage significantly affects the play's run time. The premiere production in New York had 105 seats, but a later production in Charleston, South Carolina, with 24 seats, ran just over two hours.[18] Where in the earlier plays, pauses and silences punctuated the dialogue in relatively bare physical spaces, now they seem to happen in proportion to the stuff on stage.

In *John* (2015), this is even more pronounced. Sarah Larson commented that the set introduced "a new dimension in Baker's work as I knew it—it was like seeing a richly imagined theoretical world become a lavishly physical world."[19] *John* continues to show Baker's concern with the material aspects of theater. In turn, the set is the inside of a Gettysburg, Pennsylvania, bed-and-breakfast, owned and furnished by a 72-year-old woman named Mertis who has a fondness for small objects including myriad gnomes and porcelain angels. Mertis has given the dining area a Parisian theme and has accordingly outfitted the space with all the odds and ends to make that known to her guests. In addition, there are also on stage, among many other things, a grandfather clock, a piano, a jukebox, and a large doll named Samantha. Stuff abounds in this play. My contention is that this new materially rich approach to stagecraft offers a new way for the plays to connect with the audience and to communicate the thematic concerns that generally have to do with the ways in which people relate to one another. The material elements of *John* reinforce Baker's thematic interest in interpersonal attentiveness and her practical interest in how an audience responds to a theatrical performance.

John presents two characters' lack of ethical substance in relation to an older, wiser character. Elias and Jenny stop at Mertis's bed-and-breakfast for a few days to break up their drive from Columbus, Ohio, to Brooklyn, where they live. They are having difficulties in their relationship, largely due to a history of betrayals and lies. Nonetheless, they are hoping to use this time together over Thanksgiving weekend to patch things up. As soon as they arrive in Mertis's house in the opening scene, they quickly take stock of Mertis's peculiarity and charm. She hospitably offers them peanut butter fudge, shows them "Paris," and describes a frightening diet regimen whose regular injections have allowed Mertis to shed sixty-seven pounds in four months. Elias is excited to visit Gettysburg, since he has been a Civil War buff since childhood, and Jenny is happy enough to oblige him in the spirit of improving their troubled relationship.

The stark difference between this couple and Mertis is apparent from the first moments of the play—Elias mouths "*SHE'S A TRIP*" to Jenny when they first meet—but the difference gains definition when Jenny and Mertis first spend time alone together.[20] Suffering from painful menstrual cramps, Jenny cut short her time with Elias on the battlefield tour and, instead, relaxes with Mertis in the parlor of the house. As Jenny lies on the sofa looking at her cellphone, Merits writes in her journal recording the day's sunset. Prompted by Jenny, Mertis reads her entry, which begins: "The white November sky morphed into an exquisite robin's egg blue by 4 p.m., and its welcome presence lasted but a short while" (54). Through Mertis's florid description, this passage reveals her devoted attention to the world. Further, her pen-and-paper writing gives her experience substance that contrasts sharply with Jenny's typing and scrolling on her iPhone. As part of her work, Jenny is writing on her phone trivia questions for a TV show called Cash Cow. Jenny's concern for insubstantial trivia is a world away from Mertis's investment in the physical world. Indeed, the abundance of physical things in Mertis's house concretizes that investment in the world around her. Later, her friend Genevieve comments, "Mertis takes very good care of her matter" (71). That care extends not simply to the arrangement of the menageries on her shelves but, more importantly, to the people around her. She cares for her sick husband, George, who remains offstage the entire play, and she patiently reads to her blind friend Genevieve. Jenny, in contrast, lacks such ethical attunement. For example, after Mertis tells Genevieve and Jenny that her husband isn't feeling well, Jenny tells a story about how she once got stoned in New Mexico and felt "like the universe was having sex with me. And it was really intense" (75). Jenny here echoes Rose's sexualized narcissism in *The Flick* and similarly betrays her own ethical insouciance.

Elias, for his part, fails to demonstrate care for others. By using "care," I want to emphasize an ethical practice of responding to the needs of a specific person at a specific moment.[21] He has consistently felt on unsteady ground with Jenny since, as becomes clear, she has had and perhaps continues to have a sexual relationship with John. Even as he and Jenny try to rehabilitate their strained relationship, he doesn't trust her. He confides to Mertis that he has always, after a few months, thought of women he has dated as insects. Mertis tries to soften this admission by saying that she thinks her husband sometimes looks like a marmot or a woodchuck. But the misogyny at the heart of Elias's "problem" becomes clear later that night when he and Jenny return to the house after a long day on the battlefield. As they enter, Elias comments that she is "like a statue" (134). She plays the part of a doll, allowing, for example, her arm to drop after he lifts it. But when he picks her up and carries her *"stiffly, like a mannequin,"* and then lies down next to her, he wonders if this is what "true love" feels like (134). Elias hazards that true love is the experience of a woman submitting to his demands.

Baker reasserts this idea in the dazzling final moments of the play. Mertis, Elias, and Genevieve sit quietly watching Swedish angels fly around in circles listening to *"Les oiseaux dans la charmille"* from Offenbach's opera *Tales of Hoffmann*. This aria is sung by the doll Olympia to Hoffmann, who loves her and who believes she is human when he wears special eyeglasses. Olympia sings (in translation; in the play, the aria is in the original French):

Everything that sings and sounds

And sighs, in its turn,

Moves her heart, which trembles with love![22]

Such love, as only an automaton can offer, can last neither in the opera (Olympia is torn apart) nor in the play (Mertis reveals that John had just texted Jenny). Elias's conception of love is deficient, because it fundamentally fails to acknowledge the real existence of another person, the alleged beloved. Therefore, his shortcomings in this regard are of a piece with Jenny's: both fail to respond to the real world apart from themselves.

Baker's earlier plays, *Body Awareness* and *Circle Mirror Transformation* are primarily interested in the relation between language and self-understanding; in *The Aliens*, *The Flick*, and most especially *John*, she considers how characters respond to other people who make some sort of ethical claim on them. As Baker's scope has widened to explore interpersonal relationships, her theater practice has also made much more use of props. I'd like to suggest that the material on stage activates a wider perceptual field, one that makes claims on the audience's attention.

Andrew Sofer has theorized the effect of props in theater in relation to the idea of dark matter. In physics, Sofer concisely explains, "dark matter refers to nonluminous mass that cannot be directly detected by observation."[23] Although dark matter constitutes between 80 and 95 percent of all the matter in the universe, it "can only be inferred by its gravitational effects on the motion of ordinary matter."[24] This idea is utterly fascinating in its own right, and Sofer uses it as an analogy for how material stuff works on stage in theater. In short, whatever we see on stage depends on a force field of "felt absences." "Exerting irresistible force over our imaginations in the playhouse, [dark matter] invisibly pulls the iron filings of theatrical representation into a pattern. Dark matter comprises *whatever is materially absent onstage but un-ignorable*; it is not a finger pointing at the moon, but the tidal force of gravity that pulls at the unseen."[25] *John* is chock-full of felt absences. George is there but offstage. Bedrooms with some affinity with the supernatural are upstairs and offstage. At one point, a sound like "the beating of wings" comes from upstairs (118). These plentiful felt absences emerge in relation to all the visible material in Mertis's house. To follow Sofer's argument, Mertis's matter is supported by all the dark matter that hovers on the margins of the action of the play.

From Sofer's suggestive analogy of dark matter, I'd like to develop the claim that the material stuff on stage exists within a network of relations that ultimately includes the play's audience. As has been noted, the length and the ample silences of Baker's drama affect the audience, often by creating a sense of discomfort. Baker links matter with time. Stuff takes time and is worth our attention. Just as there is value in watching a 35-mm film in *The Flick*, there is value to Mertis's practice of hand-writing a journal in a notebook in *John*. Things of the world are worth holding onto and tarrying before.

"If it's like an ethical you know–"

This is precisely the experience Baker's plays create for the audience. Critics have repeatedly commented on the plays' distinctive affective quality, on how they manage to get a certain hold on the audience. For example, in his review of *John*, Hilton Als was particularly moved by Mertis's poetic litany of the names of groups of birds: "It's hard to sit still as Mertis talks about birds, for instance; you feel airborne with the sheer effervescence of the sound she makes, building a world out of words and love."[26] Mertis's wonderful speech, which ends with her lush enthusiasm for her favorite, "an exaltation of larks," gets under the skin of the spectators to elevate and edify their spirits (84). Other critics have described the connection the plays create with the audience in terms of empathy afforded by focused attention. For example, Alexis Soloski concludes her review, "Baker approaches them all [her characters] with a kind of radical empathy, without ever softening or excusing their faults. She sees them so clearly that though the play runs more than three hours, you can't take your eyes off it."[27] In her perceptive and admiring profile of Baker, Sarah Larson maintains that this radical empathy extends to the audience: "When an artist's work is sensitive, disciplined, and well-structured, and when it listens to its subjects, portrays them thoughtfully, and treats their lives with respect, that generosity of time becomes part of the empathy, and we become part of the empathy, too. We're paying them the respect of attention."[28] The suggestion here is that Baker's empathetic creation of her characters activates the audience's capacity for empathy. This intuitively seems right, but it's difficult to demonstrate.

Rita Felski's *Hooked: Art and Attachment* proposes that one's experience of a work of art can profitably be thought of as a mediated experience of attachment. A benefit of this line of thought is that it opens up the experience of art to the many relations that constitute the experience but which are often ignored in accounts of how art works. Though Felski refers to theater only in passing, her argument jibes with ideas current in performance studies. For example, she draws on James Elkins's *Pictures and Tears*, which examines how and why people cry when looking at paintings, in order to demonstrate the variety of factors that contribute to one's experience of a work of art, what she calls art's "distributed agency":

> The [art] object does not contain its own effects: whether a viewer responds with tears or a smile of delight or turns away in indifference cannot be predicted by analyzing the painting, even though these responses define its impact for that viewer. Meanwhile, other factors also play their part in wetting the viewer's cheeks: the framing space of the museum; the proper name Gauguin; the knowledge that the thing to do in an art gallery is to stand in front of a painting and look with rapt attention.[29]

This example shows how the distributed agency of aesthetic experience consists of a range of factors that broaden the binary of object and spectator. And so, by extension, a person's experience of a play in a theater entails, among all the other factors, their presence in a given space with other people. Felski's argument indicates the capaciousness of a person's experience of a work of art and allows us to begin to theorize how empathy extends to the audience in Baker's plays.

Felski recognizes the importance of empathy in aesthetic experience but is also mindful of its limitations. She recalls the position of philosophers like Richard Rorty and Martha Nussbaum who have contended that empathy "can expand the limits of experience, engender a sense of solidarity with distant others, and do valuable civic and political work."[30] This effect of art is certainly attractive, but Felski suggests that such aims are beyond the scope of empathy, which is politically problematic and critically inexact.[31] Felski prefers a refined concept of identification to explain how readers relate to novels and, more specifically, to the characters in those novels. As she works to articulate what art does to us, she advances the concept of acknowledgment, which can more squarely help us grasp the effect of Baker's plays.

Acknowledgment differs from knowledge because it is attuned to "the relations and obligations in which [a person] . . . is entangled."[32] Developed in the work of Stanley Cavell and Toril Moi, the concept of acknowledgment tries to account for the way I respond to something or someone other than myself that does not reduce this thing or person to a definition that I impose on it. In *Revolution of the Ordinary*, Moi argues that reading a literary text is a practice of acknowledgment, and I believe Baker's plays invite the audience to participate in a similar act of engagement. What this means practically is that a spectator must pay attention to the specificity of the aesthetic experience: "To attend to something is to direct the mind or the senses toward something, to apply oneself; to watch over, minister to, wait upon, follow, frequent; to wait for, await, expect. In this concept, the idea of caring for, or serving others converges on the idea of listening, waiting, and watching."[33] The slow unfolding of Baker's plays encourages the spectator's practice of attending without knowing or determining what the play is about. A certain comfort with uncertainty is required. Elaborating this concept of acknowledgment, Moi says it complements Iris Murdoch's notion of a "just and loving gaze." Moi writes, "A just and loving gaze is open and waiting in relation to reality, but it is not passive. To be attentive is to let reality reverberate in us. Attention answers, responds and takes responsibility."[34] This is precisely the kind of ethical comportment Baker's plays value. In Mertis's daily record of the sunset, reality reverberates in her and calls to us to acknowledge it.

The spectator's acknowledgment of the play entails a response. There is no one right response, just as the plays do not convey a message. Baker said, "Of course you want your plays to say something. But you want them to say something that could never be said in a sentence, because then you'd write a sentence and not a play."[35] The experience of watching a play goes well beyond what the play communicates. An integral part of aesthetic experience for both Felski and Moi is a spectator's recognition that it takes place in the world filled with other people and not in a fanciful rarefied space. While the plays do not offer a message on how to go about living once they end, they do give us training in the art of paying attention.[36]

In order to indicate the critical territory I believe Baker's work takes us to, I would like to briefly show how the concept of attention has guided two discussions of Karl Ove Knausgaard's absorbing six-volume novel *My Struggle*. The novel is autobiographical and is filled with quotidian details of the author's life. In a 2017 essay in *The Point Magazine*, Toril Moi notes that for Knausgaard the goal of writing is "to convey not reality but 'the picture of reality, the picture that combines two entities: concretion and inexhaustibility,'" which Knausgaard, in an essay, calls "inexhaustible precision."[37] Thus, Knausgaard's novel teems with extraordinary descriptions in an effort to achieve his desired precision. At the end of a long description of a Stockholm street scene that Moi quotes, Knausgaard writes, "Writing is drawing what exists out of the shadows of what we know. That is what writing is about. Not what happens there, not what actions are played out there, but the *there* itself."[38] Knausgaard's writing, Moi says, is "an exercise of *attention*."[39] For Knausgaard, the way to mark his being there as time and hence his life pass by is to describe in language his experience as faithfully and fully as possible. Moi maintains that an attentive description reveals the presence of the creator and also serves as an invitation to a response, "an invitation to answer the question: 'This is what I see. Can you see it too?'" The attention manifested in the writing spurs the attention of the reader. In *This Life: Secular Faith and Spiritual Freedom*, Martin Hägglund says that the credo of *My Struggle* is "one must focus the gaze" or "what matters is to focus the gaze," which Hägglund prefers to translate as: "attach yourself to what you see." Given the limits of finite life, what matters to us are those things and people we're attached to and that we spend time on. Paying attention entails spending time and attending to what has value. Hägglund recalls Augustine's image of the "glue of love." In a passage in which Augustine discusses the dangers of getting drawn in too deeply by the charms of music, he writes, "Do not let my soul attach itself to these words with the glue of love [*glutine amore*] through the sensations of the body. For all these things move along a path toward nonexistence. They tear the soul apart with contagious desires."[40] Where Augustine sees the stickiness of the glue of love as dangerous, Hägglund sees it as essential and desirable in life. When we pay attention to someone, we attach ourselves to them and express love. Both Moi and Hägglund identify attention and attachment as essential to Knausgaard's writing and to the reader's engagement with the text. Attention is not simply a personal and private mode of comportment, but it is rather a way of being in the world among other people.

In ways distinct from Knausgaard's novel or from any novel for that matter, Baker's plays produce modes of attention through the audience's experience in the theater. Simply because of the nature of live theater (viz., its physicality and its temporality), the invitation to a response that Moi identifies in Knausgaard is more pressing in Baker's plays. The plays lead us to recognize the insistent realness of the lives of others. Attention prevents us from reducing other people to symbols or ideas, for example, Elias in *John* when he carries Jenny around as if she were a doll. Baker's plays call the audience to pay attention and to secure their attachments with the glue of love. Adequately attending to the specific reality of other people in our lives is the burden central to Baker's dramatic world and an urgent ethical demand the audience faces when the curtain closes.

The Drama and Theatre of Annie Baker

ANNIE BAKER'S DOMESTIC UNCANNY

Jeanmarie Higgins

Unlike the power American playwright Annie Baker's non-domestic settings usually exert over her characters—the confessional force of the acting studio in *Circle Mirror Transformation*, Avery's temporary movie theater workplace in *The Flick*, *The Aliens*'s coffeehouse picnic table and dumpster—Baker's domestic settings haunt. Paying attention to how design shapes a playwright's dramaturgy has broader implications, the most important of which is for students and audiences to notice that the history of *theatre* is usually seen (and taught) as the history of *drama*; but to understand *how* something means in time and space, we must look to scenic designers' strategies to create worlds that not only mark or indicate time and place, but create the conditions by which the play might happen. The implications of such a shift in audience attention, and the effect it could have on performance criticism, are more than a revelation of the way sign systems mean in theater. They are also an unveiling of the authorship of scenic, costume, props, and lighting designers—to produce time and space in concert with other artists on a team.

Baker includes an epigraph in the published version of *John* from Heinrich von Kleist's 1810 essay "On the Marionette Theatre": "Grace appears most purely in that human form which either has no consciousness or an infinite consciousness. That is, in the puppet or in the god."[1] Upon seeing the play's New York premiere at Signature Theatre, *New York Times* theater critic Charles Isherwood observed that "Ms. Baker's play is laced with shivery suggestions of a ghost story," that *John*'s "world of things and the world of spirits" made "the membrane between life and death . . . seem strangely permeable."[2] These "shivery suggestions" hew to Sigmund Freud's uncanny, or *unheimlich*, meaning simultaneously homelike and foreign. Freud introduces the uncanny as "that class of the frightening which leads back to what is known of old and long familiar."[3] Set in a charming if eerie bed-and-breakfast in the history-tourism town of Gettysburg, Pennsylvania, *John*'s setting is filled with things, especially dolls and other figurines that seem to exist simultaneously in the past and present.

To its contradictory qualities of time—past and present, secret and known—literary critic Nicholas Royle articulates the uncanny's spatial qualities, stating that it "has to do with a strangeness of framing and borders, an experience of liminality"; it "disturbs any straightforward sense of what is inside and what is outside."[4] This contradictory time-space event, describing a border of present and past, is an apt analytic for discussing domestic spaces, constituted as they are by the physical borders of walls, rooms, and other enclosures, and by the thresholds that mark them, thereby hosting a discussion of borders' integrity and permeability. This essay discusses uncanniness in *John* as it is brought out through the uses of domestic spaces and objects. *John*'s B&B insulates the play's characters from places that mark the town's violent histories. Haunted by its Civil War past, Gettysburg is the "outside" to the bed-and-breakfast's domestic interior. A B&B is already an uncanny space: a kind of hotel, a home away from home, it is *unheimlich*, both "homelike" and "un-homelike." I argue that Baker's uncanny domestic mise-en-scène mediates between the world of things and the world of spirits, assigning the setting of the play an agency usually reserved for dialogue or other stage languages that privilege the verbal over the visual or kinetic.

My research into *John* comes from the published script, of course, but also from the production I saw with a friend at Signature Theatre in Washington, DC. Paige Hathaway's scenic design authorized the workings of the play world, especially as key props—all of them domestic objects of some kind—governed time and space. As a professor who teaches dramaturgy and play analysis, I teach that designers create worlds built upon careful script analysis. Hathaway's set is an object lesson in this regard, embracing the uncanniness of Baker's stage directions to create collection upon collection of objects that lined the walls of Mertis's guest parlor. As Baker's author's note explains, Mertis is to open and close a curtain before and after each act, and change the time on the onstage clock. "If she isn't the last person onstage, she stealthily creeps onstage between scenes to move time forward" (5). The effect of this manipulation of props is a playful conspiracy between scenic designer and performer that inspired me to write this essay.

Furthermore, by focusing on the domestic realm, Baker brings a dimension of American character to life. Gettysburg's tourist experiences, like the Americans who visit them, repress the nation's colonial history, keeping it on the outside, while inside it bubbles up in the form of ghosts that invade its private spaces. The domestic spaces in *John*, a drama that charts the end of Millennials Jenny and Elias's relationship as it unfolds in the eerie Gettysburg bed-and-breakfast, do more than constitute the creepy setting for a breakup, they also intensify the conspiracy among stage languages in theatrical production. Whether an object is a prop follows from its human use. So says theater theorist Andrew Sofer, who adds the audience to this relationship: "The prop's status as a prop does not depend on the actor alone. An object becomes a stage prop only when it is perceived as such by a spectator who is consciously observing an actor—in other words, when an act of theater is taking place."[5] As Sofer also states, "A prop is an object that goes on a journey,"[6] meaning that props travel not only within a performance of a play but also across historical time periods. If all theater objects conspire with actors and audiences to become props, *John* offers the possibility for the reverse to be true—that scenery and props engage actors to initiate acts of theater. Drawing attention to the things of production—scenery, props, costumes, and the invisible/present workings of light—Baker's play offers an example of the design elements of mise-en-scène as prime mover.[7]

John

Jesse Green's review of Baker's Pulitzer Prize–winning play, *The Flick*, observes: "It's uncanny; rarely has so much feeling been mined from so little content."[8] Most critics remark on the simplicity of Baker's plots given the plays' length and depth of feeling. *John*'s simple plot describes a profound emotional dramatic action that unfolds in a deceptively realistic setting. On one level, it's a breakup play. Elias, 29, and Jenny, 31, are on their way home to Brooklyn from Ohio where they have been visiting family, staying overnight at 72-year-old Mertis's bed-and-breakfast. Jenny and Elias have been dating for three years, and their relationship is withering from familiarity. As the *New Yorker*'s theater critic Hilton Als observed, "They're at that point in a relationship when just seeing your partner eat can go through you like a drill."[9] But the proximate cause of their likely breakup is Jenny's cheating with a guy named John, which Elias is trying to forgive. Elias is also trying to see as much of Gettysburg as possible in the forty-eight hours they plan to spend in town—he's a history buff. But while Elias visits battlefields and takes ghost tours, Jenny stays behind (she has cramps) with Mertis (called Kitty), and Kitty's 85-year-old neighbor, Genevieve, who is blind. The two older women become witnesses to the couple's relationship demise in a series of understated scenes punctuated by some outright supernatural moments that brew over three-plus hours of stage time, with scene breaks marked by Kitty manually changing the hands

Critical Perspectives

on her grandfather clock. In the end, the young couple does break up after Elias threatens to burn a doll in front of Jenny. Believing that this doll is an embodiment of a doll she had as a child, the threat terrifies her.

The Mise-en-Scène Has Agency

As straightforward as *John*'s plot might be, the play's setting is both strange and familiar. As Isherwood observed, *John* feels like a ghost story driven by objects. I would add to this that these objects produce a theatrical time-space that is a process rather than a "container," what Bertolt Brecht scholar Sarah Bryant-Bertail calls an Epic theatrical time space:

> Space and time are ... not pre-existing containers for the dramatic event but are themselves the event—a journey toward meaning. Theatrical space is not just the set, the fictional locale, or the theater building but the way in which these present themselves through time, interrelating rhythmically with each other and with the dialogue, sound, and light to create a spatiality.[10]

Just as semiotician Patrice Pavis reframes *mise-en-scène* to encompass the integrated contributions of all theater artists and circumstances of rehearsal and production, Bryant-Bertail positions theatrical time-space as a collaboration among stage languages that does not assume the importance of one over another. *John* calls for scenery that privileges "process over container," as objects take on power to control space and time. This emphasis on process echoes feminist revisions of Freudian psychoanalysis. Just as feminist psychoanalytic theorists push back on the Freudian model of attaining subjectivity as a destination, Bryant-Bertail, in many senses of the term, begins with feminist psychoanalytic theory to form her idea of the "journey toward meaning."[11] Although it is outside the scope of this chapter's chief concern, Baker's notion of time and space is only one element of *John* that constitutes a feminist dramaturgy. For example, it is important to note that this spatiotemporal power of the setting lies with two characters in their seventies and eighties, a triumph of visibility, agency, and power for the play's elderly woman-identifying characters.

Much about Kitty seems very familiar, grandmotherly. Her history includes a deceased husband and a nursing assistant job. She likes things traditionally associated with the domestic lives of women: she collects ceramic figurines; she loves birds; she's on an extreme diet. Yet she and her neighbor Genevieve exhibit varying degrees of uncanny supernatural powers. When Kitty learns that Jenny's job is to write questions for a quiz show, she asks Jenny to test her; when she guesses all the answers correctly, she tells Jenny she can read minds. Later, when Jenny asks Kitty to tell her a scary story to keep her calm after the B&B's lights suddenly go out, Kitty instead lists the names of groups of birds as if it is an incantation. As if Kitty has cast a spell, *the Christmas tree lights flicker back on* (83–4). Most critical to Kitty and Genevieve's power is their curation of the things of history that make up *John*'s onstage world.[12]

Home-and-Not-Home in Realism and Naturalism

Isn't there something always already uncanny about theater's domestic spaces? Chairs around a dining room table, a parlor filled with domestic objects; staircases and doors that suggest the existence of additional rooms—these dominate the dramaturgies of mid- and late twentieth-century (and sometimes contemporary) American realism, just as they signaled innovation to nineteenth-century modernist drama. A lifetime immersion in the domestic spaces of Realism can make domestic interiors onstage feel foreign. Confronted by a domestic interior at pre-show, one might wonder how strange it is to leave home to go elsewhere, sit down, and look at someone else's home. Was it the same for the late nineteenth-century bourgeois and artist-class European audiences who watched the first performances of Henrik Ibsen's 1879 *A Doll's House*, whose stage directions call for a full catalogue of domestic furnishings, including "a piano," "a round table with an armchair and a small sofa," a "porcelain stove with two armchairs and a rocking chair beside it," "Engravings on the walls," and "An étagère with china figures and other small art objects?"[13] The opening stage directions of *John* are likewise filled with domestic objects. The bed-and-breakfast Jenny and Elias enter is an uncanny place made even more so for its domestic setting, which Baker details like Ibsen did. It is a playful parallel between *John* and *A Doll's House*, but another look at this description of setting reveals a puzzle with its key found in the historical role that domestic spaces have played in the conversation between realism and naturalism in the theater.

Baker's six-paragraph description of the play's setting contains references to familiar American plays' iconic objects and the ways different subgenres of realism have conceived of domestic onstage settings: the "glass menageries" that serve as lonely Laura Wingfield's companions in Tennessee Williams's 1944 play; "a bird cage with a little fake bird in it," that is a reference to Susan Glaspell's 1916 true-crime naturalistic drama, *Trifles*; and "a very large Christmas tree," the object that organizes the action of *A Doll's House*'s first scene. Finally, Baker notes: "There are two French doors upstage" which "lead to Mertis's wing of the house," placing the elderly "Kitty" in Nora Helmer's husband Torvald's space. (In contrast to Torvald's office, though, Mertis's beloved, ailing husband George lives in these offstage rooms.) As Baker notes that a 1950s jukebox plays Bach, all semiotic systems fire simultaneously to produce a familiar/unfamiliar past/present. It is a tapestry of liminality woven by domestic objects.

It is also easily argued that domestic objects hold traces of histories in the form of the residue of the people who have owned and used them in the past. As philosopher Mark Kingwell has written: "Furniture structures space. [. . .] The absent protagonists of the various human stories that room has witnessed and will witness are instantly summoned, necromantically, by the couch's human dimensions, its constant invitation to sit or lie."[14] But domestic objects can also hold complete personal histories, as in the way a child might feel that a doll is a sentient being. Kitty's spooky home is filled with countless tchotchkes that she, her friends, and her guests imbue with consciousness, or what von Kleist calls "grace." Like a lot of B&Bs, Kitty's place is filled with insentient likenesses of sentient beings—from the haunted face of an oil painting ("that's Eugenia," Kitty explains), to a cream pitcher in the likeness of a dog's head, to Edwardian-era, philanthropic-orphan American Girl Doll Samantha sitting ominously at the top of the stairs in a Samantha-sized rocking chair.

Critics have noted that Baker embraces naturalism at a time when her contemporaries are experimenting with non-realistic dramaturgies. Hilton Als says: "Baker returns us to the naturalistic and soulful theatre that many of her contemporaries and near-contemporaries have disavowed in their rush to be '"postmodern."'[15] Of course, what is meant by "naturalism" in theater is fluid and even overlaps with what is meant by "realism." It is safe to say that realism's dramas retain traces of well-made play structure, but they are geared toward serious subjects. Naturalism, in contrast, does not concern itself with structured plots, presenting instead an uncurated "slice of life." It is the frankness of this slice of life that constitutes the seriousness of the play's message. But taking Als at his critical word, consider the foundational document, "Naturalism on the Stage," where Emile Zola refutes the idea that drama, unlike fiction, is a poor form for description. He argues that description is not only possible through theater, but is also constitutive of theater: "description is a necessity which is imposed on the theater as an essential condition of its existence"; it is brought about by the "perfect exactness" of scenery in naturalism, and furthermore, this exactness is considered "proof of the unheralded task that naturalism has accomplished in the theater since the beginning of the century."[16]

The dramatic-historical allusions in *John*'s opening stage directions, especially its lists of objects and spaces, position *John* as a meditation on the things of realistic and naturalistic drama, even the tension between the two forms: the bourgeois Helmers' armchairs and étagère and Nora's real Christmas tree from *A Doll's House*, versus the dirty dishes in Minnie Wright's working-class kitchen in *Trifles*. If Baker's dialogue and choices of subjects are read as naturalism, it is because the plot she crafts diverges from the well-made play structure that realism never abandoned. But she also embraces naturalism through scenery and props. As most of us encounter theater history narratives, we tend to learn about the playwrights who mark dramaturgical shifts, but rarely do we read about how designers shift dramatic movements. Green notes that Baker's plays have "so little content"; Als associates this with Baker's divergence from her postmodern peers. To entertain the idea that Baker's plays move beyond a style of dialogue that "feels real" and to examine how the scenery produces space, is to craft an object lesson in a dramaturgy that relies on the collaboration among stage languages where the verbal sign does not reign supreme.

What is Repressed?

The dimension of the uncanny that *John* puts front and center—beyond the effect of the house filled with creepy dolls and stuffed animals—is the idea that the uncanny arises when something repressed returns. The shelves and shelves of figures within the setting collectively serve to insulate its transient residents from the gruesome Civil War history that is the economic engine of the small Pennsylvania town. The insistent charm of Kitty's B&B keeps the outside at bay, that is, the town's Civil War past. Kitty tells Jenny that her bed-and-breakfast used to house a hospital. When the doctors became overwhelmed by the number of limbs generated by so many post-battle amputations, they started throwing them out the windows, until they formed a type of moat that surrounded the house with pieces of the war dead.

But inside the house, the hundreds of figurines—what Genevieve calls Kitty's "matter"—are protected from the legacies of the war. Jenny notes that having too many little things around makes her grind her teeth. Another such scene of figurines of people living inside of containers that can only be glimpsed is what Kitty calls "a sort of slave diorama," a feature of one of Gettysburg's history tours, where visitors can watch "realistic mannequins" hidden in floorboards as the slaves themselves were (36–37).

Kitty's frankness about her house's history is repaid by young Jenny's frankness about her own supernatural experiences. With Elias out of the house on his history tour, the conversations that Jenny, Mertis, and Genevieve have happen in a women-only space. When she first meets Genevieve, Jenny tells her and Kitty a story about a mystical erotic experience in New Mexico in which she was brought to orgasm by the universe. Earlier, Mertis says that Genevieve thinks the house is haunted, that she is always hearing what might be the rustlings of ghosts or of angel wings. Later that night when the lights go out, Jenny shoots a glance at American Girl doll, Samantha; it is part fear response, part accusation.

Even Elias experiences the uncanny—through ghosts. When he returns from his battlefield tour, he is convinced that he has taken a picture of the spirit of a Civil War–era child. All the characters constantly experience or else describe memories of liminal spaces between body and spirit, between life and death. For example, when Jenny recounts that story of her universe-induced orgasm, the women find nothing odd about it. Far more dangerous repressed memories become known, though, by Elias and Genevieve. Elias breaks when Jenny reveals Elias's disturbing first memory to their hosts of something approaching sexual abuse at the hands of his hippie parents' retreat clients when he was about four years old. Where Jenny's sexual memory is transcendent, Elias's is traumatic.

But it is Genevieve, the oldest woman in the group, who moves most freely between opposed time-spaces, as in an entr'acte scene she breaks at once the most and least palpable of borders, the fourth wall. In a direct address, Genevieve tells the audience about the seven stages of her break with reality, her breakup with her husband (named John, of course), and losing her sight. The early stages of her sight loss involved hallucinations and hearing voices. The sixth stage was her awareness of "an unus mundus," that is, her ability to feel what the entire universe was feeling across all space and time and to connect with the souls of both people and objects. The seventh stage was her realization that this prolonged episode of psychic break was the work of her ex-husband, John, who although not dead was haunting her by controlling her thoughts and expanding her consciousness to untenable levels.

Conclusion

If the uncanny is the unsettling feeling brought on by the simultaneous experience of something foreign and something familiar, then I propose that the domestic uncanny is the experience of fear and longing coaxed to the surface when home is simultaneously present and absent in a theatrical representation. The domestic uncanny revisits Freud's uncanny, that is, a moment just after the dissolution of a border between the past and the present. In *John*, the house itself is a liminal space that protects its occupants not only from the outside world, not only from the snow and the cold but also the bloody history of the Civil War. This world is not only imagined and built through the scene designer's collaboration with other artists, but the scenery authorizes the movement of time and the liminality of space.

Critical Perspectives

ANNIE BAKER: BUILDING ON SAMUEL BECKETT

Katherine Weiss

When asked in interviews about her influences, Annie Baker often remembers Samuel Beckett, the Irish Nobel Laureate whose novel *Watt* she wrote an essay about in school.[1] It is no surprise, then, that theater critics quickly picked up on the Beckettian in her plays.[2] Baker's work swells with silences and pauses as do Beckett's plays. She is adamant about the length of the pauses, demanding an exactness to the unspoken—an exactness that recalls Beckett's own stage directions. Furthermore, her characters are frequently marginalized and awkward as are Beckett's characters. Her characters are steeped in boredom and habit. In Baker's plays, the daily lives of her characters are unremarkable. Each scene is a subtle repetition of what has come before. The words "Nothing happens, twice"[3]—so often quoted in relation to *Waiting for Godot*—are echoed whenever Baker has a new play. The tribute she pays to Beckett is not merely in the silences and pauses, plot, and characters, however. Her debt to Beckett is one of a shared vision that accompanies the similarities in aesthetic. Annie Baker's plays depict characters in an existential crisis. They, like Beckett's characters, need to speak and to be heard and seen. In *The Aliens* and *The Flick* most particularly, Baker builds on Beckett's angst of being seen and, in doing so, speaks to the lost ones of the twenty-first century.

The most obviously Beckettian influence in Baker's work is her use of pauses and silence onstage. Like Beckett, Baker goes so far to specify the length of pauses and silences. In *The Aliens*, for example, she writes: "At least a third – if not half – of this play is silence," and gives timing for pauses ("three seconds") and silences ("five to ten seconds").[4] Baker's use of pauses and silences represent both the inability to express thoughts and those thoughts that her "people can't—or won't—articulate."[5] As she has explained: "I guess my experience of the real world is that there are a lot of strange moments in which people don't know what to say. So that ends up in my plays."[6] These silences, according to Brendan Kiley, are "deafening." His assessment echoes Graley Herren's analysis of Beckett's *Quad*, a television play eradicated of dialogue, as an expression of the ineffable.[7] David T. Johnson has a different perspective of Baker's use of silence. He believes that they slow down her plays, drawing attention to the dialogue.[8] As with Beckett's plays, the intensity of the silence heightens our attention when characters do speak. The content of what Baker's characters say may appear to be insignificant, but often what is mistaken for banality is an awkward and pained expression. Their banter, like that of Estragon and Vladimir's in *Waiting for Godot*, speaks to the relationships of the characters and the pain points they attempt to avoid.

Yet merely tracing the influences, as journalists have done, does little more than place Baker as an American follower of Beckett. It does not sufficiently delve into Baker's extraordinary writing, nor does it give Beckett's plays the nuanced care they deserve. Baker's nod to Beckett is far more than the similarities mentioned at the start of this chapter. In fact, the differences between her aesthetic and Beckett's are worth recognizing here. Baker does not utilize Beckett's minimalism. Instead, in homage to another playwright she admires, Anton Chekhov,[9] Baker creates realistic sets, placing characters in specific locations like a rundown cinema in *The Flick* and the back alley of a café in *The Aliens*. However, Jennifer Cayer notes, Baker's theatrical realism is "*a feminist dramatics of the swerve.*"[10] For Cayer, this swerve is a departure from the pessimism of Chekhov and Beckett, as it "allows for a recognizable, naturalistically staged world to be rendered convincingly textured then quickly altered, bringing about a new estranged seeing on the part of the audience." Cayer continues, noting that "Baker emphasizes the pleasures of seeing and being seen, the powers of spectatorship, and the embodied agency of characters to re-shape their relations to provisional realities through performance."[11] Cayer's observation that Baker's plays foreground seeing and being seen for the audience and the characters ties Baker directly to Beckett's existentialism. Baker, like Beckett, explores how "we cannot exist, we cannot survive, without someone to see us."[12] For Beckett, the dilemma of seeing and being seen stemmed from his reading of the seventeenth-century Bishop George Berkeley's *esse est percipi* (to be is to be seen). For Beckett, too, existence is tied to being seen. He takes *esse est percipi* and transforms it into a motto of existential crisis. Berkeley's reassurance that we exist because God sees us is for Beckett problematic. How do we know that God sees us, and in the devastation of modern warfare and rampant poverty, how can we even be certain that there is "a merciful . . . (*Brief laugh.*) . . . God," which the character of Mouth in Beckett's *Not I* can only voice with a brief and then "*Good laugh.*"[13] Baker abandons the pessimism that is prevalent in the playwrights she most admires; as Cayer argues, Baker's plays move toward a positive and affirming space as the characters are seen by other characters and the audience. Baker's plays, on a first encounter, certainly appear to conclude with more hope than Beckett's plays do. Avery of *The Flick* speaks of returning to college after working at the rundown movie theater and KJ of *The Aliens* speaks of leaving town. However, in both plays, as in Baker's other works, the conclusions are much more ambiguous than given credit. In *The Flick*, Sam and Rose stay on despite the change in the movie theater's ownership. Furthermore, the penultimate scene, a subtle variation on the first, opens with Sam training a new employee who will become a marginalized lost one at The Venue (the new name for the theater). The conclusion of *The Aliens*, too, is a subtle Sisyphean journey. It ends with both KJ and Evan on stage; "*They stand there,*" as Baker's stage directions read,[14] much like Estragon and Vladimir at the end of *Waiting for Godot*, who stand together, gazing up at the moon. "*They do not move,*" as Beckett's stage directions reiterate.[15] Baker's and Beckett's characters are remarkably resilient as they go on, like Sisyphus, carrying on with their daily burden.[16] Cayer's assessment misses the cyclical nature of *The Flick* and Baker's other works. While in *The Flick* the young black protagonist Avery may be able to move on by going back to university, this is not the result of being seen by his co-workers, his past and current boss, or even his therapist, all of whom seem to dismiss him at key moments of his development.

The optimism of the swerve veils the ugliness of the modern world and Baker, like Beckett, works to tear the veil asunder, exposing the meaninglessness behind our existence.[17] Indeed, it is the dismissal and firing of Avery—expelling him from the marginal existence of those who clean up—that gives the erroneous appearance of helping him move on.[18] George Cotkin argues that in American existentialism, unlike its European forerunner, pragmatism has been an essential ingredient. Cotkin provides an insightful study of existentialism in American literature and philosophy, concluding:

> If there is an American existentialist tradition [. . .] then it is anchored in the recognition that life, behind the pasteboard masks, is meaningless, absurd, and contingent. But one must not – as the invisible man and other figures come to realize – rest comfortably in this ultimately empty abode.[19]

Cotkin evokes the thin veil of American optimism when he writes that the "world of the twenty-first century is pock marked by meaninglessness, absurdity, and violence masked by the language of certitude and obfuscation."[20] Unlike Cayer who views the optimism as an earnest move toward positivity, for Cotkin American existential writers hide behind a language that conveys stability. American writers may voice a certainty, but they, like their European counterpoints, are faced with the unknown: an existential crisis.

Baker's understanding of the existential crisis of twenty-first-century youth culminates in act one, scene six in *The Flick* as Avery, left alone on stage, telephones his therapist to share with her a concerning dream he has recently had in which he's in Purgatory and given an "ISBN-type scanner" to scan his entire movie collection to see—and be judged upon—the film that was most important to his life.[21] Avery's anxiety builds as the scanner remains silent, not beeping for any of the classic and renowned films he owns and loves. He explains that he fears that he will be going to hell until finally the scanner beeps at *Honeymoon in Vegas*, which is shocking and embarrassing, but at least guarantees that he'll go to heaven.[22]

Avery explains that he recalls watching the movie at his cousin's birthday when he was four years old. At that young age, he was already obsessing over films although his taste was not yet as discerning. The dream presents an inconsistency in Avery's value system. For Avery, films serve as a mirror that defines identity and existence. He is obsessed with debating the worth of films, attempting to elevate himself as a worthy critic of films. It is more than just the content of the film. He is obsessed with the medium—DVDs versus VHS and film versus digital. The film that defines his life in his dream is an old VHS, an inferior technology to DVDs. Ironically, VHS technology is closer to film reels than DVD technology. His dream throws into question his obsession with classic films and film reels, and leads him to reflect on the existential crisis of being and identity.

In act two, scene five, Avery recites the Ezekiel 25:17 episode from *Pulp Fiction*, a moment that we have been waiting for since Sam first tells Rose, the projectionist, about it in act one, scene five. In *Pulp Fiction*, the passage serves as an existential question. Jules Winnfield, played by Samuel L. Jackson, attempts to make sense of why, during the last hit job, he and his partner, played by John Travolta, did not die after being sprayed with bullets. They walk away from the scene unharmed. Avery's performance, not merely a repetition of the film, stirs an emotional response in Sam and Rose. When he finishes, "*SAM looks like he might cry,*" and Rose says, "That

Critical Perspectives

was awesome" (106). After the biblical passage, Avery speaks the lines that Jackson's Winnfield does, but rather than doing so in an inquisitive manner, Avery speaks in a tone that Baker defines as "*thoughtfully, sadly,*" coloring the sentence "I been sayin' that shit for years" (106) as a melancholic revelation that the characters Sam and Rose are stuck in a purgatorial existential crisis. Even when new technologies change in the movie theater industry, they remain marginalized, cleaning up the trash left behind. They are, like the trash, left behind. Avery walks away from the cinema, but not because he chooses to. He takes the hit, unlike Winnfield, and loses his job when the new boss discovers the Dinner Money scam that all three characters have been involved in.

Avery's dream, the purgatorial scene in which celluloid images define his existence, recalls Beckett's only venture into film, a 28-minute silent film commissioned by Barney Rosset of Grove Press and Evergreen Theatre. In 1964, Beckett worked alongside theater director Alan Schneider, who directed *Film* on location in New York City. Beckett's script, although containing no dialogue, includes Berkeley's *esse est percipi* in its general notes.[23] *Film* follows the protagonist named O, played by silent film legend Buster Keaton, who is pursued by the camera, E (perhaps for eye). O hurries through the streets of New York City until he ends up in a dingy apartment, sits in a rocking chair, and takes photographs out of an envelope. Each photograph depicts a stage in O's life, from infancy to the current day.[24] After O ponders each photograph, he tears them to pieces,[25] perhaps attempting to erase his existence—a symbolic suicidal act. Roland Barthes in *Camera Lucida* reflects on the "crisis of death"[26] that photographs impart. Each photograph "produces Death while trying to preserve life."[27] If this is so, then O's suicide is more than ending life; it is erasing any trace of having been seen.

Baker's *The Flick*, too, takes on the subject of suicide as more than ending life; it, too, is erasing a trace of having been seen. Avery, we learn, attempted to commit suicide which is the very reason he is in therapy. When Rose fails to arouse Avery in act one, scene eight, by unzipping his pants and touching him, Avery responds with agony of wanting to kill himself. His utterance is out of shame, but it is also a very chilling statement as he confesses later in the same scene that on that day a year ago he had tried to kill himself. In both cases he wanted to fade away, to erase his trace. While Rose is curious to find out what the future has in store for her, Avery is nearly paralyzed by the anxiety of change and a future. Suicide haunts *The Aliens* as well, as the teenage barista Evan and slacker KJ must come to terms with the ambiguous overdose death of Jasper and what will remain of Jasper's existence. Who will remember having seen him? In his fine analysis of *The Aliens*, Thomas Butler convincingly argues that

> friendship [is] a counterintuitive experience of distance between individuals. That distance hinges on an awareness of mortality, which is distinctive in theater where there are, among other things, live (and, therefore, dying) bodies performing on stage. Theater is both an ephemeral and a mortal experience, and enables a presentation of friendship that bears the marks of life and mortality.[28]

Jasper's death draws KJ and Evan closer together while plunging them to question their own existence. Unlike the characters in *The Aliens*, Sam, Avery, and Rose of *The Flick* never truly become friends despite the references and allusions to *Jules and Jim*, the French New Wave classic about the deep friendship between two men and their encounter with a free-spirited woman. In the play's final scene, Avery pointedly tells Sam that "we were never really friends in the first place" (114). The experience of death in these plays take on different tenors. Evan takes up smoking, a destructive act, reminiscent to Avery's own suicide attempt, but much less destructive and violent.

To return to Beckett's *Film*, each photograph speaks to O's life being without distress or friction. However, photographs, just like the memory tied to Avery's *Honeymoon in Vegas*, represent happy moments. As such, O's reaction suggests that these photographs, in fact, serve to hide a troubled life. The viewer senses what only O can know—the moments between the photographs. Beckett's camera, a character in his film by the name of E, allows us to see each image before it is destroyed, and as a result, the camera assures us that O cannot erase his existence. He is seen even though he does all he can to avoid being seen.

In *The Flick*, Avery's affirmation of his existence is tied to a technology that is on its way out: film projectors being replaced by digital technology. Likewise, in Beckett's *Film* O attempts to erase his existence with technologies on their way out: silent films and photographs. Avery composes a letter for Mr. Saranac, the buyer who intends to replace the film projector with a digital projector, in which his description of the difference between film and digital projection alludes to his own existential crises. Life is a series of events, separated by moments of darkness. Our recollections of the events that make up our existence are a series of images that are light and shadow, coming in strong and eluding us at the same time.

Baker further explores the existential crises as *The Flick's* two male protagonists Sam and Avery clean up the waste left behind. Beyond the regular spilt popcorn and candy wrappers one would expect to find between movie showings, Sam and Avery come across a single shoe. In act one, scene four, the lights come up on Sam and Avery cleaning as Avery whistles to himself "Le Tourbillon" from *Jules and Jim*. The vignette moves from the debt to French New Wave cinema, to Sam's mundane banter, and culminates in the discovery of an old shoe left behind on the movie theater floor (28–9). The shoe is a physical reminder of the existence of an audience member who we never see or hear. It is a trace of the journey made into the theater and a trace of humankind. The dirty, smelly New Balance shoe serves to rebalance the audience's focus. However, as it is left behind for Sam and Avery to clean up, it is also a reminder of the position they hold. They exist in the margins, unseen by those who attend the screenings. Those who attend the rundown movie theater, too, are marginalized, living in the liminal space of celluloid. Julie Bates tells us that Estragon's boots left on stage between acts one and two in *Waiting for Godot* serve as a visual still life as well as a symbol of death. Still life paintings are ambiguous, freezing life onto the canvas to remind its viewers just how ephemeral life is. In Beckett's writing, old boots, Bates tells us, "forcefully convey the fundamental homelessness of his characters; ultimately, this loss or lack of home means that they can speak of nowhere and nothing with authority."[29] Like Beckett's marginalized figures, Baker's onstage and phantom characters leave traces of themselves to assert their existence and absence in a world crumbling before them. Sam and Avery experience dread over the shoe that is left behind as it speaks to their own lack of authority and symbolic homelessness.

Act two, scene one opens again with Sam and Avery cleaning up. Sam, having returned from his brother's wedding, shares with Avery a story of going to the movies in which he is repulsed by the smell of a woman. To escape her smell, he moves seats and, in the process, forgets to take the bag of tamales he brought into the theater with him. He recalls with horror that in doing so, he has become that guy who brings in outside food and then leaves it behind for someone else to clean up. In Tennessee Williams's article for the opening of *A Streetcar Named Desire* published in the *New York Times*, he writes: "Maids, waiters, bellhops, porters, and so forth are the most embarrassing people in the world for they continually remind you of inequities which we accept as the proper thing."[30] Baker appears to be in dialogue with Williams here when it comes to her depiction of Avery and Sam, cleaning up after others. Sam cannot assert himself and has no agency even when he is not working.

By leaving behind the tamales, Sam unintentionally leaves a trace of himself behind. The fact that someone other than himself throws it away is an erasure of his existence, just like the shoe in the earlier scene and Beckett's boots, all of which echo the thousands of shoes found in the concentration camps. The piles of footwear, despite Nazi Germany's attempt to erase the Jewish people, remained as a statement of being there and being seen.

The most distressing episode of existential angst is in act two, scene two, when Avery bursts into the painful episode between Sam and Rose in which Sam confesses his feelings for Rose. Avery, barely able to breathe, shares his discovery that someone "took a shit on the floor" of the men's bathroom and spread it on the walls (86). This leaves Avery nauseated; he vomits, adding his own human waste to that left behind and smeared on the walls of the bathroom. In act one, scene two, Avery admits he is "kind of shit-phobic" (15). His fear and disgust of feces is a rejection of the body's need to produce waste. Sam, who is "totally cool with shit" and puke (87), leaves to clean up the mess. This episode recollects Beckett's *Krapp's Last Tape*, in which the failed writer ironically named Krapp, is both physically and mentally constipated. In Krapp's attempt to separate "the grains from the husks,"[31] he defines his existence by erasing that which he views as waste—the very messy stuff of love that would help him become a writer.[32] Avery's rejection of human waste keeps him stifled in celluloid—repeating his favorite lines from movies without moving on and living his life. Similarly, KJ and Evan in *The Aliens*, despite speaking of leaving, remain tied to the back alley by the dumpster. While Evan used to take out the trash, he more and more communes with KJ, becoming constipated in his attachment to the thirty-year-old, long-haired, bearded shroom-tea-drinking loafer.

Avery's shit-phobia is the ultimate existential crisis. Existence is dependent on the production of human waste. Even in the final scene in which Sam gifts Avery the discarded and dissembled film projector, it is unclear if Avery will be able to embrace that which would have been turned to scrap metal otherwise. He vaguely and with no conviction says that maybe he'll start a 35-millimeter society back at college (113). There is none of the positivism that Cayer wants to see in Baker and no certainty in his language that Cotkin claims is part of American existentialism.

What Annie Baker leaves us with are characters who continue to make their way through the existential crisis of the twenty-first century. They are lost ones, like so many of Beckett's characters, but of the new century—young males marginalized, unseen for the most part, and paralyzed by an existential dread. Baker thus, I contend, follows much more closely in the tradition of European existentialism, and especially that of Beckett's. She builds on Beckett's tension of being seen by concluding *The Flick* and *The Aliens* with characters who remain marginalized, unseen: young men and women who are going nowhere. Like Beckett, though, her plays ask those watching to see and empathize with those in existential crisis.

The Drama and Theatre of Annie Baker

UNDRESSING THE WOUND OF THEATERGOING WHITENESS IN ANNIE BAKER'S *NOCTURAMA*

Harrison Schmidt

Annie Baker, explaining why her plays are so thick with silence, says "I think the one thing left that really makes people uncomfortable is empty space and quiet."[1] She does not reveal precisely what she aims to make the audience uncomfortable with, and perhaps she has nothing definite in mind. My sense, however, is that Baker's quiet and empty spaces usher the audience toward a discomfort with whiteness. Her plays challenge a range of assumptions that are fundamentally bound up with whiteness. They show how the narrow scope of the white imaginary places limitation on ethical possibility, and, since ethics dovetails with politics precisely at that nexus where whiteness does its worst damage—that is, at the nexus of the social—how whiteness compromises freedom in both the personal and the political sense. Although white people enjoy the privileges afforded by this construct (and I would be remiss not to acknowledge that I count among these privileged ones), they (we) are by no means exempted from the compromise.

In my reading of Baker, I am responding to Toni Morrison's still-relevant demand that the "well-established study" of "racism and the horrific results on its objects [...] be joined with another, equally important one: the impact of racism on those who perpetuate it."[2] Morrison calls us to shift our readerly orientation away from viewing racism only as a harm inflicted by white subjects upon vulnerable nonwhite objects and instead toward viewing whiteness as a harm to which we are all vulnerable, a wound that afflicts us all, even if it is white people who bear culpability for allowing the wound to fester untreated. This negligence of the wound of whiteness occurs through what Jess Row calls a "fictive closure," his shorthand for an "American (and particularly white American) quality of innocence and unknowing." For Row, this fictive closure bears heavily on American identity and pervades the American condition as its very atmosphere. However, given that Row esteems "embodiment, engagement," and "performance"[3] as writing's more potent reparative capacities, I wonder if the playwright might not have a singular power to refine American sensibilities to this wound as a way toward redressing its harms. But even when the playwright intentionally does this kind of work, there are still no guarantees. Theatergoing whiteness, after all, is characterized by the neglect of the wound, when the sensibilities that are cultivated in the theater are repressed for the sake of numbness and comfort.

Baker undermines theatergoing whiteness by initiating a noticing of whiteness's most inconspicuous harms; she does this through an attenuated process of gradual revelation that relies heavily on the acuteness of audience attention. This noticing is no less impactful for the fact that it is understated and gradual. The naturalistic fabric of Baker's drama irrupts thread by thread, surreptitiously haunted as it is by the conventionalities—which is to say the harms—of whiteness. Meanwhile, the audience members, who bear witness to the white characters' unseeing oblivion to these harms, might come to find themselves rather ill at ease with the conventionalities of whiteness. Baker thereby shifts the emphasis from the agency of the characters to that of the audience, who might even come to relinquish their comfort with whiteness, its seeming neutrality or absence of identity, and instead confront it as a discomfiting, pervasive presence. Baker's naturalism, then, would not confirm the realities of white audience members but rather make whiteness strange. It would help white audience members to notice their supposed realities for the curiosities that they actually are, curiosities which they might even come to disown. At once absorbing and disruptive, Baker's naturalism therefore operates less like a looking glass and more like the mirror of *Circle Mirror Transformation*, titled after the acting class exercise in which a group works together to recognize and mirror one participant's action, the goal being for another participant to eventually take the leap and transform it.

But Baker in no way underestimates the obduracy of whiteness's harms, nor does she overestimate the power of performance to counteract them. This is especially true of her play *Nocturama*, which, to date, has had no fully-staged productions.[4] In *Nocturama*, Baker's naturalism works to bring down the audience's guard while training their attention on ordinary moments, moments which show the conditions of whiteness to be difficult to shake in spite of the characters' best efforts. In this play, a white mother, Judy, and her white partner, Gary, attempt to help Judy's white twenty-six-year-old burnout son, Skaggs, through the depths of despair. Baker brings whiteness into view through this family's strained conversations not only with each other but with Amanda, the play's only black character, with whom Skaggs has a one-night stand. While Skaggs' depressive broodings on the meaninglessness of everyday life certainly vie for center stage, they are eclipsed in the end by the captivating quiet of Amanda. Baker gradually turns the audience's attention toward Amanda, attuning them to the hardly discernible ways in which she manifests her irreducibility to the stifling confinements of the white imaginary. In doing so, Baker shows the conditions of whiteness as impossible to transcend but possible to refuse. More than that, Baker calls forth from the audience an ethico-political response to whiteness. Indeed, Baker's *Nocturama* is a play that not only *un*dresses the wound of whiteness but also focalizes the urgency of its *re*dress.

Emptied Spaces

In an interview, Baker explains why she locates four of her plays, including *Nocturama*, in her fictionalized town of Shirley, Vermont. "Vermont fascinates me, period. The remoteness and the self-congratulation and the embracing of diversity and the fear of diversity and the beauty and the good intentions and the old farmers and the old hippies and the new farmers and the new hippies—I love all of it."[5] Baker goes on to invent (without stretching the imagination too much) a history for the town, in which its establishment involves the use of violence against Indigenous Americans. Reading some ambivalence here in Baker's expression of love for Vermont, I take her choice of setting as a means to explore the contiguity between, on the one hand, the violent acts of removal and enclosure that white people perpetrate in order to contrive what Row calls "emptied spaces,"[6] and on the other hand, the more mundane kind of violence—we might call it indifference—that white people perpetrate every day in spite of their good intentions. Row, too, views these two kinds of violence as coextensive. Indifference, for Row, is the consequence of a sort of psychical emptied space whose vacancy the white imaginary accepts as its own pardon from responsibility:

> Guilt, helplessness, the longing for redemption, the presumption of racial benevolence marked as, or indistinguishable from, innocence—those things linger around the white subject like trace elements in the air, like our own private Idahos, and turn longings

for justice and reconciliation into something foreshortened and already foreclosed.[7]

These two kinds of violence, then, are functions of the same strategy of distanciation from others, an isolation of the white self both in terms of physical distance and in terms of an interior landscape whose wide-open spaces collude with the white conscience to permit resignation to stand as substitute for absolution.

Baker's choice of setting for *Nocturama* signals toward the ways in which whiteness is substantiated by an openness made possible by closure—both the enclosure of others and the foreclosure of ethical possibility itself. Baker hints that the very sense (or, as the case may be, the nonsense) of freedom for the white imaginary is derived from the devastating violence through which whiteness is instantiated as a racial construct. This is a construct, after all, that can be traced to the racial bifurcation by which the transatlantic slave trade presumed to rationalize and justify its brutality. The racialized meanings of black and white subtend one another out of the logic of this catastrophe, acting as each other's contradistinctive backgrounds, each making the other legible. Further, as Morrison writes, "in that construction of blackness *and* enslavement could be found not only the not-free but also, with the dramatic polarity created by skin color, the not-me."[8] In other words, the white imaginary makes its own sense of freedom intelligible by consigning blackness to unfreedom. This is what Morrison calls the "parasitical nature of white freedom"[9]: freedom for the white subject coheres against blackness as a countervailing unfree object. Whiteness, it seems, is distinguished by the violence it occasions in order to stabilize the notion of the autonomous white subject.

It is crucial to acknowledge that whiteness is deeply entangled in—perhaps even inseparably bound to—this rupture out of which it emanates. Whiteness, because of the violence by which it isolates itself as a discrete identity, is both implicated and embroiled in what the poet Dionne Brand calls "the rupture in mind and body, in place, in time"; "We all feel it," Brand writes, however much we might try to "feign ignorance."[10] Within the purview of this devastating rupture, I can't help but think that relation is by no means a straightforward affair. How am I, a white person, supposed to relate if my very identity is imbricated in rupture? But I am dissuaded from resignation by Kevin Quashie's hopeful embrace of relational possibility even in the face of uncompromising conditions. "[R]elating: it doesn't exist now, doesn't seem as if it might ever exist, though it might . . . there is always possibility in the impossibility of relation," Quashie says. "This is surely a difficult way to live, this sustained openness to what might seem closed, but such is the aspiration of relational inhabitance."[11] *Relational inhabitance*. An orientation or a towardness. Not a fixed meaning, nothing static that could ever be adequately rendered beforehand or after the fact. Not a stabilizing strategy of a subject over against the fixity of an object, but rather a continuous unfolding of meaning between you and me.

In *Nocturama*, Baker in no way downplays the difficulties; she rather foregrounds them, showing how the conventionalities of whiteness undermine ethical becoming at every turn. We see this first and foremost in Skaggs, who suffers a breakdown after his girlfriend leaves him and his livelihood (his drum kit) is stolen from him on the street. Immobilized by depression, he moves from his apartment in Brooklyn back to Shirley, Vermont, his hometown, to live with his mother, Judy, and her partner, Gary. However, as the play progresses, it is Amanda who increasingly takes the spotlight, progressively displacing the white characters in the audience's attention. Baker signals Amanda's prominence early on, orienting the audience's attention toward her at the very outset of the play. As the audience enters the theater, Amanda sits onstage on a bench alone, reading *Harry Potter and the Order of the Phoenix*, and then exits before the show begins.[12] Baker piques the audience's curiosity about Amanda, sparking their interest in her in the same way it would be sparked if they saw her reading on a park bench or at a bus stop. This naturalistic technique draws the audience into Amanda's quiet and unassuming manner, effectively attuning them to the subtle ways in which, later on, Amanda manages to step outside the bounds of whiteness's limited frame of vision. We will see how Baker engages her audience in relation with Amanda, absorbing their attention in the ways in which her life is inundated by conditions of whiteness, while also alerting them to the channels by which she navigates through and away from, even if never quite outside of, those conditions.

Silence that Speaks

Baker's *Nocturama* shows how the white self takes its cue from a peculiar notion of autonomy whose basis lies in an untenable balance between distanciation and dissociation from others, how the white self attempts to distinguish itself from others and at the same time leave others out of its account. This supposed imperviousness to others is, of course, incoherent, but this incoherence in no way weakens its insidious harm. As Grant Farred writes, the "harm" of whiteness, which is its "insularity," gains a nebulous substantiation from this "mode of being that does not 'borrow from outside the self'" or even "see the need to think itself."[13] Distanciation from others is what allows the white self to remain, unthought; it is the means by which, as Row writes, whiteness "sticks together without making sense."[14] Importantly, this is a strategy that holds up only as long as its basis in unthinking remains undisrupted by encounters with others. "The hegemony of repression," Farred writes, "is vulnerable to nothing so much as what it wants to keep locked away: the Other as the bearer of thinking that stands in contradistinction to its own not-thinking."[15] *Nocturama* works to interrupt this selective not-thinking of whiteness. The play grants the audience an opportunity to take notice of the fragile basis that both enables this notion of autonomy and at the same time guarantees its failure.

Nocturama dramatizes how even the most mundane encounters with others can unsettle the white self and shake up the assumptions on which it relies. One such encounter occurs when Skaggs goes on a guided tour of the historical home of Elizabeth Collins, a nineteenth-century poet of Baker's invention. As he recounts the highlights of this tour to Judy and Gary, Skaggs takes special note of one remarkable occurrence: that the tour guide, Amanda, was black. This is noteworthy for Skaggs because, to his knowledge, there are virtually no black people in Shirley. Both Gary and Judy object to this claim: Gary cites one black person who works in his office, and Judy professes to have noticed a black woman in public last week (254). This is the play's first direct reference to the whiteness of the town of Shirley, a whiteness so pervasive that the presence of one black colleague is viewed by Gary as evidence to the contrary. Even a passing encounter with someone who is not white, an encounter so singular that it remains prominent in the memory of Judy a week later, is for her a mark of diversity. In their attempt to rebut Skaggs' noticing of whiteness by deferring to these isolated events, Judy and Gary speak to what Row calls "the mechanics of forgetting and erasure" by which white people allow themselves "not [. . .] to feel any loss over the absence of people of color in their lives."[16] Although Judy and Gary seem to recognize the value of diversity and to desire it genuinely, they find even this bare minimum of presence to be a sufficient basis for them to not think about the absence. And not thinking about the absence is essential, for the unimpeachable normalness of emptied space is what sanctions not-thinking in the first place.

But not even Judy and Gary can come to terms on their suppositions about the diversity of Shirley. Gary, who was there with Judy and also noticed the passerby from the previous week, disputes Judy's perception that she was black. An argument ensues in which Judy and Gary's desperate attempts to racially categorize the stranger become strained and eventually frustrated, terminating in "*a pause*" (255). To make sense of this silence, I turn to Farred's close reading of his own encounter with whiteness. Farred remarks on the silence of a particular white woman whose not-thinking has countenanced a disruption:

> What does she hear in that silence? What is the silence saying, relentlessly, silently, to her? (This means, of course, that the 'silence'— the lack of anything to say in response to the response—is never without its own distinctive audibility. The silence speaks.) [. . .] What [. . .] does this silence make her confront? If anything? (The lack of thinking about the silence is the greatest failure of the white woman. In and through her silence, she stands deliberately against thinking.)[17]

Judy and Gary's silent pause bespeaks their profoundly shaken confidence in what Morrison calls "the process of establishing others in order to know them, to display knowledge of the other so as to ease and order external and internal chaos."[18] Without Skaggs' timely interruption of their silence, Judy and Gary might dwell further on their argument here. They might wonder why it matters so much whether or not Judy correctly perceived this person to be black, why it is so important that this person be decidedly settled into a more definite category than not-white, or, more broadly, why it is so important that this person be determined at all as an object of racialized knowing.

Later on, we find Skaggs, too, falling into the trap of unthinking, or falling into what Claudia Rankine calls the "retreat into a space of defensiveness, anger, silence, which is to say [. . .] [the] retreat into the comfort of control, which begins by putting me in my imagined place."[19] After Skaggs and Amanda's first and only sexual encounter, Amanda confronts Skaggs for ghosting her. Skaggs maintains that he did not know he was "*obligated*" (331) to respond to her phone calls. In spite of Amanda's objections, Skaggs remains steadfast in his stance of unaccountability to Amanda. But notably, he is unable to establish his own supposed unaccountability without reference to Amanda. He reproaches her for her obsession with "dead white women" (334), her lack of meaningful friendships, and her unremarkable sex life. By making these assertions, Skaggs attempts to delimit Amanda, to render her into something definite for his own self-satisfaction. Skaggs *knows* Amanda, and by this violence he brings his knowing self to stand, invulnerable to what he perceives as Amanda's "attack" (333). If he is guilty of anything, Skaggs continues, it is of being too "altruistic." "I was doing you a *favor*," he insists (333). At least in his own reckoning, he is a "better person" (334) for having condescended to Amanda's level. All this accounting, through which Skaggs reconciles himself and confirms his own unaccountability, occurs only after "*a long pause*" (333), a tedious silence in which the audience might attend upon Skaggs' consolidation of his own powers of unthinking. In directing the audience's attention toward this silence, Baker grants them the opportunity to notice what Skaggs does not: that he positions Amanda as the object—or the abject, whose inhumanity he insinuates when he compares her to a hobbit (334)—against which he can prop up his own dubious, far-from-satisfying, mere semblance of redemption, his own fictive closure.

Silence is a theatrical power that Baker wields with intention. All of Baker's plays, in fact, are rich with silence, and *Nocturama* is no exception. Jennifer Cayer views Baker's silences as "co-present occasion[s] for" the audience's "prolonged witnessing," occasions which bring "a shifting awareness from the show to the self-as-watcher." These silences, writes Cayer, "initiate a swerve in audience attention from invisible eavesdroppers or 'passive consumers' to involved witnesses."[20] I think, therefore, that while Judy, Gary, and Skaggs do not—perhaps cannot—direct their attention toward their own silences, the same cannot be said for the audience. Baker's silences, in fact, invite the audience into a deeper intimacy with the characters, one in which violations of that intimacy can be more deeply felt. In doing so, they allow those who are caught in the orbit of whiteness to notice with visceral immediacy the harms that they so carefully conceal from themselves in their everyday lives. Baker's silences thereby call attention to the relational rupture that is consubstantial with whiteness; they initiate a noticing of the violence of whiteness, a noticing that might even work to stun the audience into a recognition of their (our) own complicity.

Attention and Embodiment

I am tempted to think that any dramatic project that seeks to disrupt whiteness must enact a displacement of the subject's unilateral fixation upon the object for, instead, the mutuality and reciprocity of what philosopher Emmanuel Levinas envisions as "direct relation with the Other," a relation that does not "thematize the Other" or "consider him in the same manner as a known object."[21] Derrida, however, views this supposed immediacy of relation as a violence in its own right. "If I attained to the other immediately and originally, silently, in communion with the other's own experience," Derrida argues, then "the other would cease to be the other."[22] Counter to the immediacy of relation, Derrida emphasizes "the *irreducibly mediate* nature of the intentionality aiming at the other as other," an intentionality which "confirms and respects separation, the unsurpassable necessity of (nonobjective) mediation."[23] Derrida leads me to have misgivings about my own yearning for assurance about the directness or immediacy of relation, to wonder whether this yearning might spring from my discomfort with ways of looking and knowing that I know to be bound up with my whiteness. Perhaps I am resorting to yet another kind of violence in order to dispel my anxiety that these ways of looking and knowing are my legacy to bear. Perhaps I am only seeking to bring about my own fictive closure.

But Baker's *Nocturama* offers no such assurances or consolations. *Nocturama* trains my attention on the objectifying violence that animates whiteness, allowing me to notice how this violence permeates my own looking. To what degree did my own assumptions begin to congeal around Amanda as she sat there reading on that bench? The power of this noticing lies in the confluence of, on the one hand, an unsettling of the white gaze, and, on the other hand, a provocation of an ethical orientation. It lies in an emphasis on Martin Buber's sense of ethical responsibility: a receptivity to being addressed as well as a commitment to respond.

It is just this kind of response-ability, however, that white theatergoers tend to shirk the moment they exit the theater. In order to satisfy the exigencies and busy-ness of everyday life, white theatergoers turn away from the speaker that addresses them and to whom they owe a response, a sobering reminder that where there is a will to change there is not by necessity a way. But Baker intervenes in this evasive maneuver of theatergoing whiteness by making her drama contiguous with the everyday, eliciting an engagement of attention rather than a straining of will, and thereby provoking a sense of responsibility that is not so easily cast aside. In doing so, Baker actualizes a potential that resides in the theater space itself, where it is not taken for granted that decisive action follows upon intention. In the theater, it is rather understood that action and intention coalesce in the performing body. Buber calls this the "personal kinesis" of, or the "union of meaning and deed peculiar to,"[24] the stage actor. Buber's interest in theater corresponds with his ethical philosophy, which advocates for a "turning towards the other" in which action and attitude are deployed in tandem. For Buber, this turning-toward is not merely "inner" but "an essential action [. . .] round which an essential attitude is built up"; attitude, he continues, relies heavily on "the very tension of the eyes' muscles and the very action of the foot as it walks."[25] Buber here reminds us of the importance of involving the body in the cultivation of a relational attention—a turning-toward-others in both action and intention—that is less likely to falter once the curtain closes. This is a turning-toward-others that I carry along with me, in my body, beyond the walls of the theater, as my future.

Accordingly, Baker provides a theater experience that weaves itself out of and back into the fabric of the everyday, demanding, and thereby cultivating, an embodied resilience of relational attention. Baker's theater of attention, which Nathan Heller praises for its "reverent focus on the small, telling details of everyday life,"[26] invites the audience to body forth a gesture of relation that is nothing like closure, for a relation where neither party suffers the violence of fixation demands a habitual yet inexhaustible, constant reorientation of the self toward others, one that leaves room for, and yet remains attuned to, the mutuality of becoming. Yet, counterintuitively, Baker's *Nocturama* focalizes this ethical obligation, this relational gesture of turning-toward-others, by dramatizing its failure in the hands of whiteness. Baker makes whiteness aporetic for relation, emphasizing the way in which the turn toward others emerges out of and easily slip-slides back into the objectifying it-grasp. Baker thus places her audience at the center of what Derrida might call an ethical economy in which nonviolence is always already in commerce with violence. In doing so, she goads her audience to inhabit a place of risk, but a risk that must be undertaken if relation is to be possible. Without ignoring the inherent difficulties of the ethical obligation to others, Baker places the onus on the audience to enact its concrete fulfillment in their everyday lives.

Quiet and Relation

Early in the play, while guiding a tour of the Collins house, Amanda meditates on Elizabeth Collins' despondency, which she links with the disappointments of Collins' baffled efforts to find enough "redemptive meaning in the world" (233). Amanda attributes Collins' worry over redemption to her Puritan upbringing, but this is a worry that is in no way unique to Collins. Questions about the pursuit of and access to redemption linger in the background for the white characters in *Nocturama*. All of them, including the haunting persona of Collins, are situated within the same immobilizing symbolic order; they all feel it, and they all seek to recuse themselves from responsibility for it. With this in mind, we might read Amanda's comportment, which Skaggs can only understand as a withdrawal from social life, as rather an adaptation of Collins' watchful non-participation (355), but with a difference. Amanda's non-participation is different from that of Collins in that it is an alternative to, or perhaps even a refusal of, the resignation that is concomitant with the white characters' yearnings for redemption. In her engagement with Collins' non-participation, Amanda explores possibilities of being that recognize and acknowledge, yet are not subject to and do not repeat, the violence of whiteness.

After Skaggs leaves town for his new job, Amanda returns to the home of Judy and Gary in order to return a small marble bust that she earlier pilfered from their house. She is overcome with remorse for stealing this item, which she likely mistook to be an image of Elizabeth Collins' husband's lover, Winnie Rosebath. Given Amanda's excitement upon learning that Judy and Gary's house is the historical home of the Rosebaths (277, 290), we might infer that Amanda hoped to find there the rumored long-missing daguerreotype of Winnie Rosebath, the lost image of Rosebath's "incredible beauty" and "mysterious charm," of which there is otherwise no extant evidence (273). If found, this small photograph would be the only clue to Winnie Rosebath's captivating allure, which drew Alfred Collins into an affair so devastating for Elizabeth that it led her to suicide.

Without telling them all this, Amanda returns the bust and apologizes to Judy and Gary. But when she moves to leave, it becomes clear that Judy and Gary are not finished with her, that they want something more from her. Groping for any means to keep her from leaving, Gary scurries off and returns, producing a small photograph, which Amanda appears to recognize as the long-lost Winnie Rosebath daguerreotype. But when Amanda finally has this mystery item in hand, it seems that it is not what she bargained for. Baker's stage directions indicate that she trembles and breathes heavily as she struggles to find the words to thank Gary for giving it to her. But Amanda's acceptance of the gift seems to coincide with a loss: "*Amanda keeps staring at the picture, bereft*" (364–5). Baker leaves unclear exactly what it is of which Amanda is supposed to be bereft by her encounter with the daguerreotype. Amanda does not speak of her loss in this scene, and Baker's stage directions offer little more explanation of Amanda's interiority than Amanda's sparing speech.

By not giving a more direct account of Amanda's affective experience, Baker places a greater interpretive labor on her audience. "The words in affective stage directions," Bess Rowen explains, "connect bodies of character and actor"—actor, of course, being drama's most discerning reader—"over and through a playtext, reminding us of the shared feelings that connect humans across time and space, while also acknowledging that no one has precisely the same experience."[27] The ambiguity with which Baker conveys Amanda's affect invites both readers and live audience members to inhabit an embodied relational gesture toward Amanda and her loss. The contextual tidbits that Baker provides about Amanda's past—for example, her troubled relationship with her needy yet barely present father, a trauma which recurs in Skaggs' mistreatment of her (333)—act as toeholds by which we can ascend toward a sense of Amanda's affective experience without ever quite getting on top of it. Baker's economy of words stops us short of exhausting the sense of Amanda's loss, thereby showing fidelity to the unknowability of her interiority. This respect for distance is "a secrecy," according to Levinas, "which does not hold to a closure which would isolate some rigorously private domain of a closed interiority, but a secrecy which holds to the responsibility for the Other."[28] Baker at once engages us in relation with Amanda and prevents us from closing the distance between ourselves and her.

This tension between connection and distance is one that Baker opens up much earlier on. Scattered throughout the play, the audience is treated to segments of Amanda's guided tour of the Collins house. You might even say that she takes us on the tour, except Baker never specifies in her stage directions whether or not Amanda is addressing the audience directly. Since Amanda delivers her live tours to us while alone on stage, these moments have a disarming effect, pulling us into the fold of the stage-world and, beyond that, giving us a sense of intimacy with Amanda. However, midway through the first act, Baker reveals that Amanda's tour guide segments might not have been addressed to us at all. Skaggs is surprised to find Amanda alone when he first enters the Collins house, for she appeared to be giving a tour when he observed her through the window as he approached. Amanda confesses that she was only talking to herself, rehearsing her tour guide routine alone (274). In this startling disillusionment of the audience's uncertain sense that they are on the receiving end of Amanda's direct address, Baker toys with their erstwhile assumption of proximity to Amanda, abruptly substituting it with a sense of distance from her. Through this disruptive technique, which she again accomplishes through what is *not* said in her stage directions, Baker acknowledges a tension that both animates and complicates the philosophy of relation. This tension between the ethical obligation to connect with others and at the same time respect the distance between oneself and others rises to a crescendo in the final scene, where Baker provokes from us a relational gesture toward Amanda at the same time that her stage directions constrain us to respect the distance between ourselves and her interiority. Baker's stage directions invite us into both the secrecy of Amanda's interiority and into the mystery of relation itself without letting us presume to fathom the depths of either.

Perhaps Amanda's encounter with the daguerreotype startles her into despair over the way she lives unrecognized or misrecognized under the white gaze. After all, the seemingly ill-founded suspicions that earlier motivate Skaggs to hurl accusations of sexual deviance at Judy and Gary—in reference, specifically, to Judy's objectifying gaze at Amanda's beauty (317–18) and to Gary's voyeuristic peeping at Skaggs and Amanda making out (311, 327), both of which attempt to hold Amanda as their object—are now confirmed. Gary and Judy do seem, at last, to be attempting (albeit ineptly) to seduce Amanda, even in this moment when Amanda is so obviously troubled. Judy and Gary start a two-person dance party and invite Amanda to join, but Amanda remains taciturn and unyielding. Her complete absorption in the daguerreotype is interrupted only after some time by the embarrassing spectacle of Gary and Judy's dance.

Amanda watches Judy and Gary's dance but does not participate, in a manner similar to, but not precisely the same as, Elizabeth Collins. As Amanda tells us earlier, Collins' journal reports her smashing a flowerpot—in the midst of a dance party, no less, and standing at the very bay window in front of which Amanda now stands—in a desperate rage over her realization that "no one was really seeing *her* at all" (356). Here and now, during Judy and Gary's dance party, Amanda, too, seems tempted to smash the flowerpot as Collins does, but she draws back (366). She does not smash the pot, perhaps because she is not, like Collins, merely dismayed by her invisibility, but rather assailed by what Rankine calls a "visceral disappointment [. . .] in the sense that no amount of visibility will alter the ways in which one is perceived."[29] Indeed, so long as Judy and Gary perceive Amanda only as an object of their pleasure, they remain insensible to her pain. Yet their glaring incomprehension in nowise inhibits the abandon with which they give themselves over to their dance, which only grows "*more uninhibited and joyful*" (366). They continue to entreat Amanda to join them. Amanda "*shakes her head and tries to smile*," quietly rejecting their invitation, yet continuing to watch them. "*A few seconds later, the room goes black*" (366). This is where the play ends.

Amanda neither smashes the flowerpot in resistance to Gary and Judy's oblivion nor acquiesces to their invitation to dance. She instead forges a third path of quiet non-participation, like that of Collins, but with a difference that is suited to the particularity of her own situation. Amanda's quiet runs counter to the assumption—a harmful assumption, in Quashie's view—that "black subjectivity is without escape from the publicness of racialization— that blackness is always faithful to or in resistance of the projections of white culture."[30] Amanda, in taciturn refusal of the acquiescence/resistance binary, inhabits her own interiority in the face of a prescriptive social scene that threatens to rob her of her agency. She cannot even bring herself to fake a smile. Instead, with quiet, Amanda takes up what Fred Moten calls the "duty to appose the oppressor, to refrain from a certain performance of the negative, to avoid his economy of objectification, and standing against, to run away from the snares of recognition."[31] Amanda's quiet is a rejection of the narrow field of unfreedom in which whiteness attempts to enclose everything. Paradoxically, it is this seemingly passive gesture of quiet by which Baker makes legible Amanda's agency, an agency that ranges outside the bounds demarcated by the white imaginary. Amanda, in the end, summarily refuses Skaggs' offer of continued friendship (334), withdrawing from complicity in his capitulation to the illusory consolation of a fictive redemption. Even more importantly, Amanda is the character through whom the narrative itself refuses closure.

Baker's *Nocturama* shifts the attention of the audience—both readers of her play text and live spectators—toward that which the white characters are unable to see. But the play does so by putting whiteness at the periphery. Instead of directing the audience's attention toward the embarrassing exploits of the white characters, Baker directs their attention toward Amanda, provoking a listening to what Amanda's reticence speaks in the face of the harms of whiteness as they are leveled at her across the stage. Baker engages her audience in relation with Amanda, granting them an indefinite kind of access to her truth without handing her over as an object for the gratification of their will to know. And by abruptly cutting the lights in the midst of the audience's attendance upon these unsettling aspects of whiteness, Baker leaves whiteness unsettled—she leaves her audience with an unanswered question that demands response. What is more, Baker leaves the audience in the midst of a relational gesture toward Amanda without granting her or them any sort of satisfying narrative redemption, troubling the very notion of redemption and raising the question of whether the pursuit of satisfaction in redemption might be a mere desperate clamber for the fictive closure out of which whiteness presumes to substantiate itself. What Baker provides, therefore, is nothing like a one-off healing session or an epiphany of seeing that conclusively sets the audience free from whiteness. Instead, Baker leaves her audience lingering in the act of an embodied relational gesture that does not admit closure, a fluidity of mutual exchange that begs to be made habitual as an ethico-political orientation even while the continuous flowing-forth of exchange demands constant reorientation. In doing so, Baker emphasizes the way in which the ethical self always takes its cue from others, the way in which freedom and becoming always rely on one's orientation toward others, even if that orientation offers no comforting assurances.

Baker calls her audience forth into a hearkening to what is being said, an attendance upon that which is plain to hear in both speech and in silence if only one is prepared to listen. I am inclined to think that such an embodied gesture of attention might induce in those afflicted by the wound of whiteness a more resilient commitment to formulating and enacting a suitable response of redress to whiteness in their everyday lives. I am inclined to think that it is by just such a gesture that relation takes shape out of the material conditions of rupture, as it must if it is to take shape at all. By such a gesture, even freedom might be possible, and out of the very stuff of its impossibility. I am inclined to think that this is true because this wound afflicts my body, and it afflicts other bodies through my body. My response of redress must be an embodied one if I am to be able to notice and acknowledge this wound and, notwithstanding, become something other than it.

AFTERWORD
THE FRAGILITY AND IMPERFECTION OF CREATING THEATER

This ending isn't an ending. Annie Baker is still in the full swing of her career, perhaps not even at her career high. As this book draws to its close, she still has at least three major projects in the works. Her play *Infinite Life*, described in promotional materials as a play about "no end in sight" and a work "that tackles persistent pain and desire," had been scheduled to open, with Baker herself directing, at the Signature Theatre in October 2021. It would have been the third and final play of her Signature Residency but was, like so many other theater events, a casualty of the COVID-19 pandemic, postponed indefinitely. Two scenes from *Infinite Life* were excerpted in *The Paris Review*. In them, five female characters (all middle-aged or older: the age range is 40s to 70s) are lying on chaise longues outside of a medical clinic "two hours north of San Francisco."[1] The tone of the conversation is franker and more raw than Baker's earlier work, closer to *I Love Dick*. It's tempting, then, to speculate whether she might be plunging deeper into explorations of women's desire and creating opportunities for middle-aged and older female actors onstage. For a number of years she has also been working on a play about Benedictine monks and monastic time, *The Last of the Little Hours*, researched when she was a Cullman Center Fellow at the New York Public Library and a MacDowell Fellow. In a conversation with Jesse Green, she said she is resisting the urge to tell a story with it: "It would really be easy to write an annoying play about monks," she says. "'Does God exist?' Who knows! Fuck that. I want to write a play a monk would go to see. And have him say, 'Yes. My life is really like that.'"[2] Since it follows the daily life of monks, my guess would be that this play will unfold slowly, more along the lines of *The Flick* or *John*, perhaps even *more* slowly, challenging us to get ever more absorbed and attentive, suspending us in the rhythm of prayers and songs and silence. And over the summer of 2022 Baker has also been shooting her first film, *Janet Planet*, in her hometown area of Western Massachusetts. It features actors Julianne Nicholson and Sophie Okonedo and follows "11 year old Lacy, her mother Janet, and the three people who come into their lives over one summer in 1991." The casting call for Lacy describes her as "8-12 years old, any ethnicity. She is herself.

Afterword

Curious, observant, straightforward. Solid in her uniqueness, lives in her imagination. Odd birds welcome." Since Baker herself was about the age of Lacy in 1991 and seems to fit the character description, it's easy to wonder if this is an autobiographical reflection, a memory film. More important, all of these projects suggest only further richness, and more creative control, as director as well as writer, from Annie Baker.

From her earliest forays in the theater, Baker has been a playwright with a singular vision. Her quiet style has been helping to lead a new golden age of American playwriting, marked by attention and care.[3] I proposed in the Preface that Baker's plays work on us like a kind of contemplative practice, guiding us into patience, into awareness, into aliveness. Paradoxically, they do this so well because they reveal imperfection—not Baker's imperfection as an artist, but the imperfection of life, illuminated through her exquisitely crafted plays. In an interview with Greta Gerwig, Baker said that she chose writing plays over writing novels because of the room for imperfection. Novelists always had to "choose the *perfect* word," she thought, and she felt incapable of doing that; "I would choose the wrong word or I would choose too many perfect words—I wrote really purple prose." So, she says, "I ended up becoming a playwright because you can be grammatically incorrect: people speaking in bad poetry or people attempting to speak well and sometimes succeeding and sometimes failing. The whole imperfection of it suddenly felt freeing to me."[4]

Theater has perhaps always been the best artform to work in to remind us of imperfection. Alan Read, in *Theatre, Intimacy and Engagement*, calls theater "the last human venue" because of its imperfection, because it is a venue in which objects are measured by their "impotential to be realized."[5] Though Baker jokes to Marc Maron about the frustrations of working in the theater, in which something will go wrong in every performance—asking herself "*Why* did I choose to work in the most flawed, ephemeral, out-of-your-control medium?"[6]—it is precisely the disappointments, the falling-shorts, that remind us of being alive.

Her longtime collaborator, director Sam Gold, describes Baker's plays as "fragile": "A lot of writers make their plays director-proof—extremely muscular, so that, no matter what the production is, it will be the play—but Annie makes her plays really fragile," he said.[7] They remain open and vulnerable for the insights and revelations of those who embody and interpret them. This feels like an apt metaphor for the audience's encounter with a Baker play: walking out of the theater feeling for the perfect imperfection of life.

NOTES

Preface

1. Elianna Kan, "Annie Baker," *BOMB*, September 15, 2015, https://bombmagazine.org/articles/annie-baker/.
2. Jesse Green, "A Bed-and-Breakfast Weekend Gone Awkward," in Annie Baker's *John*, *Vulture*, August 11, 2015, https://www.vulture.com/2015/08/theater-review-annie-bakers-john.html.
3. Adam Greenfield, "The American Voice: When We Talk About Realism," *Playwrights Horizons*, December 14, 2012, https://www.playwrightshorizons.org/shows/trailers/american-voice-when-we-talk-about-realism/.
4. Paul Holdengräber, "The Art of Nonfiction No. 7: Adam Phillips," *Paris Review* 208 (Spring 2014): 29–54. The quotation appears on page 49.
5. Nathan Heller, "Just Saying," *New Yorker*, February 17, 2013, https://www.newyorker.com/magazine/2013/02/25/just-saying.
6. Alan Berks, email correspondence, August 4, 2022.
7. Greenfield, "The American Voice."
8. Ibid.
9. Greta Gerwig, "Annie Baker," *Interview*, March 29, 2017, https://www.interviewmagazine.com/culture/annie-baker.
10. Sam Kahn, "The Triumph of the Quiet Style," *The Awl*, November 1, 2017, https://www.theawl.com/2017/11/quiet-style-annie-baker/.
11. "Playwright Annie Baker. 2017 MacArthur Fellow," MacArthur Foundation video. YouTube, https://www.youtube.com/watch?v=90-M_pOkhEg.
12. Carlin Flora, "Eccentrics Corner: The Unpretending Player," *Psychology Today* 44 (March/April 2011), https://www.psychologytoday.com/us/articles/201103/eccentrics-corner-the-unpretending-player.
13. Jessie Thompson, "Annie Baker: 'Be Incredibly Vulnerable, But Not Necessarily Confessional,'" *Evening Standard*, January 22, 2018, https://www.standard.co.uk/culture/theatre/annie-baker-be-incredibly-vulnerable-but-not-necessarily-confessional-a3746516.html.
14. Kevin Quashie, *The Sovereignty of Quiet: Beyond Resistance in Black Culture* (New Brunswick: Rutgers University Press, 2012), 6.

Notes

15. Kahn, "The Triumph of the Quiet Style."
16. "Playwright Annie Baker. 2017 MacArthur Fellow," MacArthur Foundation video. YouTube, https://www.youtube.com/watch?v=90-M_pOkhEg.
17. Carlo Rovelli, *Helgoland: The Strange and Beautiful World of Quantum Physics*, trans. Erica Segre and Simon Carnell (New York: Penguin, 2021), 68.
18. Celia McGee, "Childhood is the Mother of the Play," *New York Times*, May 25, 2008, https://www.nytimes.com/2008/05/25/theater/25mcge.html.
19. Heller, "Just Saying."
20. April Ayers Lawson, "If You're Going to Read Plays, Read Annie Baker's," *Vice*, June 2014, https://www.vice.com/en/article/bn57q8/if-youre-going-to-read-plays-read-annie-bakers-plays.
21. Thompson, "Annie Baker."
22. "Annie Baker Discusses *Circle Mirror Transformation* with Playwrights Horizons Literary Manager Adam Greenfield," *The Huntington*, n.d., https://legacy.huntingtontheatre.org/articles/Annie-Baker-discusses-iCircle-Mirror-Transformationi-with-Playwrights-Horizons-Literary-Manager-Adam-Greenfield/.
23. Adam Szymkowicz, "I Interview Playwrights Part 38: Annie Baker," August 19, 2009, http://aszym.blogspot.com/2009/08/i-interview-playwrights-part-38-annie.html.
24. Lawson, "If You're Going to Read Plays, Read Annie Baker's."
25. Ibid.
26. Flavorwire Staff, "Exclusive: Q&A with Emerging Playwright, Annie Baker," *Flavorwire*, September 9, 2009, https://www.flavorwire.com/37906/exclusive-qa-with-emerging-playwright-annie-baker-interview-circle-mirror-transformation.
27. Alexis Soloski, "Annie Baker Returns with *The Aliens*," *Village Voice*, April 6, 2010, https://www.villagevoice.com/2010/04/06/annie-baker-returns-with-the-aliens/.
28. Gerwig, "Annie Baker."
29. Ibid.
30. Steve Suskin, "Interview: Annie Baker (Part 1)," *HuffPost*, October 26, 2015, https://www.huffpost.com/entry/interview-annie-baker-par_b_8389794.
31. "Annie Baker and Sam Gold," *Playwrights Horizons* podcast, September 1, 2009, https://www.playwrightshorizons.org/shows/trailers/annie-baker-and-sam-gold/.
32. Heller, "Just Saying."
33. Ibid.
34. As Carlo Rovelli says about physics in *Helgoland*, 116.
35. Kan, "Annie Baker."

Notes

Chapter 1

1. Adam Szymkowicz, "I Interview Playwrights Part 38: Annie Baker," *Blogspot*, August 19, 2009, http://aszym.blogspot.com/2009/08/i-interview-playwrights-part-38-annie.html.
2. John Freedman, "Annie Baker Brings 'The Aliens' to Moscow and St. Petersburg," *The Moscow Times*, November 28, 2011, https://www.themoscowtimes.com/2011/11/28/annie-baker-brings-the-aliens-to-moscow-and-st-petersburg-a34298.
3. Charles Isherwood, "Outsiders, Tender and Troubled," *The New York Times*, April 23, 2010, https://www.nytimes.com/2010/04/23/theater/reviews/23aliens.html.
4. Paul Schmidt, ed., trans., *The Plays of Anton Chekhov* (New York: Harper Perennial, 1997), 1.
5. Michael C. Finke, *Freedom from Violence and Lies: Anton Chekhov's Life and Writings* (London: Reaktion Books, 2021), 144.
6. Quoted in Schmidt, *The Plays of Anton Chekhov*, 5.
7. Elianna Kan, "Annie Baker," *BOMB*, September 15, 2015, https://bombmagazine.org/articles/annie-baker/.
8. Nathan Heller, "Just Saying," *New Yorker*, February 17, 2013, https://www.newyorker.com/magazine/2013/02/25/just-saying.
9. Rosamund Bartlett, "Chekhov and the Human Experience," *Almeida Theatre*, February 22, 2016, https://almeida.co.uk/uncle-vanya-chekhov-and-the-human-experience.
10. Schmidt, *The Plays of Anton Chekhov*, 3.
11. Ibid., 4.
12. Annie Baker, "Annie Baker's Top 10," *The Criterion Collection*, June 30, 2015, https://www.criterion.com/current/top-10-lists/241-annie-baker-s-top-10.
13. Ibid.
14. Kan, "Annie Baker."
15. Ibid.
16. Quoted in Kan, "Annie Baker."
17. Annie Baker, "Preface," in *Uncle Vanya* (New York: Theatre Communications Group, 2014), v–vi. All subsequent quotations from the play will be cited parenthetically in the text.
18. Ben Gassman, "Knocking Chekhov for a Loop," *American Theatre*, January 1, 2013, https://www.americantheatre.org/2013/01/01/knocking-chekhov-for-a-loop/.
19. Emma Brown, "Annie Baker, Sam Gold, and Uncle Vanya's Beige Socks," *Interview*, June 13, 2012, https://www.interviewmagazine.com/culture/annie-baker-sam-gold-uncle-vanya.

Notes

20. Ibid.
21. Rob Weinert-Kendt, "A New 'Vanya' for the Living Room," *The New York Times*, June 7, 2012, https://www.nytimes.com/2012/06/10/theater/annie-bakers-uncle-vanya-set-for-soho-rep.html?searchResultPosition=3.
22. Brown, "Annie Baker, Sam Gold, and Uncle Vanya's Beige Socks."
23. These are words of Vladimir Nemirovich-Danchenko, co-founder of the Moscow Art Theatre. He is quoted in Finke, *Freedom from Violence and Lies*, 11.
24. Charles Isherwood, "A Fresh Breeze in Pastoral Russia," *The New York Times*, June 17, 2012, https://www.nytimes.com/2012/06/18/theater/reviews/uncle-vanya-adapted-by-annie-baker-at-soho-rep.html.
25. Clancy Martin, "On *Uncle Vanya*: Part Two," *The Paris Review*, July 3, 2012, https://www.theparisreview.org/blog/2012/07/03/on-uncle-vanya-part-two/.
26. Isherwood, "A Fresh Breeze in Pastoral Russia."
27. Chris Jones, "*Uncle Vanya*: Why Not a Little Vodka with that Boring Life?" *Chicago Tribune*, February 22, 2017, https://www.chicagotribune.com/entertainment/theater/ct-uncle-vanya-review-ent-0223-20170222-column.html.
28. Adelaide Lee, "*Uncle Vanya*: Self-hatred and Unrequited Love Shine at the Goodman," *TheaterMania*, February 23, 2017, https://www.theatermania.com/chicago-theater/reviews/uncle-vanya-annie-baker-goodman-theatre_80129.html.
29. Andrew White, "Theatre News: Annie Baker's Fresh Adaptation of *Uncle Vanya* Liberates Chekhov," *Maryland Theatre Guide*, April 16, 2015, https://mdtheatreguide.com/2015/04/theatre-news-annie-bakers-fresh-adaptation-of-uncle-vanya-liberates-chekhov/.
30. See Vsevolod Meyerhold, "Naturalistic Theater and Theater of Mood," in *Chekhov: A Collection of Critical Essays*, ed. Robert Louis Jackson (Englewood Cliffs, NJ: Prentice Hall, 1967), 62–8.
31. See Marina Brodskaya's discussion of the various forms of the informal and formal "you" in *Uncle Vanya* in her *Anton Chekhov: Five Plays* (Redwood City, CA: Stanford University Press, 2010).
32. Isherwood, "A Fresh Breeze in Pastoral Russia."
33. Finke, *Freedom from Violence and Lies*, 197.
34. Charles Baxter, "Sonya's Last Speech, or, Double-Voicing: An Essay in Sixteen Sections," in *The Story About the Story II: Great Writers Explore Great Literature*, ed. J. C. Hallman (Portland, OR: Tin House Books, 2015), 81–96. The quotation appears on page 84.
35. Ibid., 89.
36. Ibid., 93.

Notes

37. Ibid., 95.
38. Roger Copeland, "Chekhov, Our (Distracted, Prosaic, Prophetic) Contemporary," *American Theatre*, March 30, 2015, https://www.americantheatre.org/2015/03/30/chekhov-our-distracted-prosaic-prophetic-contemporary/.
39. Kelly Younger, "*The Cherry Orchard* by Anton Chekhov," in *How to Teach a Play*, ed. Miriam M. Chirico and Kelly Younger (London: Methuen Drama, 2020), 133.
40. Ibid., 134.

Chapter 2

1. Paul Schmidt, ed., trans., *The Plays of Anton Chekhov* (New York: Harper Perennial, 1997), 4.
2. Adam Greenfield, "Annie Baker Discusses *Circle Mirror Transformation* with Playwrights Horizons Literary Manager Adam Greenfield," *The Huntington*, n.d., https://legacy.huntingtontheatre.org/articles/Annie-Baker-discusses-iCircle-Mirror-Transformationi-with-Playwrights-Horizons-Literary-Manager-Adam-Greenfield/.
3. Alan Berks, "Is Compassion Inherently Theatrical?" *Minnesota Playlist*, May 30, 2010, https://minnesotaplaylist.com/magazine/article/2010/is-compassion-inherently-theatrical. Berks is describing his response to *Circle Mirror Transformation* but his insights apply to all three of these first Vermont Plays.
4. Laura Collins-Hughes, "Fictional Town Sets Her Plays in Motion," *Boston Globe*, October 10, 2010, http://archive.boston.com/ae/theater_arts/articles/2010/10/10/fictional_town_sets_annie_bakers_plays_in_motion/.
5. Greenfield, "Annie Baker Discusses *Circle Mirror Transformation* with Playwrights Horizons Literary Manager Adam Greenfield."
6. Collins-Hughes, "Fictional Town Sets Her Plays in Motion."
7. Matt Trueman, "Just Don't Call it Ordinary: Annie Baker's Plays Distil the Unnoticed in Everyday Life," *Financial Times*, June 14, 2013.
8. Ben Brantley, "In Boston, Listening to a Young Playwright Adept at Silence," *The New York Times*, November 10, 2010, https://www.nytimes.com/2010/11/11/theater/11annie.html.
9. Ibid.
10. Ibid.
11. Celia McGee, "Childhood is the Mother of the Play," *The New York Times*, May 25, 2008, https://www.nytimes.com/2008/05/25/theater/25mcge.html.

Notes

12. Gwendolyn Rice, "Searching for Meaning with Annie Baker in *Body Awareness*," *Gwendolyn Rice*, March 20, 2018, https://www.gwendolynrice.com/post-script/searching-for-meaning-with-annie-baker-in-body-awareness.

13. Chantal Mendes, "Theater Review: *Body Awareness*—A Lesson in Human Awareness," *The Arts Fuse*, October 30, 2010, https://artsfuse.org/14870/theater-review-body-awareness-a-lession-in-human-awareness/.

14. Baker eschews assumptions that her plays are autobiographical, though her brother Benjamin Nugent has written about having been misdiagnosed with Asperger's by their psychologist mother. Benjamin Nugent, "I Had Asperger Syndrome. Briefly," *New York Times*, January 31, 2012, https://www.nytimes.com/2012/02/01/opinion/i-had-asperger-syndrome-briefly.html.

15. Annie Baker, *Body Awareness*, in *The Vermont Plays* (New York: Theatre Communications Group, 2012), 402. All subsequent quotations from the play will be cited parenthetically in-text.

16. Megan Grumbling, "On Stage: *Body Awareness* Is Much More Than Skin Deep," *Portland Phoenix*, July 27, 2022, https://portlandphoenix.me/on-stage-body-awareness-is-much-more-than-skin-deep/.

17. Greenfield, "Annie Baker Discusses *Circle Mirror Transformation* with Playwrights Horizons Literary Manager Adam Greenfield."

18. April Ayers Lawson, "If You're Going to Read Plays, Read Annie Baker's," *Vice*, June 5, 2014, https://www.vice.com/en/article/bn57q8/if-youre-going-to-read-plays-read-annie-bakers-plays.

19. Charles Isherwood, "A Household's Wounds are Raw, but No One is Willing to Ease the Tensions," *The New York Times*, June 5, 2008, https://www.nytimes.com/2008/06/05/theater/reviews/05body.html.

20. "Vancouver Theatre: *Body Awareness*," *Review from the House*, October 14, 2019, https://www.reviewfromthehouse.com/review-seat/vancouver-theatre-body-awareness.

21. Greenfield, "Annie Baker Discusses *Circle Mirror Transformation* with Playwrights Horizons Literary Manager Adam Greenfield."

22. Ibid.

23. Annie Baker, *Nocturama*, in *The Vermont Plays* (New York: Theatre Communications Group, 2012), 216. All subsequent quotations from the play will be cited parenthetically in the text.

24. *Nocturama* is also the name of a 2003 album by Nick Cave and the Bad Seeds.

25. Nugent is quoted in Nathan Heller, "Just Saying: The Anti-Theatrical Theatre of Annie Baker," *The New Yorker*, February 25, 2013, https://www.newyorker.com/magazine/2013/02/25/just-saying.

26. Annie Baker, "From *Nocturama*," *Vice*, November 30, 2009, https://www.vice.com/en/article/9bdbmp/from-nocturama-264-v16n12.

Notes

27. As it happens, Baker's brother Benjamin Nugent wrote a biography of Elliot Smith, *Elliot Smith and the Big Nothing* (Boston: Da Capo Press, 2004).
28. Kevin Quashie, *The Sovereignty of Quiet: Beyond Resistance in Black Culture* (Piscataway: Rutgers University Press, 2012), 6.
29. S. Nicole, *Mildly Bitter's Musings*, August 8, 2015, https://mildlybitter.blogspot.com/2015/08/annie-baker-and-sam-gold-in.html.
30. Elianna Kan, "Annie Baker," *BOMB*, September 15, 2015, https://bombmagazine.org/articles/annie-baker/.
31. Jennifer Cayer, "Her Town: Annie Baker's Americans," *Journal of American Drama and Theatre* 3 (Fall 2011): 37.
32. Ibid., 52.
33. Annie Baker, *Circle Mirror Transformation* (New York: Samuel French, 2009), 3.
34. Ibid.
35. Ibid.
36. Berks, "Is Compassion Inherently Theatrical?"
37. Annie Baker, *Circle Mirror Transformation*, in *The Vermont Plays* (New York: Theatre Communications Group, 2012), 87. All subsequent quotations from the play will be cited parenthetically in the body of the text.
38. Greenfield, "Annie Baker Discusses *Circle Mirror Transformation* with Playwrights Horizons Literary Manager Adam Greenfield."
39. Joe Dziemianowicz, "'The Joe D Show' Episode 9: 'The Flick' Take 2 with Playwright Annie Baker, Director Sam Gold, and Actor Matthew Maher," *Daily News*, May 7, 2015, https://www.nydailynews.com/entertainment/theater-arts/joe-show-episode-9-flick-2-article-1.2214407.
40. Greenfield, "Annie Baker Discusses *Circle Mirror Transformation* with Playwrights Horizons Literary Manager Adam Greenfield."
41. Ibid.
42. Matt Trueman, "Annie Baker's *Circle Mirror Transformation* is Every Inch a Modern Classic," *New Statesman*, July 28, 2013, https://www.newstatesman.com/culture/music-theatre/2013/07/annie-bakers-circle-mirror-transformation-every-inch-modern-classic.
43. Cayer, "Her Town," 52.
44. Ibid., 53.
45. Trueman, "Annie Baker's *Circle Mirror Transformation* is Every Inch a Modern Classic."
46. Cayer, "Her Town," 52.
47. Charles Isherwood, "Some Plays Can Twinkle Without Stars," *The New York Times*, November 4, 2009, https://www.nytimes.com/2009/11/08/theater/08ishe.html?ref=playwrightshorizons.

Notes

48. Aleks Sierz, "*Circle Mirror Transformation*, Royal Court Theatre Local," *The Arts Desk,* July 13, 2013, https://www.theartsdesk.com/theatre/circle-mirror-transformation-royal-court-theatre-local.
49. Ibid.
50. Michael Billington, "*Circle Mirror Transformation* Review," *The Guardian*, July 13, 2013, https://www.theguardian.com/stage/2013/jul/13/circle-mirror-transformation-review.
51. Ibid.
52. Clare Brennan, "*Circle Mirror Transformation* Review: Naturalism Without the Social Context," *The Guardian*, March 10, 2018, https://www.theguardian.com/stage/2018/mar/10/circle-mirror-transformation-review-home-manchester-annie-baker.
53. Trueman, "Annie Baker's *Circle Mirror Transformation* is Every Inch a Modern Classic."

Chapter 3

1. "Gordon Hempton: Silence and the Presence of Everything," *On Being with Krista Tippett*, May 10, 2012, https://onbeing.org/programs/gordon-hempton-silence-and-the-presence-of-everything/.
2. Thomas Mann, *The Magic Mountain*, trans. John E. Woods (New York: Vintage, 1996), xii.
3. Patrick Healy, "*The Flick* Prompts an Explanation from Playwrights Horizons," *The New York Times*, March 25, 2013, https://archive.nytimes.com/artsbeat.blogs.nytimes.com/2013/03/25/the-flick-prompts-an-explanation-from-playwrights-horizons/.
4. Arthur C. Danto, *What Art Is* (New Haven: Yale University Press, 2013), 21.
5. Laura Collins-Hughes, "Fictional Town Sets Her Plays in Motion," *Boston Globe*, October 10, 2010, http://archive.boston.com/ae/theater_arts/articles/2010/10/10/fictional_town_sets_annie_bakers_plays_in_motion/.
6. Ibid.
7. Ibid.
8. Simone Weil, *Gravity and Grace*, trans. Emma Crawford and Mario von der Ruhr (London and New York: Routledge, 2002), 117.
9. Tim Sanford's letter to subscribers of Playwrights Horizons is reprinted in Healy, "*The Flick* Prompts an Explanation from Playwrights Horizons."
10. Jayne Blanchard, "Review: Annie Baker's John at Signature Theatre," *DC Theatre Scene*, April 11, 2018, https://dctheatrescene.com/2018/04/11/review-annie-bakers-john-at-signature-theatre/. Although Blanchard is describing *John*, her insight feels even more applicable to *The Aliens* and *The Flick*.

Notes

11. Charles Isherwood, "Outsiders, Tender and Troubled," *The New York Times*, April 22, 2010, https://www.nytimes.com/2010/04/23/theater/reviews/23aliens.html.
12. "The Aliens by Annie Baker," *Bush Theatre*, n.d., https://www.bushtheatre.co.uk/event/the-aliens/.
13. John Freedman, "Annie Baker Brings *The Aliens* to Moscow and St. Petersburg," *The Moscow Times*, November 28, 2011, https://www.themoscowtimes.com/2011/11/28/annie-baker-brings-the-aliens-to-moscow-and-st-petersburg-a34348.
14. Annie Baker, *The Aliens*, in *The Vermont Plays* (New York: Theatre Communications Group, 2012), 5, 10. All subsequent quotations from the play will be cited parenthetically in the text.
15. Charles Kruger, "SF Playhouse: Annie Baker's *The Aliens* is a Masterpiece and Not to Be Missed," *TheatreStorm*, March 26, 2012, https://theatrestorm.com/2012/03/26/sf-playhouse-annie-bakers-the-aliens-is-a-masterpiece-and-not-to-be-missed/.
16. Martha Schabas, "Annie Baker's *The Aliens* is a Beautifully Structured Early Career Gem," *The Globe and Mail*, September 22, 2017, https://www.theglobeandmail.com/arts/theatre-and-performance/theatre-reviews/review-annie-bakers-the-aliens-is-a-beautifully-structured-early-career-gem/article36368323/. Schabas is reviewing the Toronto premiere of *The Aliens* at Coal Mine Theatre. It was only the second Baker play produced in Toronto, after 2015's *John*.
17. Christopher Soden, "Pitch Perfect, Brilliant *Aliens* at Stage West," *Sharp Critic*, May 24, 2017, https://www.stagewest.org/sharp-critic-pitch-perfect-brilliant-aliens-stage-west.
18. Charles Bukowski, "The Aliens," in *The Last Night of the Earth Poems* (New York: Ecco Press, 1992), 231.
19. Nathan Heller, "Just Saying," *New Yorker*, February 17, 2013, https://www.newyorker.com/magazine/2013/02/25/just-saying.
20. Carly Maga, "Existential Pain, Masculinity on Brilliant Display in Annie Baker's *The Aliens*," *Toronto Star*, September 23, 2017, https://www.thestar.com/entertainment/stage/2017/09/23/existential-pain-masculinity-on-brilliant-display-in-annie-bakers-the-aliens-review.html.
21. Erin Keane, "Silence is Golden in [502]'s *The Aliens*," *Louisville Public Media*, October 8, 2012, https://www.lpm.org/news/2012-10-08/review-silence-is-golden-in-502s-the-aliens.
22. Aleks Sierz, "*The Aliens*, Bush Theatre," *The Arts Desk*, September 21, 2010, https://www.theartsdesk.com/node/2247/view.
23. Robert Siegel, "*The Flick* Tells the Story of the Movies, Off the Screen," *All Things Considered*, June 11, 2015, https://www.npr.org/2015/06/11/413711303/the-flick-tells-the-story-of-the-movies-off-the-screen.

Notes

24. Henri Bergson, from *La Pensée et le mouvant*, 1934, quoted in Michael Foley, *Life Lessons from Bergson* (London: Macmillan, 2013), 26–7.
25. Foley, *Life Lessons from Bergson*, 27.
26. Charles Isherwood, "Review: In *The Flick*, Moments in the Movies, but Not on Screen," *The New York Times*, May 18, 2015, https://www.nytimes.com/2015/05/19/theater/review-in-the-flick-contemplating-a-life-of-stale-popcorn.html.
27. Michael Dale, "Podcast: *John* and *The Flick*'s Annie Baker Talks of Survival Jobs, Pandering and Not Being Influenced by Harold Pinter," *Broadway World*, podcast audio, September 1, 2015, https://www.broadwayworld.com/off-broadway/article/PODCAST-JOHN-And-THE-FLICKs-Annie-Baker-Talks-of-Survival-Jobs-Pandering-and-Not-Being-Influenced-by-Harold-Pinter-20150901.
28. Healy, "*The Flick* Prompts an Explanation from Playwrights Horizons."
29. "It's unprecedented," a spokesperson says, "for a work by a writer new to the NT to sell out so quickly." Quoted in Hermione Hoby, "From Pulitzer to Popcorn: Why Annie Baker is Making the Theatre World Pause for Thought," *The Guardian*, April 1, 2016, https://www.theguardian.com/stage/2016/apr/01/pulitzer-popcorn-playwright-annie-baker-critics-pause-thought.
30. Michael Billington, "*The Flick* Review – Echoes of Racine in a Riveting Play About Love, Lost Souls and Popcorn," *The Guardian*, April 20, 2016, https://www.theguardian.com/stage/2016/apr/20/the-flick-review-dorfman-national-theatre-london-annie-baker-cinema-play.
31. Marc Maron, "Annie Baker," *WTF with Marc Maron* (podcast), podcast audio, October 12, 2015, http://www.wtfpod.com/podcast/tag/Annie+Baker. See also Ana Fernández-Caparrós, "Intimations of Precarity in Twenty-First-Century U.S. Drama: Faltering Voices of the Precariat in Annie Baker's *The Flick*," *Cultura, Lenguaje y Representación* XXV (2021): 119–33.
32. Annie Baker, *The Flick* (New York: Theatre Communications Group, 2014), 4. All subsequent references will be cited parenthetically in the text.
33. Joe Dziemianowicz, "'The Joe D Show' Episode 9: 'The Flick' Take 2 with Playwright Annie Baker, Director Sam Gold, and Actor Matthew Maher," *Daily News*, May 7, 2015, https://www.nydailynews.com/entertainment/theater-arts/joe-show-episode-9-flick-2-article-1.2214407.
34. Adam Greenfield, "Annie Baker Discusses *Circle Mirror Transformation* with Playwrights Horizons Literary Manager Adam Greenfield," *The Huntington*, n.d., https://legacy.huntingtontheatre.org/articles/Annie-Baker-discusses-iCircle-Mirror-Transformationi-with-Playwrights-Horizons-Literary-Manager-Adam-Greenfield/.
35. Dziemianowicz, "'The Joe D Show' Episode 9."
36. Greenfield, "Annie Baker Discusses *Circle Mirror Transformation* with Playwrights Horizons Literary Manager Adam Greenfield."

Notes

37. Ibid.
38. Dziemianowicz, "'The Joe D Show' Episode 9."
39. Tim Sanford, "Tim Sanford on *The Flick*," *Playwrights Horizons,* December 16, 2012, https://www.playwrightshorizons.org/shows/trailers/tim-sanford-flick/.
40. Hoby, "From Pulitzer to Popcorn."
41. Ibid.
42. Shane Hazen, "Episode 45 – Annie Baker's *The Flick*," *Phi Phenomenon,* January 11, 2021, phiphenomenon.com.
43. Ibid.
44. James Wolcott, "Why the Audiences Who Walked Out of *The Flick* Made a Terrible Mistake," *Vanity Fair,* June 2, 2015, https://www.vanityfair.com/culture/2015/06/the-flick-annie-baker-review.
45. Jesse Green, "Theater Review: The Return of Annie Baker's *The Flick*," *Vulture,* May 18, 2015, https://www.vulture.com/2015/05/theater-review-the-return-of-the-flick.html.
46. David T. Johnson, "'A Very Very Long Amount of Time Passes': Slowness, Cinema, and Annie Baker's *The Flick* (2013)," *New Cinemas: Journal of Contemporary Film* 18, no. 1 and 2 (2021): 61–75. The quotation appears on p. 62.
47. Sarah Crompton, "*The Flick* (Dorfman, National Theatre)," *WhatsOnStage,* April 20, 2016, https://www.whatsonstage.com/london-theatre/reviews/flick-dorfman-national-sarah-crompton_40237.html.
48. Timothy D. Wilson, et al., "Just Think: The Challenges of the Disengaged Mind," *Science* 345, no. 6192 (2014): 75–7.
49. Sam Kahn, "The Triumph of the Quiet Style," *The Awl,* November 1, 2017, https://www.theawl.com/2017/11/quiet-style-annie-baker/.
50. Paula Vogel, "Sarah Ruhl," *BOMB,* April 1, 2007, https://bombmagazine.org/articles/sarah-ruhl/.
51. Tracy Bersley, "The Body Electric: Using Neuroscience and Theater to Reclaim Empathy for the Twenty-First Century," in *Text & Presentation, 2021,* ed. Amy Muse (Jefferson, NC: McFarland & Company, 2022), 199.

Chapter 4

1. MacArthur Foundation, "Playwright Annie Baker, 2017 MacArthur Fellow," *YouTube* video, 2:21, 2017, https://www.youtube.com/watch?v=90-M_pOkhEg.
2. Tyler Coates, "Are We *Supposed* to Hear Them?" *Slate,* August 12, 2015, https://slate.com/culture/2015/08/annie-bakers-new-play-john-reviewed.html.

Notes

3. J. Kelly Nestruck, "Annie Baker's John Is a Religious Experience," *The Globe and Mail*, February 1, 2017, https://www.theglobeandmail.com/arts/theatre-and-performance/theatre-reviews/annie-bakers-john-is-a-religious-experience/article33868395/.
4. Jessie Thompson, "Annie Baker: 'Be Incredibly Vulnerable but Not Necessarily Confessional,'" *Evening Standard*, January 22, 2018, https://www.standard.co.uk/culture/theatre/annie-baker-be-incredibly-vulnerable-but-not-necessarily-confessional-a3746516.html.
5. Andrzej Lukowski, "Annie Baker: 'I'm Stunned I Have a Career,'" *TimeOut*, January 19, 2018, https://www.timeout.com/london/theatre/annie-baker-im-stunned-i-have-a-career-at-all.
6. Ibid.
7. Tim Jackson, "Theater Review: Annie Baker's 'John' — A Feminist Black Comedy," *The Arts Fuse*, August 9, 2015, https://artsfuse.org/132403/fuse-theater-review-annie-bakers-john-a-feminist-black-comedy/.
8. Paul Woodruff, *The Necessity of Theater: The Art of Watching and Being Watched* (Oxford: Oxford University Press, 2008), 10.
9. Annie Baker, "Annie Baker's Top 10," *The Criterion Collection*, June 30, 2015, https://www.criterion.com/current/top-10-lists/241-annie-baker-s-top-10.
10. Ibid.
11. Jeremy Malies, "'John': Annie Baker," *Plays International & Europe*, n.d., https://playsinternational.org.uk/john-annie-baker-national-theatre-jeremy-malies/.
12. Alex Ross, "Bach's Holy Dread," *The New Yorker*, December 25, 2016, https://www.newyorker.com/magazine/2017/01/02/bachs-holy-dread.
13. Marc Maron, "Annie Baker," *WTF with Marc Maron* (podcast), podcast audio, October 12, 2015, http://www.wtfpod.com/podcast/tag/Annie+Baker.
14. Charles Isherwood, "Review: In *John*, Pondering Life's Mysteries from Gettysburg," *The New York Times*, August 11, 2015, https://www.nytimes.com/2015/08/12/theater/review-in-john-pondering-lifes-mysteries-from-gettysburg.html.
15. Lukowski, "Annie Baker."
16. Nestruck, "Annie Baker's John Is a Religious Experience."
17. Hilton Als, "The Way Station," *New Yorker*, August 17, 2015, https://www.newyorker.com/magazine/2015/08/24/the-way-station.
18. Leigh Scheps, "Best Plays of All Time," *TimeOut,* July 19, 2022, https://www.timeout.com/newyork/theater/best-plays-of-all-time. *John* is placed between Brecht's *Mother Courage* and Bruce Norris's *Clybourne Park*.
19. Lloyd Evans, "Review of *John*," *The Spectator*, February 3, 2018.
20. Annie Baker, *John* (New York: Theatre Communications Group, 2016), 36. All subsequent references will be cited parenthetically in the text. In a truth-is-

Notes

stranger-than-fiction kind of way, this is a real place in Gettysburg, with real mannequins. See http://www.dobbinhouse.com/.

21. Michael Paller, "Intimacy and the Numinous: An Interview with *John* Playwright Annie Baker Part Two," *Inside A.C.T.*, March 14, 2017, http://blog.act-sf.org/2017/03/intimacy-and-numinous-interview-with.html.

22. Charles Kruger, "Review: 'John' by Annie Baker at A.C.T." *TheatreStorm*, March 12, 2017, https://theatrestorm.com/2017/03/12/review-john-by-annie-baker-at-a-c-t/.

23. Elissa Blake, "*John*: Dread and Breakfast," *Audrey Journal*, September 13, 2019, https://www.audreyjournal.com.au/arts/john-seymour-centre-annie-baker-preview/.

24. Coates, "Are We *Supposed* to Hear Them?"

25. Jesse Green, "A Bed-and-Breakfast Weekend Gone Awkward, in Annie Baker's *John*," *Vulture*, August 11, 2015, https://www.vulture.com/2015/08/theater-review-annie-bakers-john.html.

26. Jane Bennett, "The Force of Things: Steps Toward an Ecology of Matter," *Political Theory* 32, no. 3 (July 2004): 347–72.

27. Barbara Hoffman, "In My Library: Annie Baker," *New York Post*, July 18, 2015, https://nypost.com/2015/07/18/in-my-library-annie-baker/.

28. William James, *The Varieties of Religious Experience* (London: Longmans, Green, and Co., 1902; London: Routledge Classics, 2002), 50.

29. Michael Billington, "Check into Annie Baker's Gothic Gettysburg B&B," *The Guardian*, January 25, 2018, https://www.theguardian.com/stage/2018/jan/25/john-review-annie-baker-dorfman-national-theatre.

30. Jill Dolan, "*John*, by Annie Baker, at the Signature," *The Feminist Spectator*, August 19, 2015, https://feministspectator.princeton.edu/2015/08/19/john-by-annie-baker-at-the-signature/.

31. Als, "The Way Station."

32. Emma Gray, "*I Love Dick* and the Radical Power of a Writer's Room Without Cis Men," *HuffPost*, June 23, 2017, https://www.huffpost.com/entry/i-love-dick-and-the-radical-power-of-a-writers-room-without-cis-men_n_594d2c1fe4b02734df29fa3f.

33. Alexis Soloski, "Groundbreaking TV about Female Desire, Thanks to Playwrights," *The New York Times*, June 16, 2017, https://www.nytimes.com/2017/06/16/arts/television/amazon-i-love-dick-jill-soloway.html.

34. Ibid.

35. Chris Kraus, *I Love Dick* (Los Angeles: Semiotext(e), 1997; London: Serpent's Tail, 2016), 154.

36. Hoffman, "In My Library."

37. Grillo, "Jill Soloway is a 'Weird Girl,'" *Lenny Letter*, March 30, 2018, https://www.lennyletter.com/story/jill-soloway-is-a-weird-girl.

Notes

38. Ibid.
39. Ibid.
40. Ibid.
41. Kraus, *I Love Dick*, 121.
42. Ibid.
43. Soloski, "Groundbreaking TV about Female Desire, Thanks to Playwrights."
44. Ibid.
45. Emily Nussbaum, "What Women Want on '*I Love Dick*,'" *The New Yorker*, June 19, 2017, https://www.newyorker.com/magazine/2017/06/26/what-women-want-on-i-love-dick.
46. See Hilary Bergen and Sandra Huber, "Pornography, Ectoplasm and the Secret Dancer: A Twin Reading of Naomi Uman's *Removed*," *Screening the Past*, April 2018, http://www.screeningthepast.com/issue-43/.
47. *I Love Dick*, "A Short History of Weird Girls," *Amazon Studios* video, 21:00, May 12, 2017.
48. Joey Soloway, "Joey Soloway on The Female Gaze, MASTER CLASS, TIFF 2016," *YouTube* video, 57:48, September 11, 2016, https://www.youtube.com/watch?v=pnBvppooD9I.
49. Ruth Curry, "*I Love Dick* Shows the Possibilities of the Peak TV Era—And Its Limitations," *Esquire*, May 15, 2017, https://www.esquire.com/entertainment/tv/a55080/i-love-dick-review/.
50. Rebecca Pitts, "A Short History of Weird Girls," January 6, 2019, https://www.rebeccaapitts.com/articles/weird-girls.
51. Annie Baker, *The Antipodes* (New York: Theatre Communications Group, 2018), 5. All other quotations from the play will be cited parenthetically in the text.
52. Ben Brantley mentions that there were several blackouts in the Signature Theatre production, but the script doesn't call for any. Ben Brantley, "Review: *The Antipodes* and Ambiguous Brainstorming," *The New York Times*, April 23, 2017, https://www.nytimes.com/2017/04/23/theater/the-antipodes-review-annie-baker.html.
53. Greta Gerwig, "Annie Baker," *Interview*, March 29, 2017, https://www.interviewmagazine.com/culture/annie-baker.
54. Tim Teeman, "Welcome to Annie Baker's World of Unseen Horrors," *Daily Beast*, April 23, 2017, https://www.thedailybeast.com/welcome-to-annie-bakers-world-of-unseen-horrors-review-of-the-antipodes.
55. Holly O'Mahony, "*The Antipodes*, National Theatre Review," *Culture Whisper*, October 31, 2019, https://www.culturewhisper.com/r/theatre/annie_baker_the_antipodes_london_theatre/14169.
56. Glenn Sumi, "Review: *The Antipodes* is the Play We All Need to See Right Now," *NowToronto*, April 9, 2022, https://nowtoronto.com/culture/review-the-antipodes-is-the-play-we-all-need-to-see-right-now.

Notes

57. Robert Reid, "*The Antipodes*: The Chaos of Creation," *Witness*, July 24, 2018, https://witnessperformance.com/antipodes/.
58. O'Mahony, "*The Antipodes*, National Theatre Review."
59. Andrzej Lukowski, "*The Antipodes* Review," *TimeOut*, October 31, 2019, https://www.timeout.com/london/theatre/the-antipodes-review.
60. Marie-Helene Bertino, "Annie Baker's *The Antipodes*: The Universe and the Playwright," *BOMB*, June 6, 2017, https://bombmagazine.org/articles/annie-bakers-the-antipodes/.
61. Brantley, "Review: *The Antipodes* and Ambiguous Brainstorming."
62. Gerwig, "Annie Baker."
63. Teeman, "Welcome to Annie Baker's World of Unseen Horrors."
64. Ibid.
65. O'Mahony, "*The Antipodes*, National Theatre Review."
66. Ibid.
67. Lukowski, "*The Antipodes* Review."
68. Brantley, "Review: *The Antipodes* and Ambiguous Brainstorming."
69. Bertino, "Annie Baker's *The Antipodes*."
70. Marilyn Stasio, "Off Broadway Review: Annie Baker's *The Antipodes*," *Yahoo!*, April 24, 2017, https://www.yahoo.com/entertainment/off-broadway-review-annie-baker-antipodes-141111728.html.
71. Michael Billington, "*The Antipodes* Review: Annie Baker Searches for the Sting in the Tale," *The Guardian*, October 31, 2019, https://www.theguardian.com/stage/2019/oct/31/the-antipodes-review-annie-baker-dorfman-theatre.
72. Sumi, "Review: *The Antipodes* is the Play We All Need to See Right Now."
73. Oscar Wilde, *The Picture of Dorian Gray* (New York: W. W. Norton, 2019), 5.

Chapter 5

Caring about the Matter

1. Marc Maron, *WTF with Marc Maron*, Episode 546: Annie Baker, October 12, 2015.
2. Greta Gerwig, "Annie Baker," *Interview Magazine*, March 29, 2017.
3. Annie Baker, *Body Awareness*, in *The Vermont Plays* (New York: Theatre Communication Group, 2012), 410. All subsequent citations will be cited parenthetically in the text.
4. Nathan Heller, "Just Saying," *The New Yorker*, February 25, 2013.
5. Mark Lawson, "I Like Theatre Because it is so Unprofitable," *Guardian*, October 24, 2019.

Notes

6. Ibid.
7. Annie Baker, *Circle Mirror Transformation*, in *The Vermont Plays* (New York: Theatre Communication Group, 2012), 134. All subsequent citations will be cited parenthetically in the text.
8. Heller, "Just Saying."
9. Adam Greenfield, "Annie Baker Discusses *Circle Mirror Transformation* with Playwright Horizons Literary Manager Adam Greenfield," *The Huntington*, n.d., https://legacy.huntingtontheatre.org/articles/Annie-Baker-discusses-iCircle-Mirror-Transformationi-with-Playwrights-Horizons-Literary-Manager-Adam-Greenfield/.
10. Annie Baker, *The Aliens*, in *The Vermont Plays* (New York: Theatre Communication Group, 2012), 84. All subsequent citations will be cited parenthetically in the text.
11. Sam Kahn, "The Triumph of the Quiet Style," *The Awl*, November 1, 2017.
12. Annie Baker, *Circle Mirror Transformation* (New York: Dramatists Play Service, 2010), 3.
13. Greenfield, "Annie Baker Discusses *Circle Mirror Transformation* with Playwright Horizons Literary Manager Adam Greenfield."
14. Jennifer Cayer, "Her Town: Annie Baker's Americans," *Journal of American Drama and Theatre* 23, no. 3 (2011): 39.
15. Ibid., 41.
16. Ibid., 52.
17. Ibid., 54.
18. Erik Piepenburg, "How Long is *The Flick*? It Depends on the Seats," *New York Times*, May 26, 2016.
19. Sarah Larson, "The Funny, Empathetic Genius of Annie Baker," *The New Yorker*, September 17, 2015.
20. Annie Baker, *John* (New York: Theatre Communications Group, 2016), 8. All subsequent citations will be parenthetically cited in the text.
21. I'm here drawing on Virginia Held's thinking: "The central focus of the ethics of care is on the compelling moral salience of attending to and meeting the needs of the particular others from whom we take responsibility" (10). For Held, the ethics of care contrasts with liberal individualism insofar as it is fundamentally relational and therefore always responsive to a person's relations.
22. Jules Barbier, *Tales of Hoffmann* (libretto), trans. Ann Fenney. Aria Database, http://www.aria-database.com/translations/contes12_oiseaux.txt.
23. Andrew Sofer, "Spectral Readings," *Theatre Journal* 64, no. 3 (2012): 330.
24. Ibid.
25. Ibid., 332.
26. Hilton Als, "The Way Station," *The New Yorker*, August 17, 2015.
27. Alexis Soloski, "*John* Review–A Claustrophobic Drama You Can't Take Your Eyes Off of," *Guardian*, August 12, 2015.

28. Larson, "The Funny, Empathetic Genius of Annie Baker."
29. Rita Felski, *Hooked: Art and Attachment* (Chicago: University of Chicago Press, 2020), 64.
30. Ibid., 105.
31. Some theorists have maintained that empathy is "soaked through with power and privilege," and others have described powerful aesthetic experiences people have had with novels that seem designed to thwart empathy: Camus's *The Stranger*, for example (Felski, *Hooked*, 106).
32. Ibid., 154.
33. Toril Moi, *Revolution of the Ordinary: Literary Studies after Wittgenstein, Austin, and Cavell* (Chicago: University of Chicago Press, 2017), 227.
34. Ibid., 228.
35. Jesse Green, "Watching: Annie Baker," *New York*, May 4, 2015.
36. Simone Weil conceived of attention less as an experience of intellectual focus and more as an experience of openness in which a person's desires give way to what is outside of the self. Robert Zaretsky comments, "To attend means not to seek, but to wait; not to concentrate, but instead to dilate our minds. We do not gain insights, Weil claims, by going in search of them, but instead by waiting for them" (46). The waiting and the engagement that characterize Baker's audience's experience in the theater are part of the attention that the plays attempt to nurture. Importantly, Weil argues that one's attention can and should develop through training. In her essay "Reflections on the Right Use of School Studies with a View to the Love of God," Weil argues that the primary goal of school exercises, no matter the specific subject, is "the development of the faculty of attention" (57).
37. Toril Moi, "Describing My Struggle," *The Point Magazine*, December 27, 2017.
38. Ibid.
39. Ibid.
40. Martin Hägglund, *This Life: Secular Life and Spiritual Freedom* (New York: Anchor, 2020), 85.

Domestic Uncanny

1. Annie Baker, *John* (New York: Theatre Communications Group, 2016). All subsequent references will be cited parenthetically in the text.
2. Charles Isherwood, "Review: In 'John,' Pondering Life's Mysteries from Gettysburg," *The New York Times*, August 11, 2015, https://www.nytimes.com/2015/08/12/theater/review-in-john-pondering-lifes-mysteries-from-gettysburg.html.
3. Sigmund Freud, *Psychological Writings and Letters* (New York: Continuum, 1995), 121.

Notes

4. Nicholas Royle, *The Uncanny* (Manchester: Manchester University Press, 2003), 2.
5. Andrew Sofer, *The Stage Life of Props* (Ann Arbor: University of Michigan Press, 2003), 31.
6. Ibid., 3.
7. Here, I use the term, *mise-en-scène* in Patrice Pavis's sense of the term, as including the participation of all stage languages—design and otherwise. See Patrice Pavis, *Contemporary Mise-en-Scene: Staging Theatre Today* (London: Routledge, 2013).
8. Jesse Green, "Theater Review: *The Flick* and *The Lying Lesson*," *Vulture*, March 13, 2013, https://www.vulture.com/2013/03/theater-review-the-lying-lesson.html.
9. Hilton Als, "The Way Station," *The New Yorker*, August 17, 2015, https://www.newyorker.com/magazine/2015/08/24/the-way-station.
10. Sarah Bryant-Bertail, *Space and Time in Epic Theater: The Brechtian Legacy* (Cambridge: Cambridge University Press, 2000), 7. Bryant-Bertail continues: "Likewise, theatrical time is not just a series of connected units—minutes, hours, acts, and scenes—the process by which temporal dimensions and rhythms are revealed through spatial images."
11. See Julia Kristeva, *Revolution in Poetic Language* (New York: Columbia University Press, 1984).
12. Jill Dolan, *The Feminist Spectator as Critic* (Ann Arbor: University of Michigan Press, 2012), 4–6, 10–12.
13. Henrik Ibsen, *A Doll House*, in *The Harcourt Brace Anthology of Drama*, ed. W. B. Worthen (San Diego: Harcourt College Publishers, 1996), 587.
14. Mark Kingwell, "Tables, Chairs and Other Machines for Thinking," in *Intimus: Interior Design Theory Reader*, ed. Mark Taylor and Julieanna Preston (Chichester: John Wiley & Sons, 2011), 173–9.
15. Als, "The Way Station."
16. Emile Zola, "Naturalism on Stage," in *Playwrights on Playwriting: From Ibsen to Ionesco*, ed. Toby Cole (New York: Cooper Square Press, 2001).

Building on Samuel Beckett

1. See, for example, Carly Mensch, "Annie Baker: Laughing at the Laugh," *The Brooklyn Rail*, May 10, 2010, https://brooklynrail.org/2010/05/theater/in-dialogue-annie-baker-laughing-at-the-laugh, and "Exclusive: Q&A with Emerging Playwright, Annie Baker," *Flavorwire*, 2009, https://www.flavorwire.com/37906/exclusive-qa-with-emerging-playwright-annie-baker-interview-circle-mirror-transformation.

Notes

2. Many theater critics have drawn parallels between Baker's style and Beckett's, especially in her most famous play, *The Flick*, and her Vermont Plays, such as *The Aliens*. See, for example, Jesse Green, "Theatre Review: The Return of Annie Baker's *The Flick*," *Vulture*, May 18, 2015, https://www.vulture.com/2015/05/theater-review-the-return-of-the-flick.html; Brendan Kiley, "Wasted Youth: Drama of the Unspoken Isn't Enough in Annie Baker's 'The Aliens' at 12th Ave Arts,'" *The Seattle Times*, July 11, 2018, https://www.seattletimes.com/entertainment/theater/wasted-youth-the-drama-of-the-unspoken-isnt-enough-in-annie-bakers-the-aliens-at-12th-ave-arts/; Hermione Hoby, "From Pulitzer to Popcorn: Why Annie Baker is Making the Theatre World Pause for Thought," *The Guardian*, April 1, 2016, https://www.theguardian.com/stage/2016/apr/01/pulitzer-popcorn-playwright-annie-baker-critics-pause-thought; and Jeffrey Borak, "At Chester, Annie Baker's 'The Aliens' Floats in an Undefined Ether," *The Berkshire Eagle*, August 14, 2018, https://www.berkshireeagle.com/arts_and_culture/arts-theater/at-chester-annie-bakers-the-aliens-floats-in-an-undefined-ether/article_18640169-208a-5000-8184-4a8d09c6d493.html.

3. Vivian Mercier, "The Uneventful Event," *The Irish Times*, February 18, 1956.

4. Annie Baker, *The Aliens*, in *The Vermont Plays* (New York: Theatre Communications Group, 2012), 3. Subsequent references will be cited parenthetically in the text.

5. Kiley, "Wasted Youth."

6. Hoby, "From Pulitzer to Popcorn."

7. Graley Herren, *Samuel Beckett's Plays on Film and Television* (New York: Palgrave Macmillan, 2007), 123–39.

8. David T. Johnson, "'A Very Very Long Amount of Time Passes': Slowness, Cinema and Annie Baker's *The Flick* (2013)," *New Cinemas: Journal of Contemporary Film* 18, no. 1 and 2 (2021): 68.

9. Annie Baker undertook to adapting and translating *Uncle Vanya*. This project was published in 2014 by Theatre Communications Group.

10. Jennifer Cayer, "Her Town: Annie Baker's Americans," *Journal of American Drama and Theatre* 23, no. 3 (2011): 33.

11. Ibid., 33–4.

12. Ibid., 41.

13. Samuel Beckett, *Not I*, in *The Complete Dramatic Works* (London: Faber and Faber, 1986), 377.

14. Baker, *The Aliens*, 84.

15. Samuel Beckett, *Waiting for Godot*, in *The Complete Dramatic Works* (London: Faber and Faber, 1986), 88.

16. For an insightful look at absurdism and Beckett, see Pim Verhulst's "'A Thing I Carry About with Me': The Myth(s) of Sisyphus in Beckett's Radio Play *All That Fall*," *Samuel Beckett Today / Aujourd'hui* 31 (2019): 114–29.

Notes

17. In 1937 Beckett wrote to his friend Axel Kaun that "more and more my language appears to me like a veil which one has to tear apart in order to get to those things (or the nothingness) lying behind it." See Martha Dow Fehsenfeld and Lois More Overbeck, *The Letters of Samuel Beckett, 1929-1940* (Cambridge: Cambridge University Press, 2009), 518.
18. The last scene of *The Flick* depicts Sam as the magnanimous one. He gifts the dissembled film projected and leftover reels to Avery. Avery, however, has lost trust (113) and faith (115) in people.
19. George Cotkin, "Punching Through the Pasteboard Masks: American Existentialism," in *Situating Existentialism: Key Texts in Context*, ed. Jonathan Judaken and Robert Bernasconi (New York: Columbia University Press, 2012), 140.
20. Ibid.
21. Ibid., 43.
22. Ibid., 45.
23. Samuel Beckett, *Film*, in *The Complete Dramatic Works* (London: Faber and Faber, 1986), 323.
24. Ibid., 333–4.
25. Ibid., 328.
26. Roland Barthes, *Camera Lucida: Reflections on Photography* (London: Flamingo, 1988), 92.
27. Ibid.
28. Thomas Butler, "Friends Dying Before Our Eyes in Annie Baker's *The Aliens*," in *Text and Presentation, 2014*, ed. Graley Herren (Jefferson: McFarland, 2015), 180.
29. Julie Bates, *Beckett's Art of Salvage: Writing and Material Imagination* (Cambridge: Cambridge University Press, 2017), 64.
30. Tennessee Williams, *Where I Live: Selected Essays* (New York: New Directions, 1978), 19.
31. Samuel Beckett, *Krapp's Last Tape*, in *The Complete Dramatic Works* (London: Faber and Faber, 1986), 217.
32. For further studies that examine *Krapp's Last Tape* to waste, love, and writing, see Julie Campbell's "The Semantic Krapp in *Krapp's Last Tape*," *Samuel Beckett Today / Aujourd'hui* 6, no. 1 (1997): 63–72 and Paul Stewart's *Sex and Aesthetics in Samuel Beckett's Work* (New York: Palgrave/Macmillan, 2011), 141–50.

Undressing the Wound of Theatergoing Whiteness

1. Annie Baker, "Annie Baker Discusses *Circle Mirror Transformation* with Playwrights Horizons Literary Manager Adam Greenfield," *The Huntington*,

Notes

https://legacy.huntingtontheatre.org/articles/Annie-Baker-discusses-iCircle-Mirror-Transformationi-with-Playwrights-Horizons-Literary-Manager-Adam-Greenfield/.

2. Toni Morrison, *Playing in the Dark: Whiteness and the Literary Imagination* (New York: Vintage, 1992): 11.
3. Jess Row, *White Flights: Race, Fiction, and the American Imagination* (Minneapolis: Graywolf, 2019), 9, 196.
4. Baker refers to *Nocturama* as "the play that no one will ever produce" in "Annie Baker Discusses *Circle Mirror Transformation* with Playwrights Horizons Literary Manager Adam Greenfield." Because *Nocturama* has no production history, my discussion of possibilities of staging, performance, and audience experience of the play is based purely on my reading of the play text and is therefore entirely speculative.
5. Baker, "Annie Baker Discusses *Circle Mirror Transformation* with Playwrights Horizons Literary Manager Adam Greenfield."
6. Row, *White Flights*, 105.
7. Ibid., 117.
8. Morrison, *Playing in the Dark*, 38.
9. Ibid., 57.
10. Dionne Brand, *A Map to the Door of No Return: Notes to Belonging* (Toronto: Vintage Canada, 2011), 221.
11. Kevin Quashie, *Black Aliveness, or a Poetics of Being* (Durham, NC: Duke University Press, 2021), 109.
12. Annie Baker, *Nocturama*, in *The Vermont Plays* (New York: Theatre Communications Group, 2012), 211. All subsequent references will be cited parenthetically in the text.
13. Grant Farred, *Martin Heidegger Saved My Life* (Minneapolis: University of Minnesota Press, 2015), 53. He here interprets whiteness in terms of Derrida's deconstruction of auto-affection, a term employed in Husserl's account of self-experience. For Derrida, even self-experience is not immediate, but rather suffers mediation, so what is actually referred to is something other. See Leonard Lawlor, "Auto-Affection," in *Jacques Derrida: Key Concepts*, ed. Claire Colebrook (New York: Routledge, 2015), 130.
14. Row, *White Flights*, 261.
15. Farred, *Martin Heidegger Saved My Life*, 55.
16. Row, *White Flights*, 98, 97.
17. Farred, *Martin Heidegger Saved My Life*, 52–3.
18. Morrison, *Playing in the Dark*, 53.
19. Claudia Rankine, preface to *The White Card* (Minneapolis: Graywolf, 2019), ix.
20. Jennifer Cayer, "Her Town: Annie Baker's Americans," *Journal of American Drama and Theatre* 23, no. 3 (Fall 2011): 38.

Notes

21. Emmanuel Levinas, *Ethics and Infinity: Conversations with Philippe Nemo*, trans. Richard A. Cohen (Pittsburgh: Duquesne University Press, 1985), 57.
22. Jacques Derrida, *Writing and Difference*, trans. Alan Bass (Chicago: University of Chicago Press, 1978), 123.
23. Ibid., 124.
24. Martin Buber, *Martin Buber and the Theatre*, trans., ed., and intro. Maurice Friedman (New York: Funk & Wagnalls, 1969), 68.
25. Martin Buber, *Between Man and Man*, trans. Ronald Gregor Smith (Mansfield Centre, CT: Martino, 2014), 21.
26. Nathan Heller, "Just Saying: The anti-theatrical theatre of Annie Baker," *New Yorker*, February 17, 2013, https://www.newyorker.com/magazine/2013/02/25/just-saying.
27. Bess Rowen, "Undigested Reading: Rethinking Stage Directions through Affect," *Theatre Journal* 70, no. 3 (September 2018): 317. Rowen describes affective stage directions as "lines that a playwright uses to describe the nuance and/or subtext of a given portion of the play so that the actor might catch the tone and feelings evoked"; by "providing information that does not directly translate to an agreed-upon code or interpretation in the theatrical lexicon, [. . .] affective stage directions give performers information that allow them to make choices about the feel of a particular character, movement, or overall play in a more nuanced way" (310). Rowen's remarks apply not just to performers but to any reader of the play text, as the stage directions provoke from the reader an interpretive labor that respects the character's distance.
28. Levinas, *Ethics and Infinity*, 81.
29. Claudia Rankine, *Citizen* (Minneapolis: Graywolf, 2014), 24.
30. "Quiet," writes Quashie, "is a metaphor for the full range of one's inner life—one's desires, ambitions, hungers, vulnerabilities. The inner life is not apolitical or without social value, but neither is it determined entirely by publicness." Kevin Quashie, *The Sovereignty of Quiet: Beyond Resistance in Black Culture* (Piscataway: Rutgers University Press, 2012), 15, 6.
31. Fred Moten, "The Case of Blackness," *Criticism* 50, no. 2 (Spring 2008): 211.

Afterword

1. Annie Baker, from *Infinite Life*, *The Paris Review*, no. 238 (Winter 2021): 75.
2. Jesse Green, "The Fascinator: Meet Playwright Annie Baker," *Elle*, August 2, 2013, https://www.elle.com/culture/a13908/playwright-annie-baker-profile/.
3. Charles McNulty, "Coming to an LA Stage: Proof We're in a Golden Age of American Playwriting," *Los Angeles Times*, July 16, 2021, https://www.latimes.com/entertainment-arts/story/2021-06-16/theater-reopening-branden-jacobs-jenkins-octoroon-fountain.

Notes

4. Greta Gerwig, "Annie Baker," *Interview*, March 29, 2017, https://www.interviewmagazine.com/culture/annie-baker.
5. Alan Read, *Theatre, Intimacy and Engagement: The Last Human Venue* (Basingstoke: Palgrave Macmillan, 2008), 4.
6. Marc Maron, "Annie Baker," *WTF with Marc Maron*, Podcast audio, October 12, 2015, http://www.wtfpod.com/podcast/tag/Annie+Baker.
7. Nathan Heller, "Just Saying," *New Yorker*, February 17, 2013, https://www.newyorker.com/magazine/2013/02/25/just-saying.

BIBLIOGRAPHY

"The Aliens by Annie Baker." *Bush Theatre*, n.d. https://www.bushtheatre.co.uk/event/the-aliens/.
Als, Hilton. "The Way Station." *The New Yorker*, August 17, 2015. https://www.newyorker.com/magazine/2015/08/24/the-way-station.
Baker, Annie. *The Aliens*. In *The Vermont Plays*, 1–84. New York: Theatre Communications Group, 2012a.
Baker, Annie. "Annie Baker's Top 10." *The Criterion Collection*, June 30, 2015. https://www.criterion.com/current/top-10-lists/241-annie-baker-s-top-10.
Baker, Annie. *The Antipodes*. New York: Theatre Communications Group, 2018.
Baker, Annie. *Body Awareness*. In *The Vermont Plays*, 367–480. New York: Theatre Communications Group, 2012b.
Baker, Annie. *Circle Mirror Transformation*. New York: Samuel French, 2009a.
Baker, Annie. *Circle Mirror Transformation*. In *The Vermont Plays*, 85–208. New York: Theatre Communications Group, 2012c.
Baker, Annie. *The Flick*. New York: Theatre Communications Group, 2014a.
Baker, Annie. "From *Nocturama*." *Vice*, November 30, 2009b. https://www.vice.com/en/article/9bdbmp/from-nocturama-264-v16n12.
Baker, Annie. *John*. New York: Theatre Communications Group, 2016.
Baker, Annie. *Nocturama*. In *The Vermont Plays*, 209–366. New York: Theatre Communications Group, 2012d.
Baker, Annie. "Preface." In *Uncle Vanya*, v–vi. New York: Theatre Communications Group, 2014b.
Baker, Annie. *The Vermont Plays*. New York: Theatre Communications Group, 2012e.
Barbier, Jules. *Tales of Hoffmann* (libretto). Translated by Ann Feeney. Aria Database. http://www.aria-database.com/translations/contes12_oiseaux.txt.
Barthes, Roland. *Camera Lucida: Reflections on Photography*. London: Flamingo, 1988.
Bartlett, Rosamund. "Chekhov and the Human Experience." *Almeida Theatre*, February 22, 2016. https://almeida.co.uk/uncle-vanya-chekhov-and-the-human-experience.
Bates, Julie. *Beckett's Art of Salvage: Writings and Material Imagination, 1932–1987*. Cambridge: Cambridge University Press, 2017.
Baxter, Charles. "Sonya's Last Speech, or Double-Voicing: An Essay in Sixteen Sections." In *The Story About the Story II: Great Writers Explore Great Literature*, edited by J. C. Hallman, 81–96. Portland: Tin House Books, 2015.
Beckett, Samuel. "Film." In *The Complete Dramatic Works*, 321–34. London: Faber and Faber, 1986.

Bibliography

Beckett, Samuel. "*Krapp's Last Tape.*" In *The Complete Dramatic Works*, 213–24. London: Faber and Faber, 1986.

Beckett, Samuel. "*Not I.*" In *The Complete Dramatic Works*, 373–84. London: Faber and Faber, 1986.

Beckett, Samuel. "*Waiting for Godot.*" In *The Complete Dramatic Works*, 7–88. London: Faber and Faber, 1986.

Bennett, Jane. "The Force of Things: Steps Toward an Ecology of Matter." *Political Theory* 32, no. 3 (July 2004): 347–72.

Bergen, Hilary, and Sandra Huber. "Pornography, Ectoplasm and the Secret Dancer: A Twin Reading of Naomi Uman's *Removed.*" *Screening the Past*, April 2018. http://www.screeningthepast.com/issue-43/.

Berks, Alan. "Is Compassion Inherently Theatrical?" *Minnesota Playlist*, May 30, 2020. https://minnesotaplaylist.com/magazine/article/2010/is-compassion-inherently-theatrical.

Bersley, Tracy. "The Body Electric: Using Neuroscience and Theater to Reclaim Empathy for the Twenty-First Century." In *Text & Presentation, 2021*, edited by Amy Muse, 194–209. Jefferson: McFarland & Company, 2022.

Bertino, Marie-Helene. "Annie Baker's *The Antipodes*: The Universe and the Playwright." *BOMB*, June 6, 2017. https://bombmagazine.org/articles/annie-bakers-the-antipodes/.

Billington, Michael. "*The Antipodes* Review: Annie Baker Searches for the Sting in the Tale." *The Guardian*, October 31, 2019. https://www.theguardian.com/stage/2019/oct/31/the-antipodes-review-annie-baker-dorfman-theatre.

Billington, Michael. "*Circle Mirror Transformation* Review." *The Guardian*, July 13, 2013. https://www.theguardian.com/stage/2013/jul/13/circle-mirror-transformation-review.

Billington, Michael. "*The Flick* Review – Echoes of Racine in a Riveting Play About Love, Lost Souls and Popcorn." *The Guardian*, April 20, 2016. https://www.theguardian.com/stage/2016/apr/20/the-flick-review-dorfman-national-theatre-london-annie-baker-cinema-play.

Billington, Michael. "*John* Review – Check into Annie Baker's Gothic Gettysburg B&B." *The Guardian*, January 25, 2018. https://www.theguardian.com/stage/2018/jan/25/john-review-annie-baker-dorfman-national-theatre.

Blake, Elissa. "*John*: Dread and Breakfast." *Audrey Journal*, September 13, 2019. https://www.audreyjournal.com.au/arts/john-seymour-centre-annie-baker-preview/.

Blanchard, Jayne. "Review: Annie Baker's *John* at Signature Theatre." *DC Theatre Scene*, April 11, 2018. https://dctheatrescene.com/2018/04/11/review-annie-bakers-john-at-signature-theatre/.

Borak, Jeffrey. "At Chester, Annie Baker's *The Aliens* Floats in an Undefined Ether." *The Berkshire Eagle*, August 14, 2018. https://www.berkshireeagle.com/arts_and_culture/arts-theater/at-chester-annie-bakers-the-aliens-floats-in-an-undefined-ether/article_18640169-208a-5000-8184-4a8d09c6d493.html.

Brand, Dionne. *A Map to the Door of No Return: Notes to Belonging*. Toronto: Vintage Canada, 2011.

Bibliography

Brantley, Ben. "In Boston, Listening to a Young Playwright Adept at Silence." *The New York Times*, November 10, 2010. https://www.nytimes.com/2010/11/11/theater/11annie.html.

Brantley, Ben. "Review: *The Antipodes* and Ambiguous Brainstorming." *The New York Times*, April 23, 2017. https://www.nytimes.com/2017/04/23/theater/the-antipodes-review-annie-baker.html.

Brennan, Clare. "*Circle Mirror Transformation* Review: Naturalism Without the Social Context." *The Guardian*, March 10, 2018. https://www.theguardian.com/stage/2018/mar/10/circle-mirror-transformation-review-home-manchester-annie-baker.

Brodskaya, Marina. *Anton Chekhov: Five Plays*. Redwood City: Stanford University Press, 2010.

Brown, Emma. "Annie Baker, Sam Gold, and Uncle Vanya's Beige Socks." *Interview*, June 13, 2012. https://www.interviewmagazine.com/culture/annie-baker-sam-gold-uncle-vanya.

Bryant-Bertail, Sarah. *Space and Time in Epic Theatre: The Brechtian Legacy*. Cambridge: Cambridge University Press, 2000.

Buber, Martin. *Between Man and Man*. Translated by Ronald Gregor Smith. Mansfield Centre: Martino, 2014.

Buber, Martin. *Martin Buber and the Theatre*. Translated, edited, and introduced by Maurice Friedman. New York: Funk & Wagnalls, 1969.

Bukowski, Charles. "The Aliens." In *The Last Night of the Earth Poems*, 231–2. New York: Ecco Press, 1992.

Butler, Thomas. "Friends Dying Before Our Eyes in Annie Baker's *The Aliens*." In *Text and Presentation, 2014*, edited by Graley Herren, 179–91. Jefferson: McFarland, 2015.

Campbell, Julie. "The Semantic Krapp in *Krapp's Last Tape*." *Samuel Beckett Today/Aujourd'hui* 6, no. 1 (1997): 63–72.

Cayer, Jennifer. "Her Town: Annie Baker's Americans." *Journal of American Drama and Theatre* 23, no. 3 (Fall 2011): 31–55.

Coates, Tyler. "Are We *Supposed* to Hear Them?" *Slate*, August 12, 2015. https://slate.com/culture/2015/08/annie-bakers-new-play-john-reviewed.html.

Collins-Hughes, Laura. "Fictional Town Sets Her Plays in Motion." *Boston Globe*, October 10, 2010. http://archive.boston.com/ae/theater_arts/articles/2010/10/10/fictional_town_sets_annie_bakers_plays_in_motion/.

Copeland, Roger. "Chekhov, Our (Distracted, Prosaic, Prophetic) Contemporary." *American Theatre*, March 30, 2015. https://www.americantheatre.org/2015/03/30/chekhov-our-distracted-prosaic-prophetic-contemporary/.

Cotkin, George. "Punching Through the Pasteboard Masks: American Existentialism." In *Situating Existentialism: Key Texts in Context*, edited by Jonathan Judaken and Robert Bernasconi, 123–44. New York: Columbia University Press, 2012.

Crompton, Sarah. "*The Flick* (Dorfman, National Theatre)." *WhatsOnStage*, April 20, 2016. https://www.whatsonstage.com/london-theatre/reviews/flick-dorfman-national-sarah-crompton_40237.html.

Bibliography

Curry, Ruth. "*I Love Dick* Shows the Possibilities of the Peak TV Era—And Its Limitations." *Esquire*, May 15, 2017. https://www.esquire.com/entertainment/tv/a55080/i-love-dick-review/.

Dale, Michael. "Podcast: John and The Flick's Annie Baker Talks of Survival Jobs, Pandering and Not Being Influenced by Harold Pinter." *Broadway Word*. Podcast audio. September 1, 2015. https://www.broadwayworld.com/off-broadway/article/PODCAST-JOHN-And-THE-FLICKs-Annie-Baker-Talks-of-Survival-Jobs-Pandering-and-Not-Being-Influenced-by-Harold-Pinter-20150901.

Danto, Arthur C. *What Art Is*. New Haven: Yale University Press, 2013.

Derrida, Jacques. *Writing and Difference*. Translated by Alan Bass. Chicago: University of Chicago Press, 1978.

Didion, Joan. *The White Album*. New York: Farrar, Straus & Giroux, 1979.

Dolan, Jill. *The Feminist Spectator as Critic*. Ann Arbor: University of Michigan Press, 2012.

Dolan, Jill. "*John*, by Annie Baker, at the Signature." *The Feminist Spectator*, August 19, 2015. https://feministspectator.princeton.edu/2015/08/19/john-by-annie-baker-at-the-signature/.

Dziemianowicz, Joe. "'The Joe D Show' Episode 9: 'The Flick' Take 2 with Playwright Annie Baker, Director Sam Gold and Actor Matthew Maher." *Daily News*, May 7, 2015. https://www.nydailynews.com/entertainment/theater-arts/joe-show-episode-9-flick-2-article-1.2214407.

Evans, Lloyd. "Review of *John*." *The Spectator*, February 3, 2018.

"Exclusive: Q&A with Emerging Playwright, Annie Baker." *Flavorwire*. September 9, 2009. https://www.flavorwire.com/37906/exclusive-qa-with-emerging-playwright-annie-baker-interview-circle-mirror-transformation.

Farred, Grant. *Martin Heidegger Saved My Life*. Minneapolis: University of Minnesota Press, 2015.

Fehsenfeld, Martha Dow, and Lois More Overbeck. *The Letters of Samuel Beckett, 1929–1940*. Cambridge: Cambridge University Press, 2009.

Felski, Rita. *Hooked: Art and Attachment*. Chicago: University of Chicago Press, 2020.

Fernández-Caparrós, Ana. "Intimations of Precarity in Twenty-First-Century U.S. Drama: Faltering Voices of the Precariat in Annie Baker's *The Flick*." *Cultura, Lenguaje y Representación* XXV (2021): 119–33.

Finke, Michael C. *Freedom from Violence and Lies: Anton Chekhov's Life and Writings*. London: Reaktion Books, 2021.

Flora, Carlin. "The Unpretending Player." *Psychology Today* 44 (March/April 2011). https://www.psychologytoday.com/us/articles/201103/eccentrics-corner-the-unpretending-player.

Foley, Michael. *Life Lessons from Bergson*. London: Macmillan, 2013.

Freedman, John. "Annie Baker Brings *The Aliens* to Moscow and St. Petersburg." *The Moscow Times*, November 28, 2011. https://www.themoscowtimes.com/2011/11/28/annie-baker-brings-the-aliens-to-moscow-and-st-petersburg-a34298.

Freud, Sigmund. *Psychological Writings and Letters*. New York: Continuum, 1995.

Bibliography

Gassman, Ben. "Knocking Chekhov for a Loop." *American Theatre*, January 1, 2013. https://www.americantheatre.org/2013/01/01/knocking-chekhov-for-a-loop/.

Gerwig, Greta. "Annie Baker." *Interview*, March 29, 2017. https://www.interviewmagazine.com/culture/annie-baker.

Glaspell, Susan. *Trifles*. 1916.

"Gordon Hempton: Silence and the Presence of Everything." *On Being with Krista Tippett*, May 10, 2012. https://onbeing.org/programs/gordon-hempton-silence-and-the-presence-of-everything/.

Gray, Emma. "*I Love Dick* and the Radical Power of a Writer's Room Without Cis Men." *HuffPost*, June 23, 2017. https://www.huffpost.com/entry/i-love-dick-and-the-radical-power-of-a-writers-room-without-cis-men_n_594d2c1fe4b02734df29fa3f.

Green, Jesse. "Theater Review: A Bed-and-Breakfast Weekend Gone Awkward, in Annie Baker's *John*." *Vulture*, August 11, 2015a. https://www.vulture.com/2015/08/theater-review-annie-bakers-john.html.

Green, Jesse. "Theater Review: *The Flick* and *The Lying Lesson*." *Vulture*, March 13, 2013. https://www.vulture.com/2013/03/theater-review-the-lying-lesson.html.

Green, Jesse. "Theatre Review: The Return of Annie Baker's *The Flick*." *Vulture*, May 18, 2015b. https://www.vulture.com/2015/05/theater-review-the-return-of-the-flick.html.

Green, Jesse. "Watching Annie Baker: A Playwright Who Chooses Her Movies Wisely." *Vulture*, May 4, 2015c. https://www.vulture.com/2015/05/annie-baker-the-flick.html.

Greenfield, Adam. "The American Voice: When We Talk About Realism." *Playwrights Horizons*, December 14, 2012. https://www.playwrightshorizons.org/shows/trailers/american-voice-when-we-talk-about-realism/.

Greenfield, Adam. "Annie Baker Discusses *Circle Mirror Transformation* with Playwrights Horizons Literary Manager Adam Greenfield." *The Huntington*, n.d. https://legacy.huntingtontheatre.org/articles/Annie-Baker-discusses-iCircle-Mirror-Transformationi-with-Playwrights-Horizons-Literary-Manager-Adam-Greenfield/.

Grillo. "Jill Soloway is a 'Weird Girl.'" *Lenny Letter*, March 30, 2018. https://www.lennyletter.com/story/jill-soloway-is-a-weird-girl.

Grumbling, Megan. "On Stage: *Body Awareness* Is Much More Than Skin Deep." *Portland Phoenix*, July 27, 2022. https://portlandphoenix.me/on-stage-body-awareness-is-much-more-than-skin-deep/.

Hägglund, Martin. *This Life: Secular Life and Spiritual Freedom*. New York: Anchor, 2020.

Hazen, Shane. "Episode 45 – Annie Baker's *The Flick*." *Phi Phenomenon*, January 11, 2021. phiphenomenon.com.

Healy, Patrick. "*The Flick* Prompts an Explanation from Playwrights Horizons." *The New York Times*, March 25, 2013. https://archive.nytimes.com/artsbeat.blogs.nytimes.com/2013/03/25/the-flick-prompts-an-explanation-from-playwrights-horizons/.

Bibliography

Held, Virginia. *The Ethics of Care: Personal, Political, and Global.* Oxford: Oxford University Press, 2006.

Heller, Nathan. "Just Saying: The Anti-Theatrical Theatre of Annie Baker." *The New Yorker*, February 25, 2013. https://www.newyorker.com/magazine/2013/02/25/just-saying.

Herren, Graley. *Samuel Beckett's Plays on Film and Television.* New York: Palgrave Macmillan, 2007.

Hoby, Hermione. "From Pulitzer to Popcorn: Why Annie Baker is Making the Theatre World Pause for Thought." *The Guardian*, April 1, 2016. https://www.theguardian.com/stage/2016/apr/01/pulitzer-popcorn-playwright-annie-baker-critics-pause-thought.

Hoffman, Barbara. "In My Library: Annie Baker." *New York Post*, July 18, 2015. https://nypost.com/2015/07/18/in-my-library-annie-baker/.

Holdengräber, Paul. "The Art of Nonfiction No. 7: Adam Phillips." *Paris Review* 208 (Spring 2014): 29–54.

I Love Dick. "A Short History of Weird Girls." *Amazon Studios* video, 21:00. May 12, 2017.

Ibsen, Henrik. "*A Doll House.*" In *The Harcourt Brace Anthology of Drama*, edited by W. B. Worthen, 415–40. Fort Worth: Harcourt Brace & Company, 1996.

Isherwood, Charles. "A Fresh Breeze in Pastoral Russia." *The New York Times*, June 17, 2012. https://www.nytimes.com/2012/06/18/theater/reviews/uncle-vanya-adapted-by-annie-baker-at-soho-rep.html.

Isherwood, Charles. "A Household's Wounds Are Raw, but No One is Willing to Ease the Tensions." *The New York Times*, June 5, 2008. https://www.nytimes.com/2008/06/05/theater/reviews/05body.html.

Isherwood, Charles. "In *The Flick*, Moments in the Movies, but Not on Screen." *The New York Times*, May 18, 2015a. https://www.nytimes.com/2015/05/19/theater/review-in-the-flick-contemplating-a-life-of-stale-popcorn.html.

Isherwood, Charles. "Outsiders, Tender and Troubled." *The New York Times*, April 22, 2010. https://www.nytimes.com/2010/04/23/theater/reviews/23aliens.html.

Isherwood, Charles. "Review: In *John*, Pondering Life's Mysteries from Gettysburg." *The New York Times*, August 11, 2015b. https://www.nytimes.com/2015/08/12/theater/review-in-john-pondering-lifes-mysteries-from-gettysburg.html.

Isherwood, Charles. "Some Plays Can Twinkle Without Stars." *The New York Times*, November 4, 2009. https://www.nytimes.com/2009/11/08/theater/08ishe.html?ref=playwrightshorizons.

Isherwood, Charles. "You didn't Like Our Play? You're Right. Very Sorry." *The New York Times*, March 27, 2013. https://www.nytimes.com/2013/03/28/theater/the-flap-over-the-flick-at-playwrights-horizons.html.

Jackson, Tim. "Theater Review: Annie Baker's *John* — A Feminist Black Comedy." *The Arts Fuse*, August 9, 2015. https://artsfuse.org/132403/fuse-theater-review-annie-bakers-john-a-feminist-black-comedy/.

James, William. *The Varieties of Religious Experience.* London: Routledge Classics, 2002. First published 1902 by Longman, Green, and Co. (London).

Bibliography

Johnson, David T. "'A Very Very Long Amount of Time Passes': Slowness, Cinema and Annie Baker's *The Flick* (2013)." *New Cinemas: Journal of Contemporary Film* 18, nos. 1 and 2 (2021): 61–75.

Jones, Chris. "*Uncle Vanya*: Why Not a Little Vodka with that Boring Life?" *Chicago Tribune*, February 22, 2017. https://www.chicagotribune.com/entertainment/theater/ct-uncle-vanya-review-ent-0223-20170222-column.html.

Kan, Elianna. "Annie Baker." *BOMB*, September 15, 2015. https://bombmagazine.org/articles/annie-baker/.

Keane, Erin. "Silence is Golden in [502]'s *The Aliens*." *Louisville Public Media*, October 8, 2012. https://www.lpm.org/news/2012-10-08/review-silence-is-golden-in-502s-the-aliens.

Kiley, Brendan. "Wasted Youth: Drama of the Unspoken Isn't Enough in Annie Baker's *The Aliens* at 12th Ave Arts." *The Seattle Times*, July 11, 2018. https://www.seattletimes.com/entertainment/theater/wasted-youth-the-drama-of-the-unspoken-isnt-enough-in-annie-bakers-the-aliens-at-12th-ave-arts/.

Kraus, Chris. *I Love Dick*. London: Serpent's Tail, 2016. First published 1997 by Semiotext(e) (Los Angeles).

Kruger, Charles. "SF Playhouse: Annie Baker's *The Aliens* is a Masterpiece and Not to Be Missed." *TheatreStorm*, March 26, 2012. https://theatrestorm.com/2012/03/26/sf-playhouse-annie-bakers-the-aliens-is-a-masterpiece-and-not-to-be-missed/.

Kruger, Charles. "Review: *John* by Annie Baker at A.C.T." *TheatreStorm*, March 12, 2017. https://theatrestorm.com/2017/03/12/review-john-by-annie-baker-at-a-c-t/.

Larson, Sarah. "The Funny, Empathetic Genius of Annie Baker." *The New Yorker*, September 17, 2015. https://www.newyorker.com/culture/sarah-larson/the-funny-empathetic-genius-of-annie-baker.

Lawlor, Leonard. "Auto-Affection." In *Jacques Derrida: Key Concepts*, edited by Claire Colebrook, 130–8. New York: Routledge, 2015.

Lawson, April Ayers. "If You're Going to Read Plays, Read Annie Baker's." *Vice*, June 5, 2014. https://www.vice.com/en/article/bn57q8/if-youre-going-to-read-plays-read-annie-bakers-plays.

Lee, Adelaide. "*Uncle Vanya*: Self-hatred and Unrequited Love Shine at the Goodman." *TheaterMania*, February 23, 2017. https://www.theatermania.com/chicago-theater/reviews/uncle-vanya-annie-baker-goodman-theatre_80129.html.

Levinas, Emmanuel. *Ethics and Infinity: Conversations with Philippe Nemo*. Translated by Richard A. Cohen. Pittsburgh: Duquesne University Press, 1985.

Lukowski, Andrzej. "Annie Baker: 'I'm Stunned I Have a Career.'" *TimeOut*, January 19, 2018. https://www.timeout.com/london/theatre/annie-baker-im-stunned-i-have-a-career-at-all.

Lukowski, Andrzej. "*The Antipodes* Review." *TimeOut*, October 31, 2019. https://www.timeout.com/london/theatre/the-antipodes-review.

MacArthur Foundation. "Playwright Annie Baker, 2017 MacArthur Fellow." YouTube video, 2:21. 2017. https://www.youtube.com/watch?v=90-M_pOkhEg.

Bibliography

Maga, Carly. "Existential Pain, Masculinity on Brilliant Display in Annie Baker's *The Aliens*." *Toronto Star*, September 23, 2017. https://www.thestar.com/entertainment/stage/2017/09/23/existential-pain-masculinity-on-brilliant-display-in-annie-bakers-the-aliens-review.html.

Malies, Jeremy. "'John': Annie Baker." *Plays International & Europe*, n.d. https://playsinternational.org.uk/john-annie-baker-national-theatre-jeremy-malies/.

Mann, Thomas. *The Magic Mountain*. Translated by John W. Woods. New York: Vintage, 1996.

Maron, Marc. "Annie Baker." *WTF with Marc Maron*. Podcast audio. October 12, 2015. http://www.wtfpod.com/podcast/tag/Annie+Baker.

Martin, Clancy. "On *Uncle Vanya*: Part Two." *The Paris Review*, July 3, 2012. https://www.theparisreview.org/blog/2012/07/03/on-uncle-vanya-part-two/.

McGee, Celia. "Childhood is the Mother of the Play." *The New York Times*, May 25, 2008. https://www.nytimes.com/2008/05/25/theater/25mcge.html.

Mendes, Chantal. "Theater Review: *Body Awareness*—A Lesson in Human Awareness." *The Arts Fuse*, October 30, 2010. https://artsfuse.org/14870/theater-review-body-awareness-a-lession-in-human-awareness/.

Mensch, Carly. "Annie Baker: Laughing at the Laugh." *The Brooklyn Rail*, May 10, 2010. https://brooklynrail.org/2010/05/theater/in-dialogue-annie-baker-laughing-at-the-laugh.

Mercier, Vivian. "The Uneventful Event." *The Irish Times*, February 18, 1956.

Meyerhold, Vsevolod. "Naturalistic Theater and Theater of Mood." In *Chekhov: A Collection of Critical Essays*, edited by Robert Louis Jackson, 62–8. Englewood Cliffs: Prentice Hall, 1967.

Moi, Toril. "Describing My Struggle." *The Point Magazine*, December 27, 2017a. https://thepointmag.com/criticism/describing-my-struggle-knausgaard/.

Moi, Toril. *Revolution of the Ordinary: Literary Studies after Wittgenstein, Austin, and Cavell*. Chicago: University of Chicago Press, 2017b.

Morrison, Toni. *Playing in the Dark: Whiteness and the Literary Imagination*. New York: Vintage, 1993.

Moten, Fred. "The Case of Blackness." *Criticism* 50, no. 2 (Spring 2008): 177–218.

Nestruck, J. Kelly. "Annie Baker's *John* Is a Religious Experience." *The Globe and Mail*, February 1, 2017. https://www.theglobeandmail.com/arts/theatre-and-performance/theatre-reviews/annie-bakers-john-is-a-religious-experience/article33868395/.

Nicole, S. *Mildly Bitter's Musings*, August 8, 2015. https://mildlybitter.blogspot.com/2015/08/annie-baker-and-sam-gold-in.html.

Nugent, Benjamin. *Elliot Smith and the Big Nothing*. Boston: Da Capo Press, 2004.

Nugent, Benjamin. "I Had Asperger Syndrome. Briefly." *New York Times*, January 31, 2012. https://www.nytimes.com/2012/02/01/opinion/i-had-asperger-syndrome-briefly.html.

Nussbaum, Emily. "What Women Want on 'I Love Dick.'" *The New Yorker*, June 19, 2017. https://www.newyorker.com/magazine/2017/06/26/what-women-want-on-i-love-dick.

Bibliography

O'Mahony, Holly. "*The Antipodes*, National Theatre Review." *Culture Whisper*, October 31, 2019. https://www.culturewhisper.com/r/theatre/annie_baker_the_antipodes_london_theatre/14169.

Paller, Michael. "Intimacy and the Numinous: An Interview with *John* Playwright Annie Baker Part Two." *Inside A.C.T.*, March 14, 2017. http://blog.act-sf.org/2017/03/intimacy-and-numinous-interview-with.html.

Phillips, Elizabeth M. "Chekhov, Boredom, and Pathology as Dramatic Technique." *Modern Drama* 63, no. 1 (Spring 2020): 39–62.

Piepenburg, Erik. "How Long is *The Flick*? It Depends on the Seats." *The New York Times*, May 26, 2016. https://www.nytimes.com/2016/05/29/theater/how-long-is-the-flick-it-depends-on-the-seats.html.

Pitts, Rebecca. "A Short History of Weird Girls." *Rebecca Pitts*, January 6, 2019. https://www.rebeccaapitts.com/articles/weird-girls.

Quashie, Kevin. *Black Aliveness, or a Poetics of Being*. Durham: Duke University Press, 2021.

Quashie, Kevin. *The Sovereignty of Quiet: Beyond Resistance in Black Culture*. Piscataway: Rutgers University Press, 2012.

Rankine, Claudia. *Citizen*. Minneapolis: Graywolf, 2014.

Rankine, Claudia. Preface to *The White Card*, vii–ix. Minneapolis: Graywolf, 2019.

Read, Alan. *Theatre, Intimacy and Engagement: The Last Human Venue*. Basingstoke: Palgrave Macmillan, 2008.

Reid, Robert. "*The Antipodes*: The Chaos of Creation." *Witness*, July 24, 2018. https://witnessperformance.com/antipodes/.

Rice, Gwendolyn. "Searching for Meaning with Annie Baker in *Body Awareness*." *Gwendolyn Rice*, March 20, 2018. https://www.gwendolynrice.com/post-script/searching-for-meaning-with-annie-baker-in-body-awareness.

Ross, Alex. "Bach's Holy Dread." *The New Yorker*, December 25, 2016. https://www.newyorker.com/magazine/2017/01/02/bachs-holy-dread.

Row, Jess. *White Flights: Race, Fiction, and the American Imagination*. Minneapolis: Graywolf, 2019.

Rowen, Bess. "Undigested Reading: Rethinking Stage Directions through Affect." *Theatre Journal* 70, no. 3 (September 2018): 307–26.

Royle, Nicholas. *The Uncanny*. Manchester: Manchester University Press, 2003.

Sanford, Tim. "Tim Sanford on *The Flick*." *Playwrights Horizons*, December 16, 2012. https://www.playwrightshorizons.org/shows/trailers/tim-sanford-flick/.

Schabas, Martha. "Annie Baker's *The Aliens* is a Beautifully Structured Early Career Gem." *The Globe and Mail*, September 22, 2017. https://www.theglobeandmail.com/arts/theatre-and-performance/theatre-reviews/review-annie-bakers-the-aliens-is-a-beautifully-structured-early-career-gem/article36368323/.

Scheps, Leigh. "Best Plays of All Time." *TimeOut*, July 19, 2022. https://www.timeout.com/newyork/theater/best-plays-of-all-time.

Schmidt, Paul, ed., trans. *The Plays of Anton Chekhov*. New York: Harper Perennial, 1997.

Siegel, Robert. "*The Flick* Tells the Story of the Movies, Off the Screen." *All Things Considered*, June 11, 2015. https://www.npr.org/2015/06/11/413711303/the-flick-tells-the-story-of-the-movies-off-the-screen.

Bibliography

Sierz, Aleks. "*Circle Mirror Transformation*, Royal Court Theatre Local." *The Arts Desk*, July 13, 2013. https://www.theartsdesk.com/theatre/circle-mirror-transformation-royal-court-theatre-local.

Sierz, Aleks. "*The Aliens*, Bush Theatre." *The Arts Desk*, September 21, 2010. https://www.theartsdesk.com/node/2247/view.

Smith, Zadie. "Joan Didion and the Opposite of Magical Thinking." *The New Yorker*, December 24, 2021. https://www.newyorker.com/culture/postscript/joan-didion-and-the-opposite-of-magical-thinking.

Soden, Christopher. "Pitch Perfect, Brilliant *Aliens* at Stage West." *Sharp Critic*, May 24, 2017. https://www.stagewest.org/sharp-critic-pitch-perfect-brilliant-aliens-stage-west.

Sofer, Andrew. "Spectral Readings." *Theatre Journal* 64, no. 3 (2012): 323–36.

Sofer, Andrew. *The Stage Life of Props*. Ann Arbor: University of Michigan Press, 2003.

Soloski, Alexis. "Groundbreaking TV About Female Desire, Thanks to Playwrights." *The New York Times*, June 16, 2017. https://www.nytimes.com/2017/06/16/arts/television/amazon-i-love-dick-jill-soloway.html.

Soloski, Alexis. "*John* Review – A Claustrophobic Drama That You Can't Take Your Eyes Off." *The Guardian*, August 12, 2015. https://www.theguardian.com/stage/2015/aug/12/john-review-play-annie-baker-signature-theatre-new-york.

Soloway, Joey. "Joey Soloway on The Female Gaze, MASTER CLASS, TIFF 2016." YouTube video, 57:48. September 11, 2016. https://www.youtube.com/watch?v=pnBvppooD9I.

Stasio, Marilyn. "Off Broadway Review: Annie Baker's *The Antipodes*." *Yahoo!*, April 24, 2017. https://www.yahoo.com/entertainment/off-broadway-review-annie-baker-antipodes-141111728.html.

Stewart, Paul. *Sex and Aesthetics in Samuel Beckett's Work*. New York: Palgrave Macmillan, 2011.

Sumi, Glenn. "Review: *The Antipodes* is the Play We All Need to See Right Now." *NowToronto*, April 9, 2022. https://nowtoronto.com/culture/review-the-antipodes-is-the-play-we-all-need-to-see-right-now.

Suskin, Steve. "Interview: Annie Baker (Part 1)." *HuffPost*, October 26, 2015. https://www.huffpost.com/entry/interview-annie-baker-par_b_8389594.

Szymkowicz, Adam. "I Interview Playwrights Part 38: Annie Baker." *Blogspot*, August 19, 2009. http://aszym.blogspot.com/2009/08/i-interview-playwrights-part-38-annie.html.

Teeman, Tim. "Welcome to Annie Baker's World of Unseen Horrors: Review of 'The Antipodes.'" *Daily Beast*, April 23, 2017. https://www.thedailybeast.com/welcome-to-annie-bakers-world-of-unseen-horrors-review-of-the-antipodes.

Thompson, Jessie. "Annie Baker: 'Be Incredibly Vulnerable but Not Necessarily Confessional.'" *Evening Standard*, January 22, 2018. https://www.standard.co.uk/culture/theatre/annie-baker-be-incredibly-vulnerable-but-not-necessarily-confessional-a3746516.html.

Trueman, Matt. "Annie Baker's *Circle Mirror Transformation* is Every Inch a Modern Classic." *New Statesman*, July 28, 2013. https://www.newstatesman.com

Bibliography

/culture/music-theatre/2013/07/annie-bakers-circle-mirror-transformation-every-inch-modern-classic.

Trueman, Matt. "Just Don't Call It Ordinary: Annie Baker's Plays Distil the Unnoticed in Everyday Life." *Financial Times*, June 14, 2013.

"Vancouver Theatre: *Body Awareness.*" *Review from the House*, October 14, 2019. https://www.reviewfromthehouse.com/review-seat/vancouver-theatre-body-awareness.

Verhulst, Pim. "'A Thing I Carry About with Me': The Myth(s) of Sisyphus in Beckett's Radio Play *All That Fall*." *Samuel Beckett Today/Aujourd'hui* 31 (2019): 114–29.

Vogel, Paula. "Sarah Ruhl." *BOMB*, April 1, 2007. https://bombmagazine.org/articles/sarah-ruhl/.

Weil, Simone. *Gravity and Grace*. Translated by Emma Crawford and Mario von der Ruhr. London: Routledge, 2002.

Weil, Simone. *Waiting for God*. Translated by Emma Craufurd. New York: Harper Collins, 2009.

Weinert-Kendt, Rob. "A New 'Vanya' for the Living Room." *The New York Times*, June 7, 2012. https://www.nytimes.com/2012/06/10/theater/annie-bakers-uncle-vanya-set-for-soho-rep.html?searchResultPosition=3.

White, Andrew. "Theatre News: Annie Baker's Fresh Adaptation of *Uncle Vanya* Liberates Chekhov." *Maryland Theatre Guide*, April 16, 2015. https://mdtheatreguide.com/2015/04/theatre-news-annie-bakers-fresh-adaptation-of-uncle-vanya-liberates-chekhov/.

Wilde, Oscar. *The Picture of Dorian Gray*. New York: W. W. Norton, 2019.

Williams, Tennessee. *The Glass Menagerie*. New York: New Directions, 1949.

Williams, Tennessee. *Where I Live: Selected Essays*. New York: New Directions, 1978.

Wilson, Timothy D. et al., "Just Think: The Challenges of the Disengaged Mind." *Science* 345, no. 6192 (July 4, 2014): 75–7.

Woodruff, Paul. *The Necessity of Theater: The Art of Watching and Being Watched*. Oxford: Oxford University Press, 2008.

Younger, Kelly. "*The Cherry Orchard* by Anton Chekhov." In *How to Teach a Play*, edited by Miriam M. Chirico and Kelly Younger, 133–5. London: Methuen Drama, 2020.

Yue, Genevieve. "Google Hangout with Annie Baker, Playwright 1/25/16, 2:33 p.m." *Film Quarterly* 69, no. 4 (2016): 57–64.

Zaretsky, Robert. *The Subversive Simone Weil: A Life in Five Ideas*. Chicago: University of Chicago Press, 2021.

Zola, Emile. "Naturalism on the Stage." In *Playwrights on Playwriting: From Ibsen to Ionesco*, edited by Toby Cole, 5–14. New York: Cooper Square Press, 2001.

CONTRIBUTORS

Thomas Butler is Professor of English at Eastern Kentucky University, where he teaches classes in drama and literary theory. He has published essays on Samuel Beckett and Seamus Heaney, and on Sarah Ruhl in *The Journal of Dramatic Theory and Criticism* and in *The Drama and Theatre of Sarah Ruhl*. His essay "Friends Dying Before Our Eyes in Annie Baker's *The Aliens*" was published in *Text & Presentation*.

Jeanmarie Higgins is Associate Professor in the School of Theatre at The Pennsylvania State University. She is the editor of *Teaching Critical Performance Theory in Today's Theatre Classroom, Studio, and Communities* (Routledge, 2020), the co-editor for the online journal *Prompt: A Journal of Theatre Theory, Practice, and Teaching* at www.promptjournal.org, and the 2021 recipient of the Oscar Brockett Award from the Association for Theatre in Higher Education.

Katherine Weiss is Associate Dean of the College of Arts and Letters at California State University, Los Angeles. Her scholarly publications include *Samuel Beckett: History, Memory, Archive* (co-edited with Seán Kennedy, Palgrave Macmillan, 2009), *The Plays of Samuel Beckett* (Methuen Drama, 2013), *A Student Handbook to the Plays of Tennessee Williams* (Methuen Drama, 2014), *Samuel Beckett and Contemporary Art* (co-edited with Robert Reginio and David Houston Jones, ibidem, 2017), and *Simply Beckett* (Simply Charly Press, 2020). She has published articles in the *Journal of Beckett Studies* and *Samuel Beckett: Aujourd'hui*.

Harrison Schmidt Harrison Schmidt is a graduate student at the University of St. Thomas. His paper "White and Wrong in Annie Baker's *Nocturama*" was presented at the Comparative Drama Conference, and his essay "Grief Unspoken in Martyna Majok's *Cost of Living*" is forthcoming in *Modern Drama*.

INDEX

Note: Baker's works are entered under their titles, with sustained discussions in **bold type**.

Akerman, Chantal 71
Albee, Edward xv, 79
 Who's Afraid of Virginia Woolf? 79
The Aliens xi, xvii, 3, 12, 17, 18, 32, **51–9**, 71, 95, **105–7**, 110, 116, 125–7, 129–30, 132, 133
Als, Hilton 77, 84, 111, 118, 121–2
Antaeus Theatre 5
The Antipodes xvii, 73–4, **88–97**
Atlantic Theater Company 19
Aukin, Daniel xv
Austen, Jane xv, 66

Baker, Annie
 attention, role in plays xii, xiii, 8, 14, 23, 35, 48, 51–2, 56, 66, 70–2, 76, 78, 89, 100, 109, 110, **111–15**, 126, 135–6, 138, **141–3**, 147–8, 150, 167 n.36
 Brooklyn College xv
 contemplation xiii, 49, 76, 150
 Cullman Center Fellow (New York Public Library) 149
 Drama Desk Award 19
 family xiii–xiv, xv, 20, 29, 76, 156 n.14, 157 n.27
 MacArthur "Genius" Grant xi, 73
 MacDowell Fellow 149
 naturalism xviii, 1, 2, 47, 51, 73, 77, 120–2, 135
 numinous 73, 77
 NYU xv, xvi, 23
 Obie Awards xi, 36, 53, 60
 Pulitzer Prize xi, xvii, 49, 60, 73, 118
 quiet style xii, xiii, 52, 73, 105, 150
 race, role in plays xviii, 24, 31–2, 35, 57, 59, 61, 62, 84, 90, **134–48**
 realism xii, xvii, 14, 19, 77, 86, 120–2
 Shirley, Vermont xvii, 17–18, 20, 28, 31–2, 35, 38–9, 44, 46, 53, 57, 59, 100, 103–5, 107, 136, 139–40
 silence, role in plays xiii, xvii, 14, 36–8, 39–41, 44, **51–70**, 79, 93, 95, 105–7, 111, 125–6, 134, **138–41**, 148
 Susan Smith Blackburn Prize xi, 60
 teaching xvi
 time, role in plays 37, 51, 53, 59–60, 69–73, 76, **89–96**, 97, 105, 107, 111, 112, 114, 117, 119
 writing process xv–xvi
Baldwin, Craig 78
Barrow Street Theatre 63, 69, 70
Barthes, Roland 129
Bartlett, Rosamund 2
Barton, Mark 80
Bates, Julie 131
Baumbach, Nico 83
Baxter, Charles 13–14
Bay Area Playwrights Festival 19
Beckett, Samuel xv, 66, 104, **125–33**, 170 n.17
 Film 129
 Not I 126
 Quad 126
 Waiting for Godot 58, 125–7, 131
Bennett, Jane 80
Bergman, Ingmar 65, 75
 Fanny and Alexander 65, 66, 75
Bergson, Henri 60
Berkeley, George 126
Berks, Alan xii, 17, 37
Bersley, Tracy 71
Bertino, Marie-Helene 90, 96–7
Big Dance Theater xv
Billington, Michael 47, 60–1, 84, 97
Birney, Reed 3
Body Awareness xi, xvii, 17–19, **19–27**, 30, 32, 45, 48, 53, 100–4, 107, 110
Bourgeois, Louise 86
Brand, Dionne 137

Index

Brantley, Ben 19, 90, 96
Brennan, Clare 47
Bryant-Bertail, Sarah 119
Buber, Martin 142–3
Bukowski, Charles 55, 56
Bush Theatre 53

Cage, John 51, 71, 105
Cape Cod Theatre Project 28
Cavell, Stanley 113
Cayer, Jennifer 36, 46, 106–7, 126–8, 132, 141
Chekhov, Anton xii, xiii, xv, xvii, **1–15**, 17, 19, 46, 53, 73, 126
Chernus, Michael 57
Churchill, Caryl xv
Circle Mirror Transformation xi, xiv, xvii, 3, 17–19, 31, **35–48**, 53, 58, 84, 88, 103–7, 110, 116, 135
Coal Mine Theatre (Toronto) 59, 89, 97
Coates, Tyler 69, 73, 78
Cocteau, Jean 74
Cotkin, George 127–8, 132
Court Theatre (New Zealand) 5
Crompton, Sarah 71

Danto, Arthur C. 51
Darragh, Patch 57
defamiliarization xii, 3
Derrida, Jacques 142, 143
Dickinson, Emily xv
Dizzia, Maria 3
Dolan, Jill 84

Engel, Georgia 75, 76
Epstein, Martin 23
Falls, Robert 5, 8
Farred, Grant 139, 140
Featherstone, Vicky 47
Felski, Rita 112–13
Finke, Michael 11
The Flick xi, xvii, 51, 52, **59–72**, 73, 93, 106–11, 116, 118, 125–33, 149
Foreman, Richard xiv
Fornes, Maria Irene xv
Friedman, Peter 19

Gann, Erin 57
Gassman, Ben 3

Gerwig, Greta 99, 150
Gill, Peter 51
Gold, Sam 1, 3, 4, 28, 36–8, 53, 60, 63, 69–71, 74, 96, 150
Green, Jesse 70–1, 79, 118, 122, 149
Greenfield, Adam xii, 28, 105

Hägglund, Martin 114
Hathaway, Paige 117
Heller, Nathan xii, 103, 104, 143
Herren, Graley 125
HOME Theatre (Manchester) 47
Hubley, Whip 22

Ibsen, Henrik 11, 120–2
  A Doll's House 120–2
I Love Dick xvii, 69, 72, 73, **84–8**, 90, 97, 149
Infinite Life 149
Isherwood, Charles 1, 5, 10, 27, 47, 52, 60, 76–7, 116, 119

James, William 74, 81
Janet Planet 149
Jeanne Dielman, 23, quai de commerce, 1080 Bruxelles (Akerman) 71
Jellinek, Laura 89
John xvii, 29, 31, **74–84**, 93, 96, 97, 99, 108–11, 116–18, **118–24**, 149
Johnson, David T. 71, 125
Jones, Chris 5, 27
Jones, Toby 47

Kachman, Misha 8
Kahn, Sam xii–xiii, 105
Kiley, Brendan 125
Kingwell, Mark 121
Kleist, Heinrich von 74–5, 116, 121
Knausgaard, Karl Ove 114–15
Kohlhaas, Karen 19
Kraus, Chris 84–6
Kruger, Charles 53, 78

Lamford, Chloe 75–6, 89, 96
Larson, Sarah 108, 111–12
The Last of the Little Hours 149
Lawson, Mark 103
Lee, Young Jean xv
Levinas, Emmanuel 142, 145
Liebermann, Andrew 4

Index

Lovecraft, H. P.   82
Lukowski, Andrzej   77, 89

Macdonald, James   xv, 47
Maeterlinck, Maurice   2, 73
Maga, Carly   59
Malle, Louis   2
Manhattan (Woody Allen)   70
Manhattan Theatre Club   28
Mann, Thomas   xiii, xv, xvii, 20, 51, 66, 81, 89
Maron, Marc   61, 99, 150
Martin, Clancy   5
McDonagh, Martin   51
Meyerhold, Vsevolod   9
Miller, Henry   54, 56
Moi, Toril   113–15
Monagahan, Louise   47
Morrison, Toni   134, 137, 140
Moten, Fred   147
Murdoch, Iris   113

Nabokov, Vladimir   xv
National Theatre (London)   60, 71, 75–6, 89, 90, 96
Nelson, Victoria   78
Nestruck, J. Kelly   73, 77
Neugebauer, Lila   96
New York Theatre Workshop   xv
Nicholson, Julianne   149
Nocturama   17–19, **27–35**, 48, 53, 55, 57, 95, **135–48**, 171 n.4
Nugent, Benjamin   xiv, 29, 156 n.14, 157 n.27
Nussbaum, Emily   86
Nussbaum, Martha   112

Okonedo, Sophie   149
O'Mahony, Holly   91
Otto, Rudolf   77

Parham, Keith   8
Pavis, Patrice   119
Perls, Fritz   xv
Phillips, Adam   xi
Pinter, Harold   51
Playwrights Horizons   28, 35, 37, 47, 52, 60, 61, 65
Portland Theater Festival   22
Pulp Fiction (Tarantino)   69, 128–9

Quashie, Kevin   xiii, 35, 137–8, 147
Quintessence Theatre Group (Philadelphia)   5

Rankine, Claudia   140, 146
Rattlestick Playwrights Theater   53
Read, Alan   150
Red Stitch Actors' Theatre (Melbourne)   89
Reid, Robert   89, 97
Removed (Naomi Uman)   86
Rilke, Rainer Maria   74
Rohmer, Eric   xv
Rorty, Richard   112
Rosenthal, Todd   8
Ross, Alex   76
Round House Theatre   5
Row, Jess   134, 136, 139
Rowen, Bess   145
Royal Court Theatre (London)   47
Royle, Nicholas   116–17
Rudin, Scott   60
Rukeyser, Muriel   97

Sanford, Tim   52, 60, 65
Sartre, Jean-Paul   59
Schmidt, Paul   3
Schreck, Heidi   84, 86
Shakespeare, William   xv
Shalina, Margarita   3
Shaw Festival   5
Shklovsky, Viktor   xii
Sierz, Aleks   47, 59
Signature Theatre   74–6, 78, 80, 89, 116, 117, 149
Smith, Elliot   32
Smith, Kevin   48
Sofer, Andrew   110–11, 118
Soho Rep   3–5, 10, 28
Soloski, Alexis   84–6, 111
Soloway, Joey   84, 85, 88, 90
Stasio, Marilyn   97
Staunton, Imelda   47
Steppenwolf Theatre   60
Strindberg, August   2, 73
Sundance Institute   3, 36

Tales of Hoffmann (Offenbach)   83, 110
Teeman, Tim   90
Trifles (Glaspell)   121, 122

Index

Trueman, Matt   47–8
Truffaut, François   63, 66
   Jules et Jim   63, 68, 70, 130, 131

Uman, Naomi   86
Uncle Vanya   xvii, **1–15**, 18–19, 46, 51, 56, 73, 107

Vanya on 42nd Street   2, 4
Vogel, Paula   71

Weil, Simone   52, 167 n.36
Wellman, Mac   xi, xv, 57

Wilde, Oscar   xiv, 97
Williams, Tennessee   121, 131
   The Glass Menagerie   121
   Streetcar Named Desire   131
Wittgenstein, Ludwig   x, 57
Wolcott, James   70
Women Arts (Northampton, MA)   5
Woodruff, Paul   75
Woolf, Virginia   xv

Younger, Kelly   14

Zola, Emile   121–2

www.ingramcontent.com/pod-product-compliance
Lightning Source LLC
Chambersburg PA
CBHW052117300426
44116CB00010B/1694